BECAUSE OF THEIR FAITH

CONTEMPORARY AMERICAN HISTORY SERIES
William E. Leuchtenburg, General Editor

CONTEMPORARY AMERICAN HISTORY SERIES

WILLIAM E. LEUCHTENBURG, GENERAL EDITOR

BECAUSE OF THEIR FAITH

CALCAV and Religious Opposition
to the Vietnam War

MITCHELL K. HALL

 COLUMBIA UNIVERSITY PRESS • NEW YORK

Library of Congress Cataloging-in-Publication Data

Hall, Mitchell K.
  Because of their faith : CALCAV and religious opposition
to the Vietnam War / Mitchell K. Hall.
  p. cm. — (Contemporary American history series)
Includes bibliographical references.
ISBN 0-231-07140-X (alk. paper)
1. Vietnamese Conflict, 1961–1975—Protest movements—United States.
2. Vietnamese Conflict, 1961–1975—Religious aspects.
3. Clergy and Laymen Concerned About Vietnam (U.S.)
4. Clergy and Laity Concerned (U.S.)
I. Title. II. Series.
DS559.62.U6H33   1990
959.704'37—dc20   90-30103
                    CIP

Columbia University Press
New York   Oxford
Copyright © 1990 Columbia University Press
All rights reserved

Casebound editions of Columbia University Press books are Smyth-sewn
and printed on permanent and durable acid-free paper

Text design: Susan Phillips

Printed in the United States of America
c 10 9 8 7 6 5 4 3 2 1

CONTENTS

ACKNOWLEDGMENTS

There are many people who deserve thanks for their contributions to the research and writing that has gone into this project. My research benefited from the excellent staff of the Swarthmore College Peace Collection, and from the FBI documents acquired through the Freedom of Information Act and shared by the University of Kentucky King Library. Those antiwar activists who willingly agreed to interviews rendered invaluable aid. Among those who read earlier drafts of this book, Professor George Herring of the University of Kentucky stands out for offering immeasurable support. His comments provided significant help in content, style, and organization. Professor Charles Chatfield of Wittenberg University incisively critiqued my work and graciously shared from his own project, the completion of the late Charles DeBenedetti's comprehensive study of the Vietnam era antiwar movement. Richard Fernandez of Philadelphia's Northwest Interfaith Movement added a participant's perspective that helped sharpen my own thoughts. Editors Kate Wittenberg and Karen Mitchell of Columbia University Press made perceptive suggestions and added to the book's clarity. The valued input of series editor William Leuchtenburg and Columbia's outside readers is also greatly appreciated. Final recognition goes to my wife, Ann, who has shared the years of effort and now, I hope, the satisfaction.

PREFACE

Most Americans are at least partially familiar with their nation's military history. Far fewer are aware that, from colonial days, a significant number of citizens have refused to sanction the nation's wars and have established a valuable tradition of peace through non-violence. Perhaps at no time has antiwar sentiment been greater than during the Vietnam War, when, for nearly a decade, millions of Americans publicly demonstrated their opposition to a war they believed to be ill-conceived, unwinnable, and immoral.

Fifteen years have passed since the United States ended its painful involvement in Vietnam. It has taken that long for the nation to begin to understand why it went there in the first place and how, despite its confidence and power, it failed to achieve its goals. Much of the recent attention on events of that era has focused on Vietnam veterans who have struggled to find an acceptable place in the long line of American combatants. The construction of a national war memorial in Washington, D.C. during the early 1980s went a long way toward accomplishing that. In comparison, many people have only a superficial knowledge of the Americans who worked against the war and are unaware of the complexities and accomplishments of the antiwar movement.

Popular misconceptions of antiwar activists continue to abound. One national newspaper columnist referred to the typical activist as "a hairy, filthy, ragged youth with his arm and hand raised in an angry gesture. . . . [usually] performed with a single raised finger."[1] Others frequently remember the movement, if now only vaguely, as a disorganized mass of countercultural young people bent on violence against the constituted authorities. Critics attribute American withdrawal from Vietnam to the persuasiveness of the antiwar forces and are quick to blame them for the millions of Indochinese who have been killed or imprisoned since 1975. Such a portrayal does a severe injustice both to the historical record and to the individuals who were involved in one of the largest mass movements in American history.

The American movement against the Vietnam War was not a single homogeneous effort. Millions of people from a wide variety of backgrounds had different motivations and pursued numerous strategies in trying to bring the war to an end. This study focuses on one organization within the antiwar movement, Clergy and Laymen Concerned About Vietnam (CALCAV), in order to raise questions about the movement and to provide some insight into its complexity. What was the composition of the antiwar forces? Why did they choose to protest the war? What suggestions did they offer as an alternative to escalation? What tactics did the movement use in pursuing its goals? What impact did it have? How did it change over time? In answering these questions, I hope to contribute to a fuller and more accurate assessment of the people who opposed the Vietnam War.

Clergy and Laymen Concerned About Vietnam mobilized the religious community, one of the antiwar movement's major constituencies,[2] for ecumenical social action. The group arose in response to the silence of institutional religion on the questions of America's involvement in Indochina, and emerged from its New York City origins in late 1965 to become a national network of local chapters. Initially CALCAV consisted of a uniform group that appealed to the middle class of the American religious mainstream. It mixed pragmatic with moral arguments and used moderate tactics such as petitions, vigils, electoral politics, and rallies. As the United States escalated the war, CALCAV's constituency became larger and more diversified, a transition that produced divergent views characteristic of the larger antiwar movement. The situation resulted in tension between those who wanted to focus on the single issue of Vietnam and others who favored addressing a wider range of social-justice concerns. This rivalry flowed from competing evaluations of American society. The dominant position in the mid-1960s regarded U.S. policy in Indochina as a misguided exception to the policies of a generally beneficent America. The belief that Vietnam showed a nation with fundamental flaws increasingly challenged this view as the war dragged on, and CALCAV's protest grew to include more critical rhetoric and acts of civil disobedience. As part of the movement, CALCAV helped influence public opinion against the war, limited government options in conducting the war, and defended the right of dissent, but it did not by itself bring an end to the war. When the conflict ended in 1975, the organization turned its attention to other issues.

BECAUSE OF THEIR FAITH

1

A NATIONAL EMERGENCY COMMITTEE

> Peacemaking is hard, hard almost as war.
> —DANIEL BERRIGAN

Speaking at a New York press conference in January 1966, Yale chaplain William Sloane Coffin publicly announced the formation of the National Emergency Committee of Clergy Concerned About Vietnam. "The moment is crucial," Coffin warned, "for it may well be that morally speaking the United States ship of state is today comparable to the *Titanic* just before it hit the iceberg. If we decide on all-out escalation of the war in Vietnam, then to all intents and purposes of the human soul we may be sunk. We plead therefore with our fellow clergy to support our government's effort to negotiate an end to the war and to prevent its further escalation."[1]

The National Emergency Committee emerged in the spring of 1966 as an important outlet for religious leaders who opposed U.S. policy in Indochina. The inequities of American society exposed by the civil rights movement prompted the religious community to reevaluate its acceptance of cold war attitudes. Clergy Concerned avoided the limits of denominational bureaucracies by building upon the postwar ecumenical movement that united Protestants, Catholics, and Jews in cooperative ventures. Established in New York around the vigorous defense of the right to dissent, this ad hoc organization quickly found a national constituency. Firmly rooted in the American mainstream, it argued the ineffectiveness of military escalation in Vietnam and instead advocated a negotiated settlement.

American involvement in Vietnam had gradually escalated in the 1960s. President John F. Kennedy increased the number of military advisers in Vietnam to over 16,000, but the most drastic change in America's commitment occurred under his successor. In the early

1

months of 1965, Lyndon B. Johnson initiated a bombing campaign against North Vietnam and sent in the first U.S. combat troops.[2]

As the United States became more deeply entangled in Indochina, opposition to the war increased significantly. The antiwar movement emerged as a diverse collection of organizations, each with its own methods and agenda. Peace organizations of the late 1950s and early 1960s, such as the Fellowship of Reconciliation (FOR), the War Resisters League (WRL), and the Committee for a Sane Nuclear Policy (SANE) had focused on such long-term goals as nuclear disarmament. By 1963, however, they had begun to shift their emphasis to the more immediate problem of the war in Indochina and initially served as the backbone of the new antiwar movement.

Opposition to the Vietnam conflict developed in three distinct but overlapping segments. Liberal organizations included the American Friends Service Committee (AFSC), Committee for a Sane Nuclear Policy, Women Strike for Peace (WSP), Americans for Democratic Action (ADA), and Turn Toward Peace (TTP). These groups, recalling Chinese intervention in Korea, generally viewed the conflict as unnecessarily provocative to China and advocated a cease-fire, negotiations, and arbitration by an international body. Groups such as the Women's International League for Peace and Freedom (WILPF), War Resister's League, Committee for Nonviolent Action (CNVA), and Fellowship of Reconciliation constituted the pacifist wing, which favored a nonviolent end to the war. Both the Marxist Old Left, which contained the Communist and Socialist Workers parties, and the nonsectarian New Left, best exemplified by Students for a Democratic Society (SDS), tended to view the war as a deliberate attempt on the part of the American government to blunt the Vietnamese movement for national liberation. They proposed an immediate U.S. withdrawal.[3]

Expressions of antiwar sentiment appeared in a variety of forms as peace organizations frequently cooperated in lobbying, signing newspaper ads and petitions, holding rallies, and making speeches to persuade the government to end the war. The earliest demonstrations against the Vietnam conflict grew out of traditional peace activities. In 1963, speakers criticized U.S. intervention in Vietnam at annual events such as the Easter Peace Walk in New York City in support of nuclear disarmament and the August commemoration of the use of atomic bombs against Japan. In the fall, campus demonstrations during an American tour by Mme. Ngo Dinh Nhu, the sister-in-law of South Vietnamese President Ngo Dinh Diem, protested the repression of Diem's government and Mme. Nhu's references to the self-immolation of Vietnamese Buddhists as "barbecues."[4]

National antiwar demonstrations began in the spring of 1965. Prodded by American air strikes against North Vietnam, an SDS-sponsored march on Washington on April 17 attracted the largest peace rally in the city's history, an estimated 20,000 people. In addition, a unique series of debates was being held on college campuses across the country. These teach-ins, an informal series of lectures and discussions of the Vietnam conflict, originated at the University of Michigan in late March and spread to other schools.

An ad hoc organization called the Inter-University Committee for a Public Hearing on Vietnam held a national teach-in on May 15 in Washington, D.C., hoping that a reasoned attack on the administration's policies would expose them as inadequate and stop escalation. Across the nation 122 campuses listened in on telephone hookups and heard Professors George M. Kahin of Cornell and Hans Morgenthau of the University of Chicago debate defenders of government policy such as Robert Scalapino of the University of California and Arthur M. Schlesinger, Jr. of the City University of New York.[5]

The State Department attempted to blunt the attack from the academic community by sending out a four-man unit led by Thomas Conlon to carry the official view to a number of midwestern colleges. This group, dubbed the "truth team," had little success in convincing listeners of its message, running into one cold reception after another. The result of these assaults upon the government's Vietnam policies, however, was not encouraging to those who believed that the administration was open to criticism. "Few great questions of policy had ever been debated at such length, in such detail, with so little effect," Thomas Powers has concluded.[6]

In early August 1965, while protesters on the west coast attempted without much success to block troop trains in the San Francisco Bay area, nearly 2,000 peace activists met in Washington, D.C. to consider their response to Vietnam and other issues. Discussions in one of their workshops produced the first of the national coalitions of the antiwar movement, the National Coordinating Committee to End the War in Vietnam.

The National Coordinating Committee helped plan and publicize the International Days of Protest for October 15–16, which attracted about 100,000 people in sixty American cities and over a dozen foreign countries. The largest of the local events occurred in New York City under the sponsorship of a new citywide coalition of peace groups, the Fifth Avenue Peace Parade Committee. An estimated 25,000 people participated in the march down Fifth Avenue and the rally that followed on October 16. On the previous day at the Whitehall Street Army Induction Center, David Miller became the first person arrested for burning his draft card since Congress passed a federal law making that a crime punishable by up to five years in jail and a $10,000 fine.

In the middle of the growing opposition to the war, protest sometimes became tragedy. On November 2, motivated perhaps by discouragement over the war's continued escalation and similar incidents in Vietnam itself, Norman Morrison, a Quaker, burned himself alive on the steps of the Pentagon. A week later, Roger LaPorte of the Catholic Worker movement followed his example at the United Nations building. These two were not the first Americans to die in this manner in protest of the Vietnam War. Alice Herz, a Detroit Quaker, had taken her life in March.

The last mass demonstration of the year occurred November 27 and drew about 35,000 people. Chaired by Sanford Gottlieb of SANE and usually referred to as the SANE rally, its speakers included Norman Thomas, Coretta Scott King, Dr. Benjamin Spock, and Carl Oglesby, President of SDS.

That same week, however, cracks began to appear in the antiwar coalition. The diversity of constituencies and disparate analyses of American intervention in Vietnam made it difficult to maintain permanent harmony on war-related issues.[7] At the first convention of the National Coordinating Committee to End the War in Vietnam, debate erupted on the key issues of the exclusion of communist groups from the antiwar movement and the endorsement of a policy of immediate withdrawal of the U.S. from Vietnam.

The question of participation by communist organizations in the antiwar coalition plagued the movement throughout its existence. From the outset of the cold war, peace organizations that advocated international cooperation were viewed with a great deal of suspicion by a government and society that had adopted military deterrence for its national security. Government officials considered the containment of domestic dissent essential to the maintenance of the national security state. Peace groups found themselves under increased surveillance by expanding intelligence agencies, harassed by Congress, and widely identified as subversives under communist control. To try to maintain their credibility, liberal peace organizations routinely discouraged the membership of communists and avoided even the appearance of cooperation with communist organizations. In the early 1960s, groups such as SANE continued this exclusionary policy because of their fundamental differences from the communists and in order to retain their respectability with mainstream politicians. Organizations of radical pacifists and the New Left, however, attacked this rigid anticommunism as undemocratic and insisted upon complete nonexclusion. In the end, the convention refused to prohibit participation by any organization on the basis of its political views. Although the debate over exclusion continued, the precedent generally prevailed at mass gatherings of the antiwar movement.[8] The convention delegates failed to reach a consensus on withdrawal or negotiations, agreeing only that the war must be ended.

The inclusion of the American religious community in this growing opposition to the war was greatly facilitated by the emergence of two significant trends following World War II. The first was the ecumenical movement that produced in 1948 the World Council of Churches and later the National Council of Churches (NCC) in the United States. The other built upon the civil rights movement in developing a stronger commitment to social involvement.

These changes occurred gradually and within certain boundaries. American religion was far from monolithic. The three largest religious groups, Protestants, Catholics, and Jews, had only tenuous ties with each other. Catholics and Jews in particular, as minority religions generally composed of more recent immigrants than Protestants, feared that interreligious links would result in a loss of their distinctive identities. These religious bodies differed not only on theological matters but on social issues as well, especially in the early 1960s over federal aid to parochial schools and religious observances in the public schools.

Divisions also existed within these bodies. The Protestant majority, split into numerous denominations, was divided between the mainstream descendants of eighteenth- and early nineteenth-century churches usually represented in the National Council of Churches and the rapidly growing evangelical and pentacostal branches. The evangelicals were generally southern conservatives who avoided commenting on specific political issues. Spearheaded by the Southern Baptist Convention, the single largest Protestant church,[9] and best represented by Billy Graham, evangelicals blended American nationalism with their religion and criticized the National Council of Churches as too liberal. The mainstream denominations, including the Methodist, Episcopal, Presbyterian, Lutheran, and American Baptist churches among others, also participated in the nationalistic religion of the 1950s, though to a lesser extent than the evangelicals. Generally both theologically and politically more liberal than evangelicals, mainstream churches became increasingly involved in social ministries, particularly in the field of civil rights.

The Roman Catholic Church, exemplified by Francis Cardinal Spellman, eagerly participated in the religious nationalism of the postwar years. More cohesive than its Protestant and Jewish counterparts, Catholicism nevertheless underwent its own dissonance. The Second Vatican Ecumenical Council (Vatican II), held in four sessions from 1962 to 1965, produced changes of such magnitude that their implications are still being debated within the church. The American Jewish community was divided into the Reform, Conservative, and Orthodox branches. Each had its own outlook and agenda.

Despite the differences within and among the leading American religions, the 1950s and 1960s were years of greater movement toward unity and ecumenism. Within Protestantism, closer cooperation and even denominational mergers occurred. Interfaith cooperation grew out of the opening of Protestant-Catholic dialogues, the Vatican II declaration absolving Jews from special guilt in the death of Jesus Christ, and common support of the civil rights movement.[10]

The social criticism undertaken by politically active clergy developed in spite of strong social constraints. The cold war between the United States and the Soviet Union played a major role in limiting dissent. Americans viewed their global antagonist as inherently evil, and many turned the East-West conflict into a moral crusade. So pervasive was this attitude that it encouraged the equation of U.S. strategies with godliness and consequently blinded the nation to its own imperfections. Protestants, Catholics, and Jews absorbed these ideas to varying degrees and preached a more nationalistic religion. In the stifling conformity that such perceptions can impose, the mildest objection to official policy could bring suspicion of one's loyalty to both church and state.

Conditions within the religious communities joined these external pressures in contributing to the silence of the churches regarding social issues. A substantial segment of America's church and synagogue leadership traditionally avoided extensive participation in the political process. Theological liberals were more inclined toward political activity than conservatives, but even mainstream denominations hesitated to advocate positions on controversial issues that might prove divisive. The clergy generally held more liberal social attitudes than the laity. The majority of laypeople felt the churches should stay out of political and social matters and disapproved of clerics who demonstrated for causes in those areas. These views, particularly in Protestant churches with strong congregational control over the selection of ministers, tended to mute social activism.[11]

The civil rights movement served as the catalyst to change this situation. The legal relegation of blacks to an inferior social position and the often violent methods used to enforce that system were so decidedly immoral that members of churches and synagogues were forced by conscience to oppose them. Martin Luther King, Jr. symbolized the leading role played by the clergy in the struggle for civil rights. Predictably the drive for equality drew charges of communist collusion, but jolted into acknowledging the stark existence of racism, many religious leaders were unconvinced of the existence of a monolithic communism and sensitive to injustices that existed in the United States.[12]

Once committed to the idea that political issues could have moral implications, clerics searched for appropriate channels for their social witnessing. The growth of ecumenical and denominational bureaucracies freed many church executives from direct accountability to local opinion and allowed them to comment on political matters without fear of reprisal. Local clergy often went outside their own churches and made use of ad hoc ecumenical groups where they were less vulnerable. Generally, those who took an active liberal position on racial issues took a similar stance on foreign affairs.[13]

The religious press provided an additional opportunity for Christian and Jewish leaders to address important social questions. Although denominational periodicals generally had large circulations, sometimes into the hundreds of thousands, most were narrowly focused and rarely appealed to those outside their own subscribers. More influential were smaller independent journals that provided a religious framework for important public issues. *Christian Century* with 40,000 subscribers was probably the best-known and most widely quoted journal of the Protestant press. *Christianity and Crisis* with only one-fourth the circulation had an impact well beyond its numbers by influencing opinion makers and reaching a larger public through its citations in the secular press. Both of these had a moderately liberal orientation and favored social change more than most denominational constituencies. *Christianity Today,* the chief evangelical journal, was politically conservative and resisted both the ecumenical movement and the church's social involvement. The most prestigious Catholic journal was *Commonweal* with a circulation of only 22,000. *America* was somewhat more conservative than *Commonweal,* but neither was as involved in national social issues as the Protestant press. *Commentary* was the most outstanding Jewish publication, although its link to the faith was nominal.[14]

Clerical and lay church leaders began moving outside established organizations to speak about the war in Vietnam as early as 1963. That summer a series of Buddhist demonstrations and self-immolations protesting the Diem government's religious persecution exposed the enormous social and political problems that existed in South Vietnam. In August, American-trained forces arrested hundreds of Buddhists and looted their pagodas in the major cities after Diem assured the Americans that no further repressive measures would be taken. On September 15, the Minister's Vietnam Committee placed an ad in the New York *Times* which protested the sacrifice of American lives and money for a "regime universally regarded as unjust, undemocratic, and unstable," and that denied its citizens religious freedom. The committee further condemned as "immoral" the use of chemical crop defoliants and the strategic hamlet program, which required the relocation of large numbers of peasants. The committee included Reinhold Niebuhr, probably the twentieth century's leading American theologian, and the Rev. Harry Emerson Fosdick among its twelve signees and claimed the support of over 17,000 clergy.[15]

Dr. John C. Bennett, President of Union Theological Seminary in New York and one of the nation's leading theologians, became one of the first clerics to challenge U.S. policy in Indochina, presaging an increase in antiwar clergy activism. Writing for *Christianity and Crisis* in July 1964, Bennett disputed the U.S. government's claim that the war had resulted from northern aggression against South Vietnam, instead labeling it a civil war. He further questioned those who were predisposed to view such conflicts in narrow military terms. "We are always tempted to see these struggles in terms of military activity and to assume that there must be a solution," he commented, "but what if there is no solution in military terms?" His concern about future American escalation would prove to be prophetic: "A movement away from our past policy of maintaining a holding operation could easily lead to hopeless involvement in a conflict in which our power would not be relevant."[16] The following March, Bennett would use the same forum to raise additional questions about the war.[17]

These clerical criticisms did not take place in a vacuum. Vietnam emerged as an important issue in the 1964 presidential campaign. While Republican candidate Barry Goldwater argued for an increase in military pressure, Johnson successfully presented himself as the peace candidate. Convinced that Goldwater's views threatened to engage the superpowers in Indochina, numerous religious journals such as *Christian Century* and *Christianity and Crisis* broke their tradition of not supporting particular candidates and endorsed Johnson.[18]

Despite the increased attention given the war in journals such as these and in the occasional dissent by the peace movement, a significant number of Americans remained oblivious to events in Indochina. A poll released in December 1964 by the University of Michigan's Survey Research Center revealed that one in four Americans was unaware of the fighting in Vietnam (28 percent did not even know China was communist). Of those familiar with the Vietnam conflict, slightly over half opposed a U.S. withdrawal and 24 percent favored the use of American forces if the guerrillas should threaten to win even though it risked armed conflict with the Chinese.[19]

Not until 1965 did visible religious opposition to the war occur on a regular basis. The initiation of a sustained bombing campaign over North Vietnam and the landing of American combat troops in the early months of 1965 indicated that the United States had adopted a more aggressive policy in Indochina. The Fellowship of Reconciliation drafted a letter to the White House urging a cease-fire, the withdrawal of U.S. troops, and a peace conference. On April 4, FOR's Clergymen's Emergency Committee for Vietnam ran a full-page ad in the New York *Times* signed by 2,500 ministers, priests, and rabbis opposing the bombing of North Vietnam.[20] When the Johnson administration proved reluctant to participate in unconditional negotiations, a delegation of the Clergymen's Emergency Committee traveled to South Vietnam on June 29. By contacting representatives of the various factions, they hoped to open the lines of communication and contribute to a cease-fire,[21] but they proved unable to accomplish such a task by themselves.

One of the first significant ecumenical efforts against the war occurred May 11–12, 1965, when the Interreligious Committee on Vietnam called all "religiously concerned men and women" to a silent vigil at the Pentagon. The vigil's purpose was to express a sincere desire for a peaceful settlement in Vietnam, show concern over the escalation of the war, especially the bombing of North Vietnam, urge the United States to agree to unconditional discussions with all concerned parties, and encourage the President to cooperate in a program for human welfare and economic development in Southeast Asia. In somewhat stronger language, the committee, which included John C. Bennett, Daniel Corrigan, Episcopal Bishop of New York, Dana McLean Greeley, President of the Unitarian Universalist Association of America, and Martin Luther King, Jr., noted that it was "appalled by the human tragedy and suffering involved in the struggle in Vietnam."[22]

Only a month later, the editorial board of *Christianity and Crisis* took a firm stand against the war. The board, which included Niebuhr, Bennett, Robert McAfee Brown of Stanford University, and Harvey Cox of Harvard Divinity School, feared that American actions, especially bombing north of the seventeenth parallel, could damage the improving relations with the Soviet Union, drive the North Vietnamese into the arms of the Chinese, and risk war with China. They opposed bombing population centers and viewed the conflict in South Vietnam as a civil war. The board also criticized the U.S. government for insisting on an independent South Vietnam and for failing to negotiate with the National Liberation Front (NLF), the insurgents most Americans referred to as the Viet Cong.[23]

Individual denominations sometimes joined these independent religious voices. During the summer, the General Synod of the United Church of Christ (UCC) backed U.N. Secretary General U Thant's proposal of seeking a political and diplomatic solution in Vietnam rather than a military one. This followed a similar action taken by the UCC's Council for Christian Social Action. A resolution at the American Baptist annual convention supported government efforts for a cease-fire, urged negotiations with all concerned parties, and favored greater reliance on international agencies. Later that year, the UCC executive council defended the right to protest but opposed all draft resistance beyond legally recognized conscientious objection.[24] These statements expressed doubts about military escalation and offered cautious alternatives without criticizing the government.

By the end of 1965, a handful of other organizations including the National Council of Churches, Catholic Peace Fellowship, Fellowship of Reconciliation, and Union of American Hebrew Congregations had passed resolutions at least mildly critical of U.S. policies in Vietnam.[25] The NCC's World Order Study Conference, for example, approved resolutions that called for negotiating with all interested parties, including the NLF, halting the bombing in North Vietnam, and restricting air attacks in South Vietnam to military bases.[26]

This early dissent occurred in the face of widespread public support for the President's actions, a situation that inhibited the growth of the antiwar movement at that time.[27] Criticism affected many antiwar advocates, including Martin Luther King, Jr. King, the key leader of the civil rights movement and one of the best-known religious figures in America, gave indications in the summer of 1965 that he would join other religious leaders in opposition to the Vietnam War. Doubts about America's role in Vietnam had grown until, as he told members of the Southern Christian Leadership Conference, "I'm not going to sit by and see the war escalate without saying something about it." In addition to his part in the call to the Pentagon vigil, King urged a negotiated settlement that would include the Viet Cong and a halt to the bombing of North Vietnam. He later made a futile direct appeal to President Johnson, Ho Chi Minh, the Soviets, and the Chinese to end the war in Indochina.[28]

King's public statements against the war provoked disapproval even from among his closest advisers. Those who disagreed feared that his criticism of the war would make it more difficult to gain the support of President Johnson and Congress for civil rights legislation, and could result in a loss of donations for civil rights organizations.

Moderate black civil rights leaders unanimously opposed King's pronouncements on the war.[29] The overwhelming negative response convinced King to temper his criticism of the war for over a year.

Despite the growing activism within the religious community, most mainstream church organizations were not responding to the escalating conflict. In October, A. J. Muste, probably America's most respected pacifist and among the leaders of the early antiwar coalitions, addressed this situation in a letter to John C. Bennett:

> It seems to me also that church forces—the National Council [of Churches], the denominational agencies, Christian, especially Protestant, leaders to whom we are in the habit of looking for initiative—are not saying or doing anything of real significance in relation to the problem. I have the feeling they are simply marking time and so contribute to the attitude of "going along" with the Johnson Administration, which is so widespread and, in my view, so dangerous. This represents, of course, a great contrast to what happened among church people in relation to the race situation during the past half dozen years or so.[30]

The passivity disturbed a number of prominent church leaders. Those who shared this perception looked initially to their local and denominational groups for support. Most found that local churches were ignoring the war and that denominations, even if they could reach a consensus, moved painfully slowly. Frustrated by the failure of the institutional church to effectively address the war, these individuals looked beyond religious barriers and bureaucracies for ways to express themselves.

As members of the religious community became more restless, the antiwar movement continued to make its presence felt. In the winter and early spring of 1966, the movement's first umbrella coalition, the National Coordinating Committee, was in decline. At its standing committee meeting January 8–9 in Milwaukee, a proposal calling for an immediate U.S. withdrawal was narrowly defeated, indicating the depth of disagreement between the advocates of withdrawal and those favoring a negotiated settlement. The late March demonstrations known as the Second International Days of Protest drew 50,000 in New York, 7,000 in San Francisco, 5,000 in Chicago, and smaller crowds in over 100 American cities. They proved to be the last major actions planned by the National Coordinating Committee, which divided over tactics and faded out as a national body.[31]

In the absence of new national actions, individual peace groups continued to work independently. Women Strike for Peace, formed in 1960 to organize women against the nuclear arms race, lobbied members of Congress to produce a peaceful solution to the war;

SANE sponsored a national campaign to elect congressional candidates that opposed the war; and hundreds of Quakers held a vigil at the White House. College students participated in symbolic fasts at a number of eastern schools, and on May 16, over 8,000 antiwar moderates from SANE, WSP, and other groups gathered in Washington and announced the collection of 73,000 voter pledges to support political candidates who favored de-escalation and negotiations. When the Selective Service System began testing over 750,000 male college students to help determine their draft eligibility, SDS distributed over 500,000 counterdraft exams as part of a growing draft resistance movement.[32] The New York–based Fifth Avenue Peace Parade Committee, probably the most active and influential of the local antiwar organizations, drew up to 5,000 participants in a series of rallies in the first months of 1966. In New York City 20,000 people demonstrated their opposition to the war and 10,000 more protested in San Francisco as part of a mass action on August 6–9, 1966.

The antiwar movement gained a degree of respectability as prominent political figures became disenchanted with President Johnson's policies. Chief among these was Senator J. William Fulbright (D-Ark.), Chairman of the Senate Foreign Relations Committee. Beginning January 28, 1966, Fulbright's committee held several weeks of hearings on the war that exposed to the public for the first time such critics as George F. Kennan, former U.S. ambassador to the Soviet Union, and retired Lt. General James Gavin. Former officials such as these generally favored a more limited American role in South Vietnam but stopped well short of calling for a U.S. withdrawal. While they had little in common with most other activists, they brought greater attention and credibility to the arguments of the antiwar movement.

Upon close inspection of the peace forces, most people coming out of the Protestant and Catholic churches and the various branches of American Judaism found few organizations that they could fit into comfortably. The major religious groups within the antiwar movement, the Fellowship of Reconciliation, the American Friends Service Committee, and the Catholic Worker, were predominantly pacifist. While this did not preclude nonpacifists from working with them, the division between those who rejected all forms of violence and those who did not sometimes made it difficult to agree on methods and goals.

Prominent among secular peace groups, although they had a certain religious presence within them, were the War Resisters League and the Committee for Nonviolent Action. However, their acceptance of nonviolent civil disobedience, a position known as "radical pacifism," made them too radical for the vast majority of religious leaders in 1965. Another possibility was the National Committee for a Sane Nuclear Policy, one of the most conservative of the peace organizations. SANE rejected the tactic of nonviolent civil disobedience and refused to admit, or even associate with, members of the American Old Left. SANE, though, was primarily concerned with the long-term solutions to war and emphasized disarmament and nuclear test-ban treaties rather than the more immediate problem in Vietnam.[33]

One other potential source of support was the New Left, groups who rejected the old Marxist views of society but still advanced a liberal/radical critique of American society. These groups lacked appeal because they were dominated by young, college-age people and their critique of America went beyond what the religious community as a whole was willing to accept. William Sloane Coffin was bothered by what he saw as the tendency of the New Left to oppose right-wing violence and totalitarianism while sometimes overlooking similar behavior when committed by the left. He was also disturbed by the anti-American rhetoric that was becoming fashionable in SDS circles and felt that America's behavior in Vietnam should be condemned by the standards of Americans such as Thoreau instead of modern foreign revolutionaries such as Ho Chi Minh, Mao Zedong, and Che Guevara. Although convinced that the political left was correct in its view of the Vietnam War, Coffin felt that it was incapable of persuading the vast American center of its arguments.[34]

By late 1965, a significant number of religious leaders had concluded that the war in Vietnam was wrong and must be opposed. Acting as individuals or as members of ad hoc organizations, they became frustrated with their lack of influence and with the apparent neglect of the issue by denominational bodies that they normally turned to in times of crisis. While established organizations already existed where they might pursue a concern about Vietnam, none seemed to fully meet the needs of those coming out of the dominant American religious traditions. The time was right for a new instrument that would make it possible for a common religious voice to speak out against the war. Clergy and Laymen Concerned About Vietnam would fill this need.

If any single issue spurred the formation of the group that developed into Clergy and Laymen Concerned About Vietnam, it was the attempt to discredit the antiwar movement. James Reston of the New York *Times* claimed that antiwar demonstrations were "not promoting peace but postponing it."[35] Typical of the government's response was FBI head J. Edgar Hoover's view that "Anti-Vietnam demonstrators in the U.S. represent a minority for the most part composed of halfway citizens who are neither morally, mentally nor emotionally mature."[36] A number of government officials sharply criticized the nationwide protests of October 1965, including Attorney General Nicholas Katzenbach, who commented that "there are some communists involved in it. We may very well have to prosecute." Even President Johnson expressed his "surprise that any one citizen would feel toward his country in a way that is not consistent with the national interest."[37]

In response to these attacks, an ad hoc group of about 100 Protestant, Catholic, and Jewish clergy from New York City organized an ecumenical forum to evaluate America's Asian policy. Representatives of the group held a news conference in the United Nations Church Center on October 25, 1965. The Rev. Richard Neuhaus, pastor of the Lutheran Church of St. John the Evangelist, commented, "It concerns us that the President should be amazed by dissent." The Rev. William A. Jones of Brooklyn's Bethany Baptist Church added that "Any attempt to silence voices of dissent is not only morally wrong but in defiance of Christian tradition" and denounced efforts to squelch dissenters as "a prelude to despotism."[38] The clerics presented a declaration signed by over 100 New York clergy that supported the right to protest the government's conduct in Vietnam. It asserted that "To characterize every act of protest as communist-inspired or traitorous is to subvert the very democracy which loyal Americans seek to protect." Noting Jewish objections to the term "churchmen"[39] this group took the name Clergy Concerned About Vietnam. In the years that followed, the maintenance of the American tradition of dissent would be one its most notable successes.

Responding to a reporter's question at the press conference, Rabbi Abraham Heschel, a professor at Jewish Theological Seminary, declared that the group would organize and continue its efforts, a statement that caught Neuhaus by surprise.[40] Clergy Concerned was so encouraged by its success at rallying support for the declaration, however, that it formulated a program under the leadership of Reverend Neuhaus, Rabbi Heschel, and Father Daniel Berrigan, a Jesuit priest, to mobilize opposition to United States intervention in Southeast Asia. Over the next few months, this group of New York clergy sponsored rallies, demonstrations, vigils, pickets, and fasts in the city.

One of the most successful of these early actions occurred in late November when Clergy Concerned invited 5,000 New York–area clerics to a study conference on Vietnam. In calling for the conference, Rabbi Heschel explained, "For many years I felt that the Federal government had all the facts and was competent to make the necessary decisions. But in the last few weeks I have changed my mind completely. I have previously thought that we were waging war reluctantly, with sadness at killing so many people. I realize that we are doing it now with pride in our military efficiency."[41] Several hundred attended the meeting at New York's Methodist Christ Church and passed a resolution declaring that "the conflict in Vietnam, according to our religious convictions, is not a just war."

One glaring omission at the study conference, his absence marked by an empty chair, was Daniel Berrigan. The harassment of Berrigan by the Catholic Church was indicative of the pressures with which antiwar clergy could be subjected. His religious superiors, perhaps at Cardinal Spellman's direction,[42] ordered him to end his association with groups or individuals involved in discussions of the Vietnam War and then sent him on assignment to South America. Two other Jesuits, Francis Keating and Daniel Kilfoyle, were also ordered to remove their names from the list of Clergy Concerned. Heschel and Neuhaus expressed their "sorrow and shock" in a joint statement released when Berrigan was removed as a cochair of the organization. "We find it difficult," they continued, "to appreciate a form of religious authority that is exercised in a manner offensive to our common Jewish and Christian understanding of human dignity. We are also saddened because an injury has been done to the ecumenical character of the conferences' leadership."[43]

Reaction to this apparent exile occurred quickly. In early December, fifty Fordham students picketed Cardinal Spellman's residence and other pickets followed at Marquette, St. John's, and Fordham universities demanding Berrigan's return. The Protestant *Christian Century* bluntly stated, "These actions appear to be a high-handed exercise of ecclesiastical authority to silence priests who champion unpopular views. . . ."[44] In mid-December a Committee for Daniel Berrigan took out a full-page ad in the New York *Times* protesting the priest's transfer to Latin America. *Commonweal* called the move "a shame and a scandal, a disgustingly blind totalitarian act," and several hundred young Jesuits threatened to leave the order if he was not recalled. Finally in mid-February Berrigan was permitted to return to the United States.[45]

Encouraged by the support attracted by the Berrigan incident and their success in local activities, the leadership of the New York clergy recognized the potential for a national organization that would encourage and facilitate religiously motivated efforts to end the war. To discuss the possibility of expanding the New York group nationwide, several clergy met in the apartment of John C. Bennett on January

11, 1966. Among those present were Bennett, Neuhaus, Heschel; Harold Bosley, minister of Christ United Methodist Church; Rabbi Maurice Eisendrath, President of the Union of American Hebrew Congregations (UAHC); Rabbi Balfour Brickner, who directed Interfaith Activities for the UAHC; and Dr. David Hunter, Deputy General Secretary of the National Council of Churches. They decided to ask clergy across the country to mobilize their congregations around support for an indefinite bombing halt and a negotiated settlement. They called themselves a National Emergency Committee of Clergy Concerned About Vietnam.[46]

The committee hoped to augment the national board with about twenty more names, including at least one cardinal. Most of the people they approached were willing to associate with them, but adding a member of the Catholic hierarchy was more difficult. They came close when Richard Cardinal Cushing, archbishop of Boston, originally agreed to join the organization in mid-January, but he withdrew his name a week later.[47]

The Emergency Committee could not be dismissed as an insignificant protest inspired by communists. By late January, it was composed of many of the most prominent religious leaders in the nation. The forty men on the national committee of Clergy Concerned presented an interesting profile of antiwar activists. Most of them, and most antiwar clergy in general, were theological liberals. Not surprisingly, liberal theology and liberal politics were strongly related, just as individuals from a conservative religious tradition tended to hold conservative political views.[48] Theological conservatives emphasized individual salvation, fulfillment in a future life, and the supernatural aspects of God. Liberals placed greater emphasis upon God's presence in the world and believed salvation included social as well as individual transformation.[49]

The 28 Protestants represented a large majority of the national committee. Of those whose denominations are on record, most came from the liberal moderate theologies of the Methodist, Episcopal, Presbyterian, and United Church of Christ bodies. Less than half a dozen belonged to the moderately conservative Lutheran and American Baptist churches. Only one was a member of a fundamentalist group, the Missouri Synod Lutherans.[50] The Protestants in the National Emergency Committee show strong similarities to a sample of Protestant clergy in California studied by Harold Quinley. In that group fundamentalists and conservatives favored military escalation over complete withdrawal by 76 percent to 3 percent and 50 percent to 12 percent respectively, while neo-orthodox and liberals preferred withdrawal over escalation by 30 percent to 15 percent and 42 percent to 8 percent respectively. Methodists and the United Church of Christ held the strongest antiwar views, while the Southern Baptists and Missouri Synod Lutherans were the most ardent supporters of military escalation.[51]

Jews represented the second largest religious group, with seven committee members. Of the five whose faith is on record, three were Reform Jews, the most liberal of the American branches of Judaism, and two were Conservatives. Roman Catholics held the smallest representation on the national committee, with five. The disproportionate number of Jews, large majority of Protestants, and relatively small group of Catholics were roughly in line with public opinion. Jews were much more likely to oppose the war than were Protestants, who opposed the war slightly more than Catholics.[52]

Over half of the national committee members lived in New York City, and nearly three-fourths resided on the eastern seaboard corridor that stretches from Boston to Washington. Five came from the Chicago area and two each lived in St. Louis and the San Francisco area. Only Martin Luther King, Jr. of Atlanta lived in the south. This again reflects a broader trend. Easterners were consistently less likely than people from other regions to endorse escalation of the war.[53]

Gallup polls indicate that people fifty years old and over were generally more supportive of de-escalation in Vietnam than other age groups. By April 1968, a plurality of people fifty and up (43 percent) viewed themselves as doves on the war, even more than did people in their twenties (38 percent). More hawkish than these two groups, although not substantially, were people in their thirties and forties.[54] The age distribution of the National Emergency Committee is the most difficult component to identify. Of those board members whose ages are accessible, nearly half, the average virtually matches the median of fifty. The youngest was 29, the oldest 73. Although the ages of half of the group are not available, the advanced positions that most of them held in educational and denominational hierarchies would indicate that an average near the age of fifty is a reasonable assumption.

Perhaps the most significant aspect of the national board's composite profile is occupation. Overwhelmingly board members fall into one of two categories. Fully three-fourths, almost equally divided, served either as officials of denominational and ecumenical hierarchies or in education. These included several bishops and university faculty, the presidents of two national rabbinical assemblies and three theological seminaries, and key figures in the NCC. Only two other occupations are specifically mentioned, publishing and the ministry. Two men worked as editors, of *Christian Century* and *Christianity and*

Crisis. A third was the former editor of *America.* Five others served on the editorial boards of either *Christian Century* or *Christianity and Crisis,* while two more had served in similar capacities in the past. Altogether one out of every four had strong ties to these independent publications, especially the two Protestant journals. Five of the remaining seven ministered to local parishes, and, although not specifically identified, the other two probably did as well. The positions held by these men indicate a remarkable amount of influence within the religious community and the ability to use that influence without the threat of significant institutional restrictions.

The national board differs from the broader antiwar movement in two crucial areas. While blacks and women opposed the war more than any other segments of the population, the leadership of Clergy Concerned was strictly male and nearly 100 percent white. Otherwise the makeup of the board parallels antiwar public opinion. However, passive public opinion and active participation in the antiwar movement are not necessarily the same. Millions of people who opposed the war never acted. What set the men of the National Emergency Committee apart was that, for most of them, Vietnam was an important stage in a lifetime of active concern for making moral choices in the political world.

Many of the individuals crucial to the development of Clergy Concerned over the following years were with the organization from those earliest days. William Sloane Coffin, a Presbyterian, was probably the most visible of those involved in the committee's daily workings. He entered the United States Army in 1943 where he served in military intelligence and learned to speak Russian. As a Russian liaison officer he was involved in the forced repatriation of Russians to the Soviet Union at the end of the war, an event he remembers as one of the most painful of his life. His view of Christianity was the product of a gradual, thoughtful process which led him to enroll at Union Theological Seminary in 1949. At the outbreak of the Korean War he joined the CIA, where he was eventually used to train Russian volunteers to return to the Soviet Union as spies. Leaving the agency in 1953, he entered Yale Divinity School, where he developed a liberal theology mixed with social activism. In 1958 he accepted the position of chaplain at Yale. While there he participated in the freedom rides through the deep south and other civil rights activities and trained Peace Corps volunteers.[55]

In contrast to Coffin's dashing style, John C. Bennett was quiet and methodical. Born in Canada of American parents in 1902, he earned master's degrees in theology from both Oxford University and Union Theological Seminary. He was ordained in the Congregational church in 1939 and taught as a professor at the Pacific School of Religion for five years. He moved to Union Theological Seminary in 1943, serving as a professor and Dean of Faculty before assuming the position of president of that New York school. Bennett was a strong proponent of the American ecumenical movement and was active in both the World Council of Churches and the National Council of Churches in the USA. He was one of the leaders in the denominational merger that produced the United Church of Christ. As the author of several books, Bennett addressed the important social, political, and economic issues of modern America. He wielded much influence through his duties as president of Union and chair of the editorial board of *Christianity and Crisis,* two positions that earned him a description as "the most important of the early anti-Vietnam voices."[56]

The youngest of the national board members was 29-year-old Richard John Neuhaus. Born a Canadian, he came to the United States in 1950 at age fourteen and later became a naturalized citizen. He received his Master of Divinity degree from Concordia Seminary in St. Louis in 1960 and was ordained in the Lutheran church that same year. In 1961 Neuhaus became the pastor of St. John the Evangelist Church in the Bedford-Stuyvesant district of the Bronx, New York, a position he held throughout the war years. Also deeply involved in the civil rights movement, he was one of the relatively few activists to come out of the conservative theology of the Lutheran Church.[57]

Perhaps the most influential Jewish leader on the National Emergency Committee was Abraham Heschel. Born and raised in Poland, Heschel earned a Ph.D. from the University of Berlin before he was thirty. He fled Germany in 1938, moving to Warsaw and London before arriving in the United States and becoming a citizen in 1943. He taught briefly at Cincinnati's Hebrew Union College before becoming professor of Jewish ethics and mysticism at New York's Jewish Theological Seminary in 1945. A member of the Conservative branch of Judaism and one of the most respected of Jewish writers, he provided the Emergency Committee with its leading prophetic voice.[58]

Rabbi Balfour Brickner was among the most active members of the national board. An articulate speaker, he was responsible for building Christian-Jewish relations for the Union of American Hebrew Congregations, the association of Reform synagogues. Much of his earlier work succeeded in organizing around the southern civil rights movement.[59]

The most visible member of Clergy Concerned on the west coast was Robert McAfee Brown. An Illinois native educated in the east, he was ordained into the Presbyterian church in 1944. After learning of the plight of Polish Jews, Brown abandoned his belief in pacifism and served as a naval chaplain during the end of World War II. After a brief stay as an associate pastor in Massachusetts, he earned a Ph.D. at Columbia and a D.D. from Union Theological Seminary during the 1950s, working under John Bennett and Reinhold Niebuhr. Brown taught at Union for ten years before moving to Stanford University in 1962. By the time the National Emergency Committee was formed, he had already written over half a dozen books and served on the editorial board of *Christianity and Crisis*.[60]

These men along with the rest of the national board set the direction for the National Emergency Committee. One of the primary goals of Clergy Concerned was to encourage the President to move toward a negotiated settlement.[61] Its first step was to try to extend indefinitely the halt in the bombing of North Vietnam announced by Johnson on December 24, 1965. After the January 11 meeting in Bennett's apartment, the committee telegraphed its position to the President. The members expressed their dismay at the war's inhumanity but praised Johnson for his recent efforts at peace. They urged that the bombing halt be maintained, that the President pursue a negotiated settlement that included the National Liberation Front, that he resist further escalation, and that humanitarian aid be given priority over military spending.[62]

Two days later following President Johnson's State of the Union address, the National Emergency Committee sent a telegram supporting his efforts to achieve a negotiated peace and opposing critics who called for escalation and military victory.[63] A third statement on January 18 reiterated the committee's support for negotiations and its opposition to calls for military victory. Clergy Concerned anticipated pressure to escalate if Hanoi did not respond favorably to the bombing pause within a few weeks. Careful to note its respect for the loyalty and courage of U.S. soldiers in Vietnam, the committee argued that, even if military victory could be achieved, it could cause political and moral defeat by destroying the nation America was trying to defend and damaging Vietnam's capacity to maintain its independence from China.[64]

The points of view expressed in these statements identified Clergy Concerned as a moderate peace organization. By advocating a holding action it avoided the extremes of immediate withdrawal and military escalation. Its tactics of petitioning and demonstrating, while offensive to some, were long established methods of expressing grievances. It was not deliberately antiadministration, supporting any positive movement toward negotiations. By rejecting civil disobedience and expressing favorable regard for America's martial capabilities, the National Emergency Committee revealed the limits of its opposition as well as its commitment to reaching the American political center.

To begin building a national network, Coffin as acting executive secretary volunteered to spend a week organizing local chapters in major cities around the country. The National Council of Churches provided a desk at its Interchurch Center on Riverside Drive. Other individuals raised money to install a WATS line for one month or solicited volunteers, including students from Union and the Jewish Theological seminaries. Each person in the committee contributed a list of clergy who might be against the war, including many veterans of the civil rights movement.[65] Working out of the office at night, the volunteers, led by Union student Timothy Light, called all over the country, beginning with Boston on the east coast at 7:00 P.M. and moving west until they reached Anchorage at 2:30 A.M. They followed the same procedure each night for the next two weeks. New people were added to the national committee and local clergy were encouraged to organize in their general areas. As Coffin later explained, "The strategy was to locate by phone two or three clergy in communities in every state, put them in touch with each other, urge them to go to work and ask them to report back in a week what they had done."[66]

The response was enthusiastic. Organizing took place in northern industrial cities such as Philadelphia and Cleveland, in the more conservative areas of Memphis, Wichita, and Austin, in smaller towns like Chapel Hill, North Carolina, and Grinnell, Iowa, and in the state councils of churches in Maine, Vermont, and Delaware. Within days, activities took place in over twenty states. Committees around the country sent telegrams supporting Johnson's bombing pause and passed resolutions opposing escalation. At the University of Chicago, 850 people signed a resolution that called for the inclusion of the NLF in negotiations and submission of the Vietnam issue to the United Nations. Some committees sent letters and telegrams on a weekly or even daily basis. The group in Portland, Oregon, one of several to hold a press conference, received coverage from four television stations, several radio stations, and both Portland daily newspapers. Other groups held public meetings, luncheons, or discussion groups. The Boston committee, for example, invited over 4,000 area clergy to a meeting that featured Bennett as the principal speaker.

Within those first few weeks nearly 165 small local committees were organized. Roughly half of those had initiated some action within the first few months after the National Emergency Committee was formed.[67] One reason for their success was that the Emergency Committee was correctly viewed as a complementary rather than a competing movement. As Robert McAfee Brown recalled, "All of us, in effect, had one foot in CALC and the other foot in our denominational or . . . secular activist groups." Many hoped that Clergy Concerned would prod denominations into action.[68]

To attract support, the national committee had to fight the reluctance of most clergy to become actively involved in social and political matters. The clergy also faced the frequent disapproval of local congregations. In a letter to clerics across the nation, Coffin defended the committee's actions, stressing that peace was a legitimate subject for the clergy to address. Calling the war self-defeating, he urged clerics to oppose the herd mentality and question the morality of the Vietnam War, a cause made no more sacred simply because Americans had died there.[69]

Bennett followed up on that theme three weeks later, defending Clergy Concerned from possible questions related to the violation of the separation of church and state. He disavowed any view of separation that required the removal of Christian ethics from political action. That churches were bringing pressure against the state, he claimed, was evidence that they were separate, not one and the same.[70]

Volunteers staffed the desk in New York for a month, but they failed to realize their initial goals to maintain the bombing halt and prevent further escalation. The resumption of the bombing on January 31, 1966 jolted the National Emergency Committee's hopes. The steering committee of the national office responded by restating its staunch opposition to any escalation of the war. Although "shocked by the intransigence of the Hanoi government" in failing to open negotiations, the committee was disturbed with the American government's refusal to talk with the NLF, its continued troop buildup, and its "self-righteous," misleading claim that the war was solely the result of northern aggression. The committee urged Americans to resist pressures to conform and stressed that true patriotism did not necessitate surrendering individual judgment and conscience.[71]

This declaration encapsulated the basic position of the National Emergency Committee in the spring of 1966. A consensus emerged in a series of articles and official statements from the steering committee. Bennett spoke for many on the committee when he distinguished between his strong support for America's entry into World War II and his opposition to its intervention in Vietnam. His fight against pacifism in the churches in 1941 was based on the belief that Nazism meant permanent slavery for its victims and posed a threat of military conquest that precluded any peaceful relationship. Vietnam was a different type of conflict. Bennett felt communism had the capability of evolving into a more humane system, and since its primary threat was revolutionary rather than military, it was capable of competitive coexistence with its neighbors.[72]

Since the resumption of the bombing, the primary objective of Clergy Concerned was to try to stop further military escalation. The editorial board of *Christianity and Crisis* opposed a military solution and registered its "emphatic protest" against American policies in Vietnam.[73] Central to the organization's support of de-escalation was the war's potential impact on U.S.-Chinese relations. Since military conflict with China had already been provoked during the war in Korea, many felt that a major war in Vietnam would agitate the Chinese into a military response. If the United States truly desired to block Chinese influence in Indochina, this new war made little sense. If Vietnam were threatened with destruction, it would be driven toward China, one of its traditional enemies. In March, the steering committee reiterated its opposition to further escalation and called for an end to the American government's hostile policy toward China.[74]

Equating military victory with moral and political defeat, Clergy Concerned declared that if successful, U.S. policy would require an indefinite occupation. At worst, it could escalate to the use of nuclear weapons. An intensification of the war threatened détente with the Soviet Union, distracted attention from more important domestic and foreign problems, and alienated America's allies while it presented the world with an image of neocolonialism.[75]

Once escalation was stopped, the committee sought a negotiated peace settlement. Clergy Concerned recognized the roles played by North Vietnam and China and welcomed the President's peace initiatives, but it placed much of the responsibility for the absence of negotiations upon the United States. The U.S. government, by insisting that the conflict was initiated by northern aggression against the south, failed to recognize that the struggle was largely a civil war. The American refusal to participate in talks with the NLF and its virtual demand of a Viet Cong surrender made negotiations highly unlikely. The steering committee urged the government to recognize the internal dimensions of the conflict in South Vietnam, include the NLF in any peace talks, and accept arbitration of the entire issue by the United Nations.[76]

The National Emergency Committee cast doubt on the government's credibility on the war by attacking several of its basic assumptions. Bennett denied that a "communist regime is the worst fate that can come to any country" and that Vietnam should be seen as a universal test case for stopping wars of national liberation. He rejected criticisms that experts knew far more about the situation than groups of private citizens and thus would make better decisions. An editorial in *Christianity and Crisis* contested government claims that South Vietnam was a viable political unit and that Asian communism was monolithic. In advocating an alternative to escalation, Bennett stopped well short of a call for immediate withdrawal and urged "a reduction of violence, a negotiated end to the fighting, and a political settlement that does not depend on the defeat of the other side."[77]

The arguments used by Clergy Concerned stressed the practical effects of the war and claimed that American actions were self-defeating. Only occasionally did someone address the war from a moral perspective. At the end of April, Bennett attacked as "morally intolerable" the bombed population centers, poisoned water, and tortured prisoners that were part of the conflict. Even this position was qualified when he admitted that these abuses might be acceptable in a war fought to overcome a greater evil. He claimed, however, that the government had been unable to prove that this was the case.[78]

Through all its criticisms of American policy in Indochina, Clergy Concerned emphasized the antiwar position as being in the nation's best interest. "Do not let the hawks monopolize patriotism," Coffin wrote to the local groups. Distancing the committee from the tactic of direct action, he explained that "As a committee we cannot now call for withholding of income tax or other acts of civil disobedience, but should such acts take place our job should be not to condemn or necessarily condone, but rather to point again to the situation that produced them."[79]

Robert McAfee Brown typified the increasing frustration with "the apparent unwillingness of the Administration to take seriously the voices of dissent." He noted that the earlier protests were ignored and later ones attacked as trivial. He concluded, "I myself am close to the point where I would welcome the emergence of a serious rival to president Johnson in the 1968 campaign . . . unlikely as this may be. . . ."[80]

Individuals and groups occasionally made more demonstrative protests. Speaking just before Vice-President Hubert H. Humphrey at the annual *Christianity and Crisis* dinner, Bennett took advantage of his position to oppose the government's policies in Vietnam.[81] On March 29, Berrigan, recently returned from South America, Neuhaus, and Lloyd Tennenbaum led over sixty people in a two-hour peace march in New York City. They visited Central Synagogue, Christ Church Methodist, the United Nations Church Center, and lastly St. Patrick's Cathedral, where a ten-minute prayer service was believed to be the first interfaith observance in the cathedral's history.[82]

For the next few months, the Emergency Committee sought to educate itself and public opinion by distributing pertinent bibliographies of the Vietnam conflict, holding news conferences, placing ads opposing the war, and conducting letter-writing campaigns. The national office remained loosely organized. Meetings were called on an ad hoc basis, usually by Neuhaus, and in between, Light served as coordinator.[83]

The National Emergency Committee flourished during the first months of 1966. It put together an impressive list of prominent clergy and organized local groups on a national scale. The moderate tone of its opposition to the war was unmistakable. Clergy Concerned claimed for itself a share of the patriotic label, supported President Johnson's peace initiatives, and upheld the traditional American right of dissent. Its members generally argued along pragmatic lines that stressed the government's failure to adequately explain its intervention and the resultant damaged relations with friends and enemies alike. Unlike some within the antiwar coalition, Clergy Concerned advocated neither an immediate withdrawal of U.S. troops from Vietnam nor civil disobedience as a protest tactic. The already evident concern with government misrepresentations, however, foreshadowed a stronger position. In the wake of the President's renewed escalation, the National Emergency Committee began to plan for a longer struggle.

2

TAKING THE MIDDLE GROUND
(MARCH 1966 to SEPTEMBER 1967)

> . . . Peace, peace; when there is no peace.
> —JEREMIAH 6:14 (KING JAMES)

"For generations the image of America has been associated with the defense of human rights and the hope for world peace," wrote Abraham Heschel in 1967. "And now history is sneering at us."[1] This growing perception that America had abandoned its ideals in Vietnam characterized the direction taken by Clergy Concerned through the summer of 1967. The National Emergency Committee grew steadily from the spring of 1966 to mid-1967. It established itself as a permanent organization, developed a formal network of local chapters, sponsored its first national convocation, and encouraged the emergence of further opposition to the war from the Catholic clergy and the leading black spokesman in America. Although maintaining its moderate antiwar position, Clergy Concerned increasingly denounced U.S. policy as immoral and not simply as a mistake.

The National Emergency Committee had originally been established as a temporary lobbying group to take advantage of the bombing pause and push for a negotiated peace. The renewal of the bombing of North Vietnam and mounting pressure from the Joint Chiefs of Staff for expanded military action revealed the vulnerability of such short-term goals. Concerned that the government would gradually escalate the war, the Emergency Committee announced on February 14 that it would remain in existence, and on April 1 it decided to operate for the duration of the war.[2] The uncertainty of the length of its commitment, reflecting both realism and faith in the democratic process, was made painfully clear by its decision to maintain the national office for "at least a year (unless the war ends sooner.)"[3] Clergy Concerned called upon the local groups to remain active and recommended that they organize formally and affiliate with the national committee. The New York office promised to provide information and coordination and urged a continuous stream of letters and telegrams to executive and legislative leaders. The relationship between the national office and local committees remained informal as each group raised its own financial support and decided for itself what actions were most appropriate. Cautious in its approach to middle America, the steering committee carefully noted its public separation even from moderate peace organizations such as the Fellowship of Reconciliation and SANE. It did, however, acknowledge the benefits of cooperation with the antiwar movement and observed that the National Emergency Committee would undoubtedly influence some people in that direction.[4]

Composed of Bennett, Heschel, Coffin, Neuhaus, and Hunter, the steering committee recognized the need for a full-time executive director if the organization was to grow and exert influence nationally. Coffin phoned Richard Fernandez, a friend who only a few weeks earlier had contacted him about finding a job. Fernandez recalled Coffin's job description, spoken only partially in jest: "If you take it you'll never have to worry again about getting another job in a local church."[5] Bennett chaired the august group that made up the interviewing committee. During the questioning, Bennett asked, "If you were trying to convince a group of businessmen to be against the war, how would you go about it?" Fernandez responded, "Well, the last thing I would do is to hand them the editorial that you just wrote in *Christianity and Crisis.*" Despite his cockiness—or perhaps because of it—Fernandez impressed the committee and was hired. After the interview, Bennett remarked, "He's a rough diamond, but he's a diamond all right."[6]

Nothing in Fernandez's career had quite prepared him to head a fledgling national organization. An ordained minister of the United Church of Christ, he had served two years in the United States Army before leaving as a second lieutenant. He graduated from the University of New Hampshire in 1960, then moved on to Andover-Newton Theological School, where he finished in 1964. In 1962–63 he served as the campus minister at Ohio University, and the following year he became director of the Christian Association at the University of Pennsylvania. During the early 1960s, his activities in the civil rights movement earned him an arrest on more than one occasion. He resigned his position at Pennsylvania in the spring of 1966 shortly before Coffin contacted him.[7]

Coinciding with the arrival of Fernandez in May 1966, the steering committee changed the organization's name to Clergy and Laymen Concerned About Vietnam (CALCAV). This change reflected the decision to include laypeople, largely but not entirely because most Catholic opposition came from the laypublic. Despite initial reservations that mixing clergy and laity might not be the most effective way to build, Fernandez took advantage of the expanded recruiting opportunities.[8]

During his first weeks at work, Fernandez spent much of his time organizing the national office, which consisted of a small room at the National Council of Churches building with a part-time secretary. During the next several months, he acquired additional space in the NCC business building at 475 Riverside Drive. The CALCAV office consisted of an open floor with no interior walls and about twenty workers who had to cope with crowded conditions, constant noise, and ringing telephones. Volunteers collected and duplicated antiwar articles, added them to instructions for organizing local groups, and mailed the packets out to the various chapters. All financial contributions to CALCAV were channeled through the NCC as tax deductible donations.[9]

Perhaps the most pressing need was to give CALCAV a broader scope by establishing permanent chapters across the country. At this time a handful of local religious groups had already affiliated with the national organization and provided a base of local support to build upon. Boston's Committee of Religious Concern for Peace, for example, one of CALCAV's oldest and most active chapters, originated in March 1966 after John Bennett spoke to a group of 300 people in nearby Newton, Massachusetts. Draft resistance served as the focus of many of its early activities after a draft resister was beaten by angry bystanders on the steps of the federal courthouse while police watched. The Eliot United Church of Christ of Newton housed CALCAV's office, and its minister, Harold Fray, Jr., chaired the group's executive committee.[10]

From May to November, Fernandez spent a great deal of time traveling to different cities organizing local chapters. "I planned incredible trips" he later recalled, during which he would "get through at nine or ten at night and take a bus to the next [city], go to the Y[MCA], get up and do it again."[11] One such trip lasted seventeen days as he moved up the west coast from San Diego to Seattle, spending a day or two in each of the major cities. His efforts were quite successful. The number of CALCAV chapters rose from 8 in May to 17 in September to 68 by the end of his first year on the job.[12] The prestigious names on the CALCAV letterhead gave him access and credibility that he would not otherwise have had. Fernandez speculated that the ease he found in starting Clergy and Laymen chapters stemmed from the perception among recruits that it was not a new organization to join but was instead "a way of expressing their religious convictions which in the life of their own congregations they couldn't do, or they couldn't do effectively."[13]

Individuals moved into CALCAV for numerous reasons, but for many the decision to join the peace forces followed an experience similar to their religious conversion.[14] "I saw a picture of a Vietnamese child walking with a crutch," explains Ann Arbor's Barbara Fuller of the event that galvanized her to work against the war. "A homemade crutch, head bandaged and crying her heart out. . . . Her face looked just like my six-year-old daughter when she cried, and the world just shrank. . . . All I could think of was, if I were in Vietnam I couldn't protect my children."[15]

The enthusiasm generated in cities across the country was encouraging to the national office, but local workers often encountered difficulties in spreading their message. In Seattle, the antiwar movement divided between the conservative World Without War Council (WWWC) and moderate groups such as CALCAV and the AFSC. The Seattle *Times* covered the WWWC but ignored CALCAV activities, even a speech by Robert McAfee Brown that drew over 500 people. Having spoken to a supportive group of forty at nearby Highlands University, two New Mexico ministers returned to their hometown for a meeting where hawks outnumbered doves six to one.[16]

The process of building CALCAV naturally required some adjustments. In what sometimes seemed to be an endless series of meetings, Fernandez struggled with a cumbersome decision-making process. "I wrestled with these steering committee meetings," he recalled, "where these people would come and talk and talk and I couldn't figure out, God why do they come to these meetings, I mean I find them boring . . . half the time we don't make decisions, other times we vacillate on this and that, and Balfour [Brickner] would say . . . 'these people are working in other areas [and] this is the one time a month where they feel they can make a considered contribution to stopping a war they hate. . . . It may at times sound clubby, and other times you're not quite sure what came out of the meeting, . . . [but] for their participation, this is one of the prices.' "[17]

In spite of such problems, antiwar activity drew people closer together. The intense concentration of activists focusing on the war produced a strong sense of community among people who at first did not know each other well.

While Fernandez was preoccupied with building the national structure, activities in the New York area continued on a limited basis. Neuhaus, Heschel, and Daniel Berrigan led about 150 people in a two-day fast over the Fourth of July holiday. Neuhaus described the fast, held at the Community Church on Park Avenue, as "a call for repentance, to turn away from the madness that we see at least in the Administration's determination for a military victory." Heschel claimed that America had been "enticed by her own might," and added, "there is nothing so vile as the arrogance of the military mind." The committee reiterated its position: an end to the bombing of North Vietnam; immediate de-escalation of the war; and negotiations with all concerned parties, including the Viet Cong.[18]

That same month, after American bombs were dropped within three miles of Hanoi, Bennett again criticized the administration's expressed unwillingness to open unconditional negotiation. "An air of unreality has always pervaded our talk of negotiations. . . . we did in effect insist on the surrender of the Vietcong. . . . The escalation of the war in Vietnam," he added, "makes it difficult to be an American."[19]

Bennett's personal dilemma between love for his nation and disgust over its policies typified the feelings of many other national committee members. The growing belief within CALCAV was that military escalation in Vietnam and verbal attacks on war protesters at home indicated that the U.S. government was not genuinely interested in seeking a political solution to the war, despite statements to the contrary. Reinhold Niebuhr, a dedicated cold war liberal, confessed in the spring of 1966 that "For the first time I fear I am ashamed of our beloved nation."[20] "Six months ago," Fernandez wrote in September, "most of us would have said that some very good men in Washington had made some very bad mistakes from which they should try to extricate themselves as soon as possible. Today it seems that this kind of judgment is both out of date and inaccurate." The administration's apparent deception of the public led to a growing erosion of trust in the government for many Americans, including those in CALCAV. For many this loss of faith indicated that the war could be prolonged indefinitely. "The war," Fernandez noted, "is not going to end quickly."[21]

The growing urgency shown by CALCAV occurred as established religious institutions paid increasing attention to the war. Vietnam Christian Service, a cooperative effort by Lutheran World Relief, the NCC's Church World Service, and the Mennonite Central Committee supplemented U.S. government aid to refugees. The Central Conference of American Rabbis attacked American military policy and wanted pressure on the South Vietnamese government to hold its promised fall elections. The United Church of Christ's social action agency referred to the bombing near Hanoi and Haiphong as "intolerable," and urged negotiation and resistance to further escalation. Calling for an American bombing halt and negotiation, the Methodist Board of Christian Social Concerns also supported the right of dissent, a position shared by the Disciples of Christ. At their annual assembly, the Disciples suggested legal status for selective conscientious objection but avoided a firm position on the war.[22]

Most official pronouncements were more congratulatory than the mild criticism of these statements. The National Conference of Catholic Bishops affirmed its acceptance of U.S. policies, while the Episcopal House of Bishops commended the American government for its attempt to negotiate. American Baptists pushed for continued pursuit of a just and peaceful settlement. At its convention, the Lutheran Church in America passed a resolution that opposed both escalation and unilateral withdrawal and amended it to include a warning not to underestimate the threat of international communism.[23]

As the religious community exercised a cautious approach throughout 1966, Richard Fernandez began to investigate the possibility of cooperation with the antiwar movement at large. He represented CALCAV at an invitational antiwar conference called by the Cleveland-based University Teach-In Committee. Held in Cleveland in late July, this gathering of fifteen moderate organizations was designed to eliminate wasted energy and duplication of effort by coordinating events nationally. After holding preliminary discussions, a larger group reconvened in mid-September. Overcoming their differences, the various organizations formed a temporary coalition, the November 5–8 Mobilization Committee, to coordinate local antiwar actions prior to the fall elections. A. J. Muste, whose strong support helped make the coalition possible, was named chair, while Fernandez served as treasurer.[24]

A third Cleveland conference on November 26 drew 180 delegates to evaluate the earlier demonstrations. Despite the continued debate over the desirability and effectiveness of mass demonstrations, the participants agreed to preserve the coalition. Retaining Muste as chair, the delegates established the Spring Mobilization Committee to End the War in Vietnam (Spring Mobe) as an umbrella agency for all groups opposing the war. To keep the various factions from moving in different directions, the coalition scheduled new national actions at New York and San Francisco for April 15, 1967. Organizing in late December as a separate body was the Student Mobilization Committee to End the War in Vietnam (SMC). The Student Mobe supported the April 15 demonstrations but focused on issues such as the draft that were especially important to the college community.[25]

While Fernandez continued his involvement with the mobilization, CALCAV's steering committee remained cautious about becoming too closely identified with the larger movement. At Bennett's suggestion, Fernandez kept his name from being publicly linked with the Spring Mobe, reasoning that CALCAV's primary constituency might perceive it as too far to the left.[26] Fernandez felt the Cleveland meetings served a useful purpose, but he was not particularly impressed with their achievements. Having been raised on cold war platitudes like most Americans, however, he found them to be learning experiences. Shortly after the second Cleveland gathering, he wrote, "Some of the Communists who spoke at the meeting were a heck of a lot more relevant than I ever thought they might be. . . ."[27]

The national executive committee of CALCAV voted not to endorse the April 15 demonstrations, believing that the presence of radical pacifists and others who favored isolationism would not change American military policy in Vietnam or appeal to the majority of the American public. However, the national office did urge members to participate as individuals if they so desired. Many did.[28] Fernandez personally supported the Spring Mobe and worked to modify its position so that CALCAV could endorse the national action. In the end, he failed, largely because of a lack of support from Mobe administrators. The differences are revealed in a conversation between James Bevel, national director of the Spring Mobilization Committee, and Bennett as recalled by Fernandez: "Bevel called up Bennett and said, 'Do you know my brother died today in Vietnam?' Of course, John, being a rather pragmatic type, took this at face value and began to pity poor Mr. Bevel. As it turned out, Mr. Bevel was of course referring to all of his brothers who died that day in Vietnam and there wasn't very much personal content in that remark."[29]

CALCAV remained very concerned about its moderate image, and repeatedly stressed that it was not connected to radical, pacifist, or traditional peace organizations.[30] This was, of course, true. In responding to a proposal to smuggle prominent Americans into U.S. bombing targets in North Vietnam to force a halt to the bombing, Fernandez described CALCAV's position: "I am caught in the middle of some very thoughtful and courageous clergy who have yet to become radicals in the true sense of that word. I must confess, in all honesty, that I have not yet obtained that particular goal either."[31]

CALCAV's image consciousness was well founded. The emergence of nearly 100 antiwar candidates in the fall elections and a voter referendum in Dearborn, Michigan that revealed surprising popularity for a U.S. withdrawal from Vietnam[32] were still exceptions to the rule. The antiwar movement continued to be the victim of a constant stream of criticism and harassment from the government, news media, and prowar groups. This vehement response from institutions that seemed impervious to antiwar arguments sometimes frustrated and discouraged activists. Despite these occasional setbacks, however, the movement continued to endure and even thrive. As the venerable A. J. Muste asked, "Did we really think the job would be easy and attained at a modest price?"[33]

Having chosen to remain formally independent of the antiwar coalition, CALCAV considered holding its own national gathering. In December the executive committee made a momentous decision, calling "American clergymen of all faiths" to meet in Washington, D.C. for two days beginning January 31, 1967. Growing out of earlier discussions, this mobilization of the religious community would give CALCAV the opportunity to meet the heads of social action groups of the various denominations and to educate clergy in more effective methods of pressuring politicians and raising a significant protest against the war.[34] In bringing antiwar clergy together from across the country, CALCAV hoped to provide the participants with mutual support and furnish policymakers with evidence of a substantial opposition to the war in the American religious community. By ending what they saw as the silence of the churches, national leaders hoped to spark further antiwar activity on the local level.

CALCAV established contacts in about seventy cities to publicize the mobilization and to arrange transportation in their areas. It solicited local and national organizations to help distribute over 20,000 pieces of direct mail. Some of the AFSC regional peace secretaries encouraged local clergy to attend, and SANE sent out a letter supporting the convocation.[35]

To try to present an ecumenical front, CALCAV spent several weeks before the mobilization attempting to attract at least one Roman Catholic bishop or cardinal. It conferred with a number of bishops who were considered most likely to attend. Bishop John J. Wright of Pittsburgh seemed the best hope, but after a week of discussions, he decided not to come. With only four or five days left before the mobilization, the executive committee sent overnight letters to all 250 bishops in the United States urging their approval and participation. Only about a dozen responded, a few of them in very "hawkish" terms, Fernandez noted, and none was willing or able to attend.[36]

At least some CALCAV leaders viewed the success of the mobilization as critical to the survival of the organization. With the difficulty in trying to build a national network plus ongoing financial problems, a national conference that failed to draw a significant number of clergy might be too much to overcome. As Gerhard Elston later put it, "If it had snowed, that would have been the end of CALC."[37]

While Fernandez and a number of volunteers made arrangements for housing and feeding the participants and scheduled visits with congressional and administrative officials, members of the executive committee assembled to write an official statement. Robert McAfee Brown took the collective ideas and produced a rough draft overnight. After further discussions the next day, he revised and finished the official position paper, which eloquently summarized the major points made over the previous months. Entitled "The Religious Community and the War in Vietnam," it began solemnly:

> A time comes when silence is betrayal. That time has come for us in relation to Vietnam.
>
> Our allegiance to our nation is held under a higher allegiance to the God who is sovereign over all nations. . . . Each day we find allegiance to our nation's policy more difficult to reconcile with allegiance to our God.
>
> Both the exercise of faith and the expression of the democratic privilege oblige us to make our voices heard. . . . and we speak out of a loyalty that refuses to condone in silence a national policy that is leading our world toward disaster.
>
> We are unable to support our nation's policy of military escalation, and we find those to whom we minister caught as we are in confusion and anguish because of it.[38]

The clerics' opposition to the war stemmed from the immorality of the conflict, the inconsistency between the government's stated aims and the consequences of its policies, and the discrepancy between what the public was told by the government and what it discovered to be actually taking place. Brown listed two realistic alternatives: a long, bitter war that the United States might win militarily but at a price so terrible as to negate its victory; or immediate pursuit of a negotiated peace that would have no clear winner or loser. Brown believed that, given the choice, the American people would choose negotiation and that "the risks involved in such a choice are well worth taking." To achieve successful negotiations, however, certain preconditions were necessary. These included assurance from the American government of a genuine willingness to negotiate; an unconditional bombing halt in North Vietnam; acceptance of the National Liberation Front as a partner in the peace talks; and pursuit of the full cooperation of international agencies, especially the United Nations, to aid American withdrawal. The position paper urged both the United States and North Vietnam to show greater concern for prisoners of war and to provide greater relief for victims of the bombings. It also argued that Vietnam be allowed to settle its own disputes. "We must not seek to export the American way of life," it went on, "or impose an alien culture on the Vietnamese. . . . We know that millions of Americans share the anguish we express. . . ."[39] CALCAV mailed out nearly 50,000 copies of this statement in the three months following the mobilization.[40]

Upon arriving in Washington, the participants assembled at the New York Avenue Presbyterian Church, which served as headquarters. Kyle Haselden, editor of *Christian Century,* described the mood as things got under way:

> At the beginning of this mobilization the basement and halls of the New York Avenue Presbyterian Church . . . were cluttered with bedrolls, sleeping bags, box lunches and general bedlam. But the confusion was organizational, physical, external; the participants, so far as their main objective was concerned, were not confused. They knew why they were here, what they wanted to say to their government and what they needed to learn from each other if they are to arouse a lethargic or fatalistic nation and divert it from a tragic course in southeast Asia. Almost immediately, I sensed an underlying unity of purpose and resolution, a common commitment and a steady current of practical wisdom about Vietnam deeper than any presently flowing through the White House, the state department or the Pentagon. In this assembly there was no wishful thinking, no wistfulness, no impractical idealism, no naiveté. Rather, there was more tough common sense on Vietnam than Washington has been exposed to in many a month.[41]

After some opening remarks and a briefing on how to conduct visits with members of Congress, nearly 2,000 participants gathered at the White House shortly after noon. The religious vigil went on for nearly an hour as the crowd stretched out along Pennsylvania Avenue in a slow-moving circle on the sidewalk in front of the White House. The silent demonstration was devoid of the singing and chanting, even the signs and placards that usually accompanied public protests. CALCAV officials believed that public marches should try to persuade those watching, either in person or through the news media, of the correctness of their point of view on the war. To accomplish this, the marchers were asked to be orderly, to ignore any counterdemonstrators, and to remain silent during the march itself.[42] Protest leaders delivered a copy of CALCAV's position paper to William Jorden, an aide to National Security Adviser Walt Rostow.

The vigil at the White House attracted some minor opposition. Carl McIntire, a defrocked Presbyterian minister who headed the

American Council of Christian Churches, led about 100 counter-demonstrators who marched nearby carrying signs with messages such as, "Unleash Chiang" and "Fight to Win in Vietnam."[43] McIntire's group also picketed other meetings and services during the two-day mobilization.

Shortly after 1:00 P.M., the CALCAV demonstrators walked to the Capitol to lobby their representatives. Each state at the mobilization had a delegation that tried to meet with its elected officials. Their receptions varied from cordiality and patience to the command of Senator Everett Dirksen (R-Ill.) to "hush up!" Senator J. William Fulbright (D-Ark.), whose criticism of the President's Vietnam policies was well known, seemed genuinely pleased to be visited by over 150 persons in the Senate Foreign Relations Committee Office. The impact of the lobbying was revealing to the clergy, however. Many concluded that "most of the congressmen feel powerless to determine the direction in which the nation will go. . . ."[44] Having surrendered much of their authority with the passage of the Gulf of Tonkin Resolution, they seemed unable to apply any effective leverage on policies in Indochina.

That evening the conference participants joined for a meal of reconciliation of rice and tea and collected an offering to benefit a new refugee program established by the Fellowship of Reconciliation. Following the meal, a service of witness featured meditations by Brown and Heschel, addresses on the dilemma of the clergy by Coffin, John Cronin, and Jacob Weinstein, and prayers from George Docherty, Paul Moore, Jr., and Donald Campion. Rabbi Heschel expressed the underlying reason that members of the religious community were assembled. "In a free society," he pointed out, "some are guilty but all are responsible." Coffin attested to the value of the mobilization as he remembered the tremendous sense of togetherness: "Now instead of feeling alone and isolated, we were all together in the church. . . ."[45]

The still uncommon experience of interfaith meetings deeply affected many of the participants. "Nothing was said about it," Haselden observed, "perhaps nothing was thought about it—but Roman Catholics, Jews and numerous varieties of Protestants sang, prayed and worshiped together in penitence, in shared suffering and in a common commitment to peace. Unity on this occasion was no designed formality; it was a vital experience."[46]

On the following day, after a morning worship service, the group spent three hours in workshops to develop policies and tactics in presenting the Vietnam issue to local religious congregations, communities, and public officials. The closing session of the mobilization began just after noon, and the sanctuary of the New York Avenue Presbyterian Church was packed with people lining the walls and sitting on floors. Three senators delivered the addresses. Wayne Morse (D-Ore.) denounced the war as immoral, illegal, unjustifiable, and needlessly prolonged. Ernest Gruening (D-Alaska) agreed: "There is no justification for our being in Vietnam and no good will come of it. Any way out would be an improvement over what we are doing." Eugene McCarthy (D-Minn.) was less outspoken than his colleagues but received a standing ovation for his concluding remark, "We must be prepared to pass a harsh moral judgment on our nation's commitment."[47]

CALCAV's association with the American religious mainstream earned it greater respect in the Johnson administration than most other groups in the antiwar movement. It was even able to gain access to highly placed officials within the executive branch. On the afternoon of February 1, a group of clergy including Dana McLean Greeley, Harold Fray, James Miller, Robert Reed, and Hugh Anwyl met with Rostow and White House staffer Douglass Cater.[48] In discussing whether or not to receive the CALCAV delegation, William Jorden noted that the mobilization involved "leading church figures and theologians, not irresponsible agitators." CALCAV's reception by government officials, however, was based less on a desire to debate issues or share information than to placate public opinion. Jorden further noted: "The gathering here this week will attract some attention. On balance, it would seem desirable for you to see them, particularly since they are a responsible element. To ignore them might hurt our public relations."[49]

On February 2, Secretary of Defense Robert McNamara met with Bennett, Coffin, Brown, Heschel, Neuhaus, Rabbi Jacob Weinstein, President of the Central Conference of American Rabbis, and Catholic layman Michael Novak. In an off-the-record meeting that afternoon, Coffin had barely finished summarizing the contents of Brown's position paper when Rabbi Heschel erupted in an emotional speech that revealed his deep anguish over the war. McNamara heard him out and replied that he was doing his best to use restraint in conducting the war, but if the other side would not negotiate, pressure to escalate would mount. Once outside the clerics agreed that "it was a dangerous world when so much evil could be done by a man who was really a 'nice guy.' "[50]

Though government officials frustrated CALCAV leaders, the antiwar movement concerned the Johnson administration. The President feared that it strengthened Hanoi's diplomatic resolve and influenced public and foreign opinion. To avoid losing his political consensus, Johnson counterattacked by combining conciliatory public moves with secret efforts to undermine the antiwar forces. As historian Melvin Small indicates, the executive branch designed its occasional bombing halts to placate dovish political opponents as well as to solicit a response from North Vietnam. These actions failed to stop a growing number of defections from key constituencies, including organized religion. The administration wanted badly to maintain support among the mainline denominations and the National Council of Churches.[51]

The organizers considered the mobilization a success, gauged by the nearly 2,500 people from 47 states and Canada that attended.[52] It broke down the feeling of isolation many activists felt in their own communities, taught them practical strategies for local organizing, and gave them a renewed confidence in working as part of a national effort. The mobilization also made a positive impression upon dovish members of Congress. Senator McCarthy later referred to it as "the most significant early protest" against the war because of its broad religious and geographical representation. Lobbying established a visible constituency within the social mainstream that served antiwar legislators as a political base from which to build further opposition to Johnson's Vietnam policy. The news coverage given in the major media centers conveyed that fact to the general public.[53]

The mobilization resulted in the establishment of ten to fifteen new chapters. Californians from Palo Alto took CALCAV's position paper home and within two months had used it to start discussion groups on the Vietnam War in more than fifteen area churches. More than sixty Minnesotans returned from Washington and established a state affiliate centered in Minneapolis. Minnesota became one of CALCAV's strongest chapters and was among the first to hire full-time staff personnel. A small group of Buffalo clergy put together a temporary steering committee that sponsored a citywide fast for peace and followed with a debate between William Sloane Coffin and a member of the State Department that drew nearly 1,000 people.[54]

To capitalize on this momentum, the national office encouraged a second national action suggested by laymembers of the Berea Presbyterian Church in St. Louis, a three-day "Fast for the Rebirth of Compassion." Organizers hoped to draw attention to the victims of the war and to their call for a peace without victory. They specifically urged a halt to the bombing of North Vietnam and a decrease in the ground actions to create a better climate for peace talks. Participants took only fruit juice and water or a small amount of tea and rice from February 8 to 10, which coincided with the lunar New Year ceasefire in Vietnam and the beginning of Lent. Carl S. Dudley, 34-year-old pastor of the St. Louis Berea Church and coordinator of the fast, estimated that one million people in 412 cities and 37 states took part in some way.[55]

In the wake of the mobilization, the representatives of the Catholic hierarchy that CALCAV had tried to get to Washington finally began to speak out. At a CALCAV-sponsored ecumenical study conference during the first week of March on "Vietnam and the Religious Conscience," Archbishop Paul J. Hallinan of Atlanta affirmed that "Our conscience and our voice must be raised against the savagery and terror or war." The *Christian Century,* which reported on the conference, spoke bluntly on the issue of Catholic participation. "The address was fortunately timed," it editorialized, "since Protestants and Jews had begun to wonder—indeed, to complain—about the silence of high level Roman Catholic clergy in the debate on the morality of the armed conflict in Vietnam."[56]

Less than two weeks later, Auxiliary Bishop James P. Shannon of St. Paul–Minneapolis joined ten Roman Catholic college presidents in endorsing an open letter to American Catholics. The signees called for a "reassessment of American involvement in Vietnam" and noted the incongruity between "the moral principles enunciated by the Church and the uncritical support of this war by so many Catholics." They expressed reservations about the indiscriminate bombing of civilians, the human misery caused by napalm and fragmentation bombs, the crop destruction which deprived the population of food, and the torture of prisoners. Despite its moderate tone, the letter marked a significant departure from a statement released by the U.S. Conference of Catholic Bishops the preceding November that had supported American policy in Vietnam.[57]

Shannon would become one of the leading Roman Catholic voices within CALCAV. He had been the only bishop to march with Martin Luther King, Jr. at Selma, and his criticism of America's Vietnam policies again placed him well ahead of the U.S. Catholic hierarchy on this issue. Until his controversial resignation and marriage in 1969, he was highly regarded, enjoying, as John Sheerin wrote, "a unique prestige in the Catholic Church in America. . . . It can be said of him, in a way that it cannot be said of any other American bishop, that he is the hope of the future."[58]

Father John B. Sheerin, editor of *Catholic World,* would also become one of the most prominent Catholic voices within CALCAV. The previous year he had chastised his fellow believers for their silence on the war. "The great majority of American Catholics," he wrote in March 1966, "seem to have no particular moral convictions with regard to the war in Vietnam. Is it not strange that so many of our clergy who have no hesitation about making positive moral judgments week after week in confession have no opinions on the great moral problem of our generation?"[59] Sheerin provided a more consistently moral appraisal of the war earlier than most other clerics. He found the conflict unsupportable when judged by the traditional Catholic doctrine of the "just war." This doctrine demanded that an acceptable war be defensive and fought for a moral reason, but Sheerin questioned claims of an invasion by North Vietnamese that served as an extension of Chinese policy. Saving American prestige or stopping Chinese expansion were not adequate reasons for going to war. He doubted American adherence to natural and international law and questioned whether even a U.S. victory would outweigh the negative consequences of the war. He concluded that "the morality of our involvement in Vietnam is very doubtful" and opposed any form of escalation. He did not advocate immediate withdrawal, fearing that could lead to even greater problems, but declared that "all American citizens, but especially all who profess to be Christians, should reaffirm their demands for negotiations and for cessation of this seemingly interminable slaughter in Asia."[60] The following month he advocated representation for the NLF at any peace negotiations.[61]

Nevertheless, Catholics remained relatively quiet on Vietnam, and antiwar statements such as these continued to be exceptions. Even Sheerin, who in April 1967 reiterated his call for greater Catholic concern for peace, remained very cautious in his approach. This was evident in his continued support for President Johnson and his preference for study groups over antiwar protests, since "most peace demonstrations seem to attract bearded beatniks whose presence does a disservice to the cause."[62] This hesitation on the part of Catholics moved Fernandez himself to note that "we have had substantial trouble in our relationships with Roman Catholics at almost every level except local parish priests."[63]

Despite barriers such as these and resistance from a hostile or apathetic public, activists remained determined to voice their opposition and work for an end to the war. Fernandez captured this spirit. "I find in my own mind," he confessed to an acquaintance, "no real pragmatic answer to your question—how do we keep from getting frustrated—because I don't see any termination to the war. On the other hand, it is my judgment that we must persevere no matter what the odds against us."[64] He was convinced CALCAV filled an essential role within the religious community. Later that summer, he wrote enthusiastically to Tim Light in Hong Kong, "The work of our committee continues to grow and expand at a rate that even I, in my wildest dreams, did not think possible."[65]

Antiwar forces achieved some impressive gains in the spring of 1967. Among the most significant was Martin Luther King, Jr.'s unqualified support for the movement. King had spoken out against the war as early as July 1965, but turned cautious when moderate civil rights leaders criticized him for risking the loss of the support of the Johnson administration. As the years went by and civil rights programs were postponed because of the attention and funds diverted to the war, however, King saw a relationship between ending the war and refocusing on the problems of black Americans. By the middle of 1966, he was making carefully chosen references to Vietnam in his civil rights speeches, and even these guarded criticisms cost him the favor of President Johnson.[66]

Finally, on February 25, 1967 at the *Nation* Institute held in the Beverly Hills Hilton, King delivered his first speech devoted entirely to Vietnam, "one of history's most cruel and senseless wars." Much of his opposition to the war stemmed from its perceived effects on the War on Poverty. "The promises of the Great Society have been shot down on the battlefields of Vietnam," he declared. Noting American violations of the United Nations Charter and the principle of self-determination, he warned of the threat to America's traditional right to dissent. He observed "an ugly repressive sentiment to silence peace-seekers" that identified supporters of negotiations and bombing halts as "quasi-traitors, fools, and venal enemies of our soldiers and our institutions" and threatened to make free speech one of the war's major casualties. He also described his goals for a better America:

> I oppose the war in Vietnam because I love America. I speak out against it not in anger but with anxiety and sorrow in my heart, and above all with a passionate desire to see our beloved country stand as the moral example of the world. . . . We must combine the fervor of the civil rights movement with the peace movement. We must demonstrate, teach and preach, until the very foundations of our nation are shaken.[67]

At that time King was under pressure from Bevel and the Spring Mobilization Committee to serve as the keynote speaker at their April 15 rally at the United Nation's building. Because of the participation of radicals and leftist groups, nearly all King's advisers opposed his appearance, fearing that his identification with communists might destroy the civil rights movement. King decided to attend the demonstration. To clarify his position on the war and to assure his constituents of his independence of the far left, however, he approached CALCAV about speaking at Riverside Church in advance of the Spring Mobilization demonstration. To protect King, Andrew Young,

Fernandez, Heschel, and Coffin agreed to surround him with other speakers that no one could possibly associate with communist influence.[68]

The speech that King delivered at Riverside was written by Young in Atlanta and Allard Lowenstein in New York and edited by Fernandez and Fred Sontag, a publicist hired by CALCAV especially for this event. Sontag made sure that the newspapers had advance copies of the speech.[69]

King's address at Riverside Church in New York City was given on April 4. Sharing the platform with him that evening were Bennett, Heschel, and Amherst College historian Henry Steele Commager, but it was King's presence that turned the gathering of over 3,000 people into a major news event.

A standing ovation greeted King that night when he rose to speak. Noting the personal struggle that had been required to "break the betrayal of my own silences," he defended his public concern with the war. Stressing what he saw as an obvious connection between the civil rights struggle and the war in Vietnam, he used as examples the abandonment of the poverty program and the disproportionately high number of blacks who were fighting and dying in the war. King found it ironic that black Americans were being asked to guarantee liberties in Vietnam that were not available to them in the United States. Whites and blacks could kill and die together but could not live or be educated together.[70]

King's commitment to nonviolence was well known and had led him to speak against the rioting and destruction that occurred in black ghettos during the "long, hot summers" of the mid-1960s. His silence on the war, however, had made him feel inconsistent. In perhaps the most quoted line of his speech, King declared, "I knew that I could never again raise my voice against the violence of the oppressed in the ghettos without having first spoken clearly to the greatest purveyor of violence in the world today—my own government."[71]

Martin Luther King's opposition to the war was, of course, rooted in his position as a Christian minister, a position where a deep concern for peace should be so natural that "I sometimes marvel at those who ask me why I am speaking against the war." To King, the Christian commitment went deeper than the goals and positions of any single nation or political system. Because of this higher loyalty, Christians were "called to speak for the weak, for the voiceless, for victims of our nation and for those it calls enemy, for no document from human hands can make these humans any less our brothers."[72]

"They must see Americans as strange liberators," King stated as he recounted the history of American involvement in Vietnam. He wondered aloud how the National Liberation Front and North Vietnam must think of America's accusations of violence and aggression in the face of its unmatched destructive capacity, and how they must view America's halfhearted attempts to open negotiations. "Somehow this madness must cease," he declared. "The great initiative in this war is ours. The initiative to stop it must be ours."

King suggested five steps the United States should take to begin "extricating ourselves from this nightmarish conflict." These included an end to the bombing of both North and South Vietnam, a unilateral cease-fire to create an atmosphere for negotiation, the curtailment of military interference in Thailand and Laos, acceptance of the NLF as a partner in any future Vietnam government, and a specific date for the removal of all foreign troops from Vietnam in accordance with the 1954 Geneva Agreement. For Vietnamese who feared for their safety under a new regime that included the NLF, King suggested granting them asylum and urged reparations for the damage done in Vietnam. To "all who find the American course in Vietnam a dishonorable and unjust one," he recommended conscientious objection.

To King, the Vietnam conflict was only one symptom of deeper problems in American society, and he concluded with a call for action: "Now let us re-dedicate ourselves to the long and bitter—but beautiful—struggle for a new world. . . . The choice is ours, and though we might prefer it otherwise we must choose in this crucial moment of human history."[73]

According to author Thomas Powers, King's Riverside speech marked "a kind of turning point in the country's attitude toward the war."[74] Though not by itself responsible for turning around public opinion, it added respectability to the movement and helped to legitimize dissent against the war. The CALCAV leaders were especially enthusiastic. Fernandez referred to it as the most important antiwar endorsement the movement had received to that point, calling the attack on the war by the nation's leading black voice "a sledgehammer against the side of the administration."[75] The executive committee offered King the position of cochair of the organization, a position he accepted on April 11, and it distributed over 100,000 copies of a 35-page booklet containing the Riverside speeches.[76]

Outside the antiwar movement, the most common response to King's Riverside address was stinging criticism. With rare exceptions, the national press rebuked his "slanderous rhetoric" and "bitter and damaging allegations." Individually, critics in the media opposed his call to boycott the war, and denied the validity of linking the civil rights and antiwar movements. The New York *Times* accused him of whitewashing Hanoi, while the Chicago *Tribune* blasted him for taking "the communist side in the war in Viet Nam."[77] It was not surprising that members of Congress or the FBI would be brutal in their attacks. FBI documents in fact referred to him as "a traitor to his country and to his race." With some notable exceptions such as Stokely Carmichael, many of the nation's black leaders disagreed with him publicly, including Carl Rowan, Ralph Bunche, Roy Wilkins, Edward Brooke, and Whitney Young. On April 12, the national board of the NAACP unanimously rejected any effort to fuse the civil rights and antiwar movements.[78]

While this debate continued, the April 15 demonstrations sponsored by the Spring Mobilization Committee took place in New York and San Francisco. The demonstrations were endorsed by a broad coalition of peace and multi-issue organizations, but typically, a shared opposition to the war would only do so much to unify the diverse points of view. For different reasons, both national SANE and the Progressive Labor Party refused to endorse the events, although local chapters did participate. SDS also hesitated, but finally approved the protest on April 5.[79]

King's follow-up speech at the April 15 rally was relatively lackluster. Compared to the moderate position of most clerical activists, the anti-American rhetoric of some radicals made him uncomfortable.[80] King's reservations aside, the April 15 rallies were enormously successful. An estimated 400,000 people made the New York march from Central Park to the United Nations, and the rally in San Francisco drew about 75,000. In New York, protesters burned between 150 and 200 draft cards in a significant act that demonstrated the willingness of some to move "from protest to resistance." Because many groups within the coalition were unwilling to support such acts of civil disobedience, organizers did not list this particular action as an official part of the mobilization.[81]

During the summer of 1967, various factions of the antiwar movement opened two major new initiatives. A coalition of liberals headed by Normal Cousins of SANE, Joseph Rauh, Jr. of Americans for Democratic Action (ADA), Victor Reuther of the United Auto Workers, John Kenneth Galbraith, and Arthur Schlesinger, Jr. established a program called Negotiation Now. Its tactical approach was to place ads and petitions in major newspapers to support congressional doves. To end the war, it proposed that the United States initiate a halt to the bombing of North Vietnam followed by a multilateral cease-fire. In general, liberals opposed immediate withdrawal and nonexclusion of communists, and remained independent of the National Mobilization Committee. Though this cautious approach held little appeal for radicals, Negotiation Now did attract support from moderates, including a number of religiously oriented groups.[82]

The second new project was Vietnam Summer. Organized by Boston-area activists, it was an ambitious attempt to recreate the activism of Freedom Summer but with the war as the focal point instead of civil rights. King and Dr. Benjamin Spock announced Vietnam Summer at a Boston press conference on April 23. With a budget of several hundred thousand dollars, organizers hoped to recruit 10,000 volunteers and 2,000 full-time workers to educate and organize within their own communities and develop a grassroots political base for the elections in 1968. In this way they hoped to pressure the Johnson administration to de-escalate the war, negotiate, and eventually withdraw American military forces from Vietnam.[83]

Clergy and Laymen Concerned had especially strong ties to Vietnam Summer since Fernandez served as one of its codirectors, and local CALCAV chapters frequently spearheaded organizing efforts in their communities. Other supporting organizations included SANE, SDS, the Student Nonviolent Coordinating Committee (SNCC), and the Southern Christian Leadership Conference (SCLC). Volunteers canvassed local neighborhoods, staffed draft counseling programs, and conducted speaking tours. Teachers in Boston, Baltimore, and Madison developed curricula dealing with the war for use in the schools, focusing on dissent in American history, literature on Southeast Asia, and a socioeconomic history of Vietnam. Draft counselors and public speakers sought access to schools to counter military recruiters there. Vietnam Summer reached many people who had previously felt isolated in their opposition to the war.[84]

The thrust toward a highly coordinated national work based on community organizing in middle-class areas impressed Fernandez as being the key to the future effectiveness of the movement. His work in Vietnam Summer would spur a similar effort within CALCAV. Although satisfied that the project was helpful to the peace movement, Fernandez believed that it could have accomplished a great deal more. Like Negotiation Now, Vietnam Summer appealed primarily to the moderate and liberal segments of the movement. Many radical groups, such as the Socialist Workers Party, opposed the emphasis on liberal electoral politics and pushed their own programs. Ideological competition within the national office bothered Fernandez, who commented that "this sometimes nearly pathological but more often juvenile way of responding to people and organizations left an old fogey like myself always gasping for air, wondering who was safe from criticism or above reproach beyond the national staff members themselves."[85] The inability of the entire coalition to work together left a promising idea unrealized, a situation that caused Gerhard Elston to recall wistfully: "Vietnam Summer could have turned the country around if it hadn't been split, I'm still convinced of that."[86]

The nation may not have turned around completely in 1967, but that year marked a significant shift in how American churches viewed the war. The National Council of Churches set the tone with a statement that called for greater candor from the U.S. government and independence for South Vietnam, and defended dissent from charges of disloyalty. It specifically recommended a halt to the bombing of North Vietnam, a general cease-fire, negotiation with the NLF, an international peacekeeping force to allow a phased U.S. troop withdrawal, and congressional economic development funds for Southeast Asia.[87]

Individual denominations did not yet accept all these positions, but many now clearly opposed official policy in Indochina. A Methodist Board of Missions resolution virtually matched the NCC's major points. The United Church of Christ questioned the bombing of North Vietnam, while the American Baptists and United Presbyterians specifically condemned both the bombing and military escalation. The Disciples of Christ annual assembly urged study and discussion concerning U.S. escalation and the "basic justice" of entering the conflict. Delegates to the Episcopal triennial convention sought U.S. military restraint and new alternatives for a just and durable peace, but 24 of its bishops went further and petitioned President Johnson to stop the bombing of North Vietnam. By more than two to one, the General Synod of the United Church of Christ approved selective conscientious objection.[88]

Several churches still refused to take a forthright stand on Vietnam, but their conventions included major debates on the war. The Presbyterian Church of the United States affirmed its "loyalty to the government in this current conflict" but posed war-related questions for church study. Southern Baptists resolved to pray for world peace and a negotiated settlement in Vietnam, while the Lutheran Church —Missouri Synod encouraged prayers, counsel, and study without endorsing or condemning the war. At their annual assembly, the Disciples of Christ reversed the previous year's decision and opposed selective conscientious objection.[89]

The statements that emerged from these bodies ranged from cautious to moderate. Credit for the goodwill of American leaders and impatience with antiwar protests mixed with dismay over the erosion of military restraint and affirmations of dissent. Floor debates that pitted groups such as social action committees against military chaplains produced a good deal of tension, but there were few reports of lingering resentment. CALCAV kept abreast of these developments through its members who attended the conventions. Robert McAfee Brown, for example, was one of the people responsible for the United Presbyterian Church's Declaration of Conscience on Vietnam. The results certainly did not guarantee a consensus. The President of the United Church of Christ defended the General Synod's approval of legal status for selective COs when at least one church threatened to withdraw unless the resolution was rescinded.[90]

Although CALCAV was active in a number of cooperative actions, it focused on its own programs. The national office urged local groups to pressure their congressional representatives to oppose escalation of the war. As part of its emphasis on educating the public, CALCAV served as a major literature distribution point for peace groups across the country. From January to July of 1967, it distributed over 1.4 million pieces of literature, much of that to churches and synagogues. It mailed out over 100,000 copies of "The Religious Community and the War in Vietnam," which was reprinted in at least nine newspapers.[91]

In addition to its pamphlets and reprints, CALCAV played an integral part in the publication of two books. The national committee commissioned freelance journalist Dorothy Dunbar Bromley to write a book for laypeople on the moral and political issues of the war. Bromley had originally approached CALCAV about distributing a pamphlet she would write on the background of the war, but it grew into a more ambitious project. The national committee promoted and distributed *Washington and Vietnam,* published in November 1966, and sold 9,000 copies by midsummer 1967.[92]

A second book, *Vietnam: Crisis of Conscience,* was written by Brown, Heschel, and Michael Novak and was published at the end of May 1967. This collaborative effort grew out of their belief, developed at the 1967 CALCAV mobilization, that many policymakers wanted to push for a negotiated settlement but were unsure that public opinion made that politically feasible. The book urged the religious community to take the lead in creating a climate of opinion that would allow, indeed pressure, those policymakers to act. In just over a year, it sold over 50,000 copies.[93]

By June 1967, CALCAV had grown into a national organization with 78 local chapters and a mailing list of 12,000 people.[94] Despite its growth, it remained a remarkably cohesive organization. Its position on the war had changed little since its inception. Although CALCAV did not offer a single comprehensive solution to the situation in Vietnam, certain points emerged consistently from different leaders. Clergy and Laymen Concerned continued to oppose an American military solution, claiming that victory could be achieved only at unacceptable costs and would be accompanied by moral defeat.[95] At the center of CALCAV's position was its call for direct negotiation between all interested parties, including the NLF. As a prelude to these talks, various persons suggested United Nations supervision of disengagement and negotiations,[96] an unconditional halt of the bombing of North Vietnam, withdrawal of U.S. forces to some geographical perimeter, or removal of all U.S. troops over the following twelve months.[97] Although a negotiated settlement remained the preferred policy, CALCAV leaders were under no illusions about that approach. As Brown noted:

> No one should assume that a genuine declaration of intent to seek peace would magically clear up misunderstandings, that it would immediately end hostilities, that it would not demand constant scrutiny and the highest order of diplomatic expertise. Just as there has been frustration and heartache in our gradual escalation, so too there would be frustration and heartache in the development of new initiatives leading to a negotiated peace. Just as the risks of extending the war are great, so too the risks of seeking new initiatives for negotiated peace are great. But they might be the most important risks the American people have ever taken.[98]

Still sensitive to charges that moral concerns were irrelevant to political decisions and that clergy had no place making political statements, CALCAV worked diligently to collect accurate information before making public statements. Brown acknowledged that religious leaders who offered specific political proposals risked equating a particular political stance with the Gospel. He noted, however, that the Gospel's prophetic bite came from being specific, and that religious leaders often deliberately used generalities to evade important issues.[99] More than once Brown compared Vietnam to Germany in the 1930s when the churches did not speak up until it was too late. "I am haunted by the realization that as later generations look back on the late 1960s, they are going to ask, 'As the war was escalating, as civilian casualties were mounting, as the right of dissent was being stifled, as the world was moving perilously close to World War III, where was your voice, why did you not speak up?' The question is not," Brown concluded, "what right have we to be speaking, but what right have we to be silent."[100]

Defending the right to dissent remained one of CALCAV's main concerns. Attacks on antiwar protesters by their critics suggested a demand for silence and unquestioning support of government policies. During an April 1967 speech in New York City, General William Westmoreland expressed his dismay at "recent unpatriotic acts here at home" that would encourage North Vietnam to continue the war and "inevitably . . . cost lives."[101] This reasoning not only attempted to stifle one of the most important aspects of a democratic system but it placed worship of the state above one's obligation to God. CALCAV's choice, as expressed by Brown, was clear: "Our ultimate loyalty can never be to nation—it must be to God."[102]

Neuhaus stressed that dissidents operated within the American tradition, and claimed that the vast majority of religious liberals maintained faith in America's democratic institutions.[103] Brown elaborated:

> To insist that criticism is unpatriotic is already to have started down the path to totalitarianism, and to have forgotten that the right of public expression and the right of dissent are among the most honorable modes of democratic expression. . . . Nothing would be more fatal to a democracy than to succumb to the notion that its citizens must give unquestioning support to the policymakers. For the policymakers may be wrong—politically and technically as well as morally.[104]

CALCAV continued to use moderate tactics to appeal to its middle-class constituency, largely through the traditional American channel of electoral politics. To convince the government to accept their position, the churches and synagogues must "articulate a position that can command the support of 51 percent of the voters. . . . Tactically, this means no lessening of moral indignation and concern, but it means also a mode of speech that is not so emotional or judgmental that it serves only to alienate those whom it should attract."[105] To achieve maximum effectiveness, many made a conscious effort to avoid the appearance of radicalism, dressing in coats and ties during public appearances. Indeed, few accepted the radical critique of American society and most were annoyed by leftist sectarianism. Some favored aiding the postwar reconstruction of Vietnam, but there was no support for the most popular radical position. As Brown wrote, "We must not be persuaded that the only alternative is to pull out tomorrow."[106] While CALCAV did participate in antiwar coalitions, it carefully avoided close ties to organizations other than those that were religiously oriented. The reason for maintaining a 'respectable' image was that policymakers could safely ignore "antiwar sentiment among the far, far left, among certain pacifist groups, among the beatnik and hippy crowd." CALCAV represented, as Brown pointed out, "the American middle class. It is here that the voters are found, and it is from here that must come the kind of pressure that can make a difference."[107]

Several CALCAV leaders continued to attack the cold war myths that had helped push the nation into Vietnam and the government's rationale for intervention. They rejected the division of the earth into the apocalyptic camps of godly democracies and ungodly communists. They denied the idea of monolithic communism and the validity of the domino theory. Some believed revolutions were sometimes needed to eliminate social, political, and economic problems and counseled the U.S. government to respond to each individual situation rather than blindly interpret them all as communist inspired.

Members of the steering committee rejected the claims of the State Department and the Pentagon that since the policymakers had access to more information, private citizens were "not competent to evaluate the situation." Even the "experts" disagreed, they pointed out. In assailing America's growing militarism and bureaucratic decision making, Heschel asked, "Is it not possible that the minds of those involved in a certain policy become addicted to it, and are hardly capable of undertaking an agonizing reappraisal that may prove how wrong the premises are?"[108] Specifically, Clergy and Laymen Concerned claimed that the conflict in Vietnam did not result from communist aggression from the north but had begun as a civil war in the south. Some refuted government arguments that American treaty commitments imposed a military obligation in Vietnam.[109] Responding to calls for a quick military victory, Brown denied that a nation should resort to coercion simply because it had the power to do so. He similarly brushed off the argument that, although getting into the war may have been a mistake, the nation had to stay and win once it had committed troops. "It is fatalistic and wrong," he stated, "to argue that because we have made a series of mistakes in the past we should compound those mistakes by making more of the same kind in the future."[110]

More than one observer reluctantly concluded that America was betraying its own ideals. Elston pinpointed U.S. violations of the Atlantic Charter and the principle of national self-determination as the beginning of its problems in Indochina.[111] Heschel observed a loss of the "sense of moral integrity, the equation of America with the pursuit of justice and peace. . . ." Support of repressive governments in South Vietnam subverted America's commitment to democratic governments. "Is it the destiny of our youth," Heschel asked, "to serve as mercenaries in the service of military juntas all over the world?"[112] Critics detected the inconsistency between American goals and the consequences of its actions. More important, the discrepancy between what the government told the public and what actually occurred, such as the inflation of body count figures, led to cynicism and distrust among growing numbers of the public. This deception produced a widening credibility gap.

If any significant change occurred in CALCAV's position on the war, it was that it increasingly argued against the war in moral terms. Brown in particular detected a growing moral numbness among the American population. People were taking for granted the deaths of an estimated quarter of a million children. If the public accepted actions by Americans that were condemned as war crimes when committed by foreign armies, the nation was in danger of becoming brutalized.[113] Novak even detected a degree of racism in America's actions in Southeast Asia, noting the common attitude that "God favors the pure of heart, who are also, in the main, the white of skin."[114] Growing numbers of people no longer accepted that U.S. intervention in Vietnam was merely a mistake in judgment but felt it to be a deliberate choice of an immoral policy.

A second issue that began to attract more attention was the draft and the right of the individual to refuse military service. The idea of selective conscientious objection, which the government did not recognize, gained increasing support. Expressing the convictions of many nonpacifists, Novak argued:

> Many of us who love our country are sad to see its flag carried in *this* war. We might be as brave as anyone else in other wars, and as eager to leap to the defense of the values dear to our nation. But in regard to this war many have felt, from year to year, increasing shame. It was not in order that our flag might be carried in wars like this that men of the generations before us suffered and died for liberty, for bravery, for justice.[115]

In its first year and a half as a permanent organization, CALCAV had made impressive strides. The success of its mobilization and the growing number of local chapters testified to its grassroots appeal. Clergy and Laymen Concerned continued to champion the preservation of dissent, de-escalation, and a negotiated settlement. Working within the religious community, it became an influential component of the antiwar movement. Its programs helped to stimulate some of the first important sources of Catholic opposition to the war, and in Martin Luther King, Jr., it enjoyed a national figure who placed Vietnam in the larger context of American society. Encouraged and aided by CALCAV members, mainline Protestant churches examined the war more closely and increasingly adopted positions critical of government policy. The Johnson administration gave its watchful attention to the peace forces as consensus on the war eroded. The mutual attraction of CALCAV and congressional doves signaled other changes. Mass antiwar demonstrations were larger in 1967 than in previous years, and an October Gallup poll was the first to reveal a plurality that believed the U.S. had made a mistake in sending troops to fight in Vietnam (46 percent to 44 percent). Beneath the surface, however, the frustration of having its arguments ignored by most policymakers combined with a greater moral emphasis to produce a subtle shift in CALCAV's approach to ending the war.

3

"IN CONSCIENCE I MUST BREAK THE LAW"

(SEPTEMBER 1967 to DECEMBER 1968)

> I am for peace, but they are for war, and my
> voice goes unheeded in their councils.
>
> —PSALMS 120:7 (LIVING BIBLE)

Just before dawn on July 2, 1968, about 200 people emerged from a worship service at St. Paul's Chapel in New York City. Eight men and women chained themselves to Barry Johnson, a former Union student who had left the seminary to work with CALCAV. His seminary draft deferment gone, and his request for conscientious objector status denied, Johnson chose to burn his draft card and join the draft resistance. He was obligated to report to the Whitehall Street induction center later that morning. The chained protagonists and a few hundred supporters walked silently toward the induction center, carrying flags and antiwar signs and enduring occasional derisive comments from construction workers. Officials at the induction center refused to admit Johnson because of the chains, but the crowd remained for several minutes in case the military changed its mind. As she waited on the steps, Mrs. Robert Ransom, whose son had been killed in Vietnam, briefly addressed the gathering. "We who have lost a son," she declared, "want him [President Johnson] to know that we feel it is wrong to justify that sacrifice by killing yet more Americans and Vietnamese in a war which our dead son bitterly opposed. Mike will have died in vain if his tragic loss does not bring us to our senses to stop all further killing."[1]

This event tells much of CALCAV's evolution in the last year and a half of the Johnson administration. The continuation of the conflict pushed many members to adopt civil disobedience. This, combined with CALCAV's advocacy of unpopular positions such as amnesty for war resisters and its investigation of American war crimes marked the first departures from the traditional liberal approach and limited its appeal to its middle-class constituency. The organization, however, remained rooted in the religious community and diligently pursued moderate forms of dissent, particularly through electoral politics.

Throughout 1967, the war at home escalated. During the spring, antiwar activists were the targets of a series of violent reprisals. Terrorists bombed the headquarters of antiwar organizations in San Francisco and Berkeley. Other assailants attacked antiwar demonstrators in New York and Boston.[2] President Johnson, General William Westmoreland, and several members of Congress publicly criticized the antiwar movement following the April 15 demonstrations. Government officials from both major political parties portrayed it as communist controlled and blamed the protests for lengthening the war. Representative Mendel Rivers of South Carolina tried to suppress the debate, commenting that "It's too late to question whether it's [the war is] right or wrong."[3] Government agencies such as the FBI and CIA constantly monitored peace groups and tried to influence their activities.

CALCAV's actions brought it into direct conflict with these efforts. For example, two incidents occurred in the Norfolk, Virginia area in the last months of 1967. A naval reservist on active duty was transferred from the USS Independence to the USS Dewey shortly after he began working with a local CALCAV chapter's draft counseling program. When he refused to sail with the Dewey to Vietnam, military officials arrested him and advised that he would be court martialed. A second incident involved two VISTA workers who were called to Washington, D.C. to explain their involvement with CALCAV. The following day both men were transferred out of the Norfolk area.[4]

Protesters responded to harassment with an escalation of their own. Perhaps the most visible change was the emergence of a strong antidraft movement led by groups such as the Resistance. Isolated instances of draft card burning had occurred for a number of years, but it was not until 1967 that draft resistance became an organized movement. Small but growing numbers of young men burned or turned in their draft cards to resist induction and implication in the war. The price for such actions could be high. The courts sentenced David Miller, the first draft card burner prosecuted under the 1965 law prohibiting draft card destruction, to two and a half years in federal prison.[5]

Having failed to convince the government to change its policy, activists sought other means to stem the flow of American supplies and personnel to Vietnam. Some pressured defense contractors to stop producing war materiel and harassed war-related corporate recruiters on college campuses. Others blocked military buses from carrying draftees to induction centers, or attempted to separate ROTC programs from the universities.

The March on the Pentagon on October 21 was the culmination of this transition from protest to resistance. With Jerry Rubin serving as project coordinator for the National Mobe, tensions increased within the antiwar coalition. Rubin's countercultural clothing and hair style annoyed more conservative leaders of the Mobe, and his exaggerated rhetoric threatened to disrupt the careful plans that had been laid. Pacifists and moderates insisted upon nonviolence and threatened to withdraw if it could not be guaranteed. To attract the broadest possible support for the coalition, Mobe leaders planned a mass rally to satisfy the moderates and an opportunity to commit civil disobedience for the radicals, with the two distinctly separated to avoid involving people in actions they preferred not to join.[6]

The morning rally at the Lincoln Memorial attracted an estimated 100,000 people. At its conclusion, roughly 30,000 participants marched across the Arlington Memorial Bridge where a second, abbreviated rally preceded the tense confrontation at the Pentagon itself. "The vast majority of the 100,000 marchers demonstrated without untoward incident or visible effect," comments historian Charles DeBenedetti. "Yet their very irrepressibility heightened the electric atmosphere that was pervading the country. Here were white middle-class Americans staring down the gunbarrels of their government."[7] An uneasy standoff ensued that evening and the next day. Military police and federal marshals arrested a total of 683 demonstrators during the weekend.[8]

Discussions on Vietnam within religious circles turned increasingly to the effectiveness of protests alone in ending the war. With so many young men willing to defy the government for their consciences, adults beyond the draft age looked for ways to show their support. Pressure from several religious bodies failed to win any provisions for selective conscientious objectors in the Selective Service Act of 1967. Arthur Waskow and Marcus Raskin drafted "A Call to Resist Illegitimate Authority" for those not subject to the draft. This document implicated its signers in draft evasion and made them subject to charges of conspiracy for counseling men to violate the draft laws.[9]

Just as the March on the Pentagon marked a transition from protest to resistance in the antiwar movement at large, CALCAV's "Statement of Conscience and Conscription" marked the acceptance of civil disobedience by many of its leading figures. Brown best described this transition in charting his own personal route

from unconcern
to curiosity
to study
to mild concern
to deep concern
to signing statements
to genteel protest
to marching
to moral outrage
to increasingly vigorous protest
to . . . civil disobedience.[10]

Most members of CALCAV believed that the rights of conscience
were more compelling than arguments against selective conscientious
objection. Acting on this assumption, the executive committee gave
Richard Neuhaus the job of composing a statement. The national
office sent a preliminary version to contact people around the country. The major objection from the local groups was an offer of
"churches and synagogues as places of refuge, in accord with the
ancient tradition of religious sanctuary." In general, local church
boards objected to using their churches in that manner and the controversial line was deleted.[11]

The executive committee sent the "Statement on Conscience and
Conscription" in late October to a select group of prominent religious leaders soliciting their signatures and support. Recognizing the
controversial nature of its newest project, CALCAV told its membership, "We do not expect total unanimity on this particular statement
of the draft from our local groups and/or individuals."[12]

At a Detroit press conference on October 25, 1967 CALCAV
released the statement signed by eighteen clergymen, among them
Brickner, Brown, Coffin, Elston, Heschel, Neuhaus, Sheerin, Harvey
Cox, Daniel Berrigan, David Hunter, Martin Marty, and Colin Wil-
liams.[13] The document claimed that vocal support for the rights of
conscience was no longer adequate and urged those who supported
conscientious, nonviolent resistance to the Vietnam War to take a
more active role. It denied the right and the competence of the
government to judge the conscience of its citizens. Criticizing the
government's definition of a conscientious objector, the statement
argued that since ethical decisions were made in the context of particular events, those who refused participation in a particular war deserved equal respect with those who refused participation in any war.

Citing the concept of selective objection as a long-standing Jewish
and Christian tradition, the signers viewed their civil disobedience as
a form of religious obedience. The document implicated its support-

ers in violation of the Selective Service Act. "We hereby publicly counsel all who in conscience cannot today serve in the armed forces to refuse such service by non-violent means. . . . in the sight of the law we are now as guilty as they."[14] For CALCAV, the "Statement of Conscience and Conscription" provided a specific method of civil disobedience for those who wished to go beyond the legally accepted means of dissent. The decision to participate was not always an easy choice. One early signer changed his mind for fear of exposing his family to further abuse and criticism.[15] Despite the risks, by February 1968 over 1,300 clergy had signed the statement, including many seminarians who were normally exempt from the draft.[16]

Robert McAfee Brown was among the leaders of this transition to civil disobedience within CALCAV. "The longer we were in the war, the worse our abandonment of moral standards became," he later commented. "The escalation of moral numbness demands the escalation of moral protest."[17] With the President publicly ignoring demonstrations, Congress reluctant to challenge the President, and public protests written off as unpatriotic or treasonous, Brown viewed legal protest as ineffective. While many people counseled waiting and working for change in the 1968 elections, he concluded that this was not enough. It was unlikely that any Democrat would be able to challenge the President, and the most likely Republican candidates were even more hawkish than Johnson. Regardless of who was eventually selected, the elections were still a year away, and in the meantime the war continued. Seeing no alternatives and undergoing increasing moral anguish, Brown expanded his own protest to include nonviolent civil disobedience, concluding that "In conscience, I must break the law." Recognizing the limited appeal of this position and the uncertainty of its achieving any concrete results, he reasoned, "There comes a time when . . . one has to oppose evil even if one cannot prevent it, when one has to choose to be a victim rather than an accomplice. . . ."[18]

Others arrived at the same conclusion. In December, John Bennett defended a sober decision to commit civil disobedience, noting: "To disobey a particular law and take the consequences, allowing that law to run its course in exacting punishment, is not to engage in an act against public order."[19] In the summer of 1968, John Sheerin came to support acts of civil disobedience such as the "Statement on Conscience and Conscription," although he opposed acts of property destruction such as the Berrigans' burning of draft files at Catonsville.[20]

In February 1968, Coffin advocated massive civil disobedience and proposed that seminarians and young clergy give up their draft exemptions and declare themselves conscientious objectors. He urged older clergy to publicly advocate draft resistance and subject themselves to the penalties of the Selective Service Act.[21]

Coffin pointed to the submissiveness of Congress as the primary motive for his conversion to civil disobedience. "If Johnson could be forced to arrest not a handful of young people but hundreds of older ones," he explained, "if we could pack the jails, Congress might act, if not for the sake of our dying soldiers then for the sake of the domestic tranquility it so feared to disrupt."[22] Coffin's actions evidently had some impact. Following a collection of draft cards at a church service on October 15, John Chancellor commented on NBC television: "If men like this are beginning to say things like this, I guess we had all better start paying attention."[23]

Coffin was one of many to back up his words with action. He feared the potential for violence in the March on the Pentagon, and to help ensure peaceful protest he joined the national draft card turn-in sponsored by the Resistance. On October 16, he and fellow CAL-CAV member Dana McLean Greeley led 4,000 Boston-area people in a ceremonial turning-in of draft cards. Other groups collected cards from war resisters across the country, and on October 20 a delegation including Coffin, Dr. Benjamin Spock, Raskin, and Mitchell Goodman loaded 1,000 draft cards into a briefcase and delivered them to the Justice Department. Although Deputy Assistant Attorney General John McDonough refused to accept them, the protesters left the briefcase behind anyway.[24]

After a period of indecision over how to respond to the draft resistance movement, the government finally reacted. On January 5, 1968 a Boston federal grand jury indicted Spock, Coffin, Goodman, Raskin, and Michael Ferber for conspiring to counsel, aid, and abet draft resisters. According to the grand jury, the conspiracy consisted of circulating the "Call to Resist Illegitimate Authority"; promoting the call and announcing events of Stop the Draft Week at a New York press conference on October 2, 1967; receiving draft cards from young men eligible for conscription; and presenting those cards to the Justice Department. On January 29, the men, referred to as the Boston Five, were arraigned in Boston where they pleaded not guilty and were released on $1,000 bond. That evening they returned to New York where a rally at Manhattan Center sponsored by CAL-CAV and several other organizations drew about 4,000 supporters.[25]

The adoption of civil disobedience by CALCAV leaders did not imply their agreement with antiwar radicals. Coffin's views that the war threatened to undermine American instincts of decency and weakened crucial antipoverty programs were well known, and yet he did not call for immediate withdrawal from Vietnam. He preferred instead a negotiated withdrawal in which "the implementation can be very carefully phased and deliberate, but the intent must be very clear." [26]

Likewise, Neuhaus' criticism of Lewis Hershey, Director of the Selective Service System, rejected radical solutions. In a memo of October 26, 1967 Hershey had suggested to local draft boards that previously deferred registrants who participated in illegal protest activities be reclassified 1-A. Sensing a threat to democratic traditions from the right, Neuhaus was unwilling to swing to the far left to combat it. "We do not need to be alarmists or pronounce the American democratic experiment dead," he wrote, "to recognize the signs of ascendancy among the anti-democratic forces in the country. . . . Fascism is not an entirely adequate category," Neuhaus added, "but its characteristic marks are related to what is happening. . . . Those of us who believe in America's promise of democratic experiment, work to disprove the radical indictment, or, acknowledging its partial basis in fact, to correct what is distorted." [27]

Sheerin's tacit approval of civil disobedience hardly made him a strong advocate. His editorials, however, frequently went beyond the opinion of most Catholics as he pushed the church hierarchy to assert its moral judgment on the war, advocated selective conscientious objection, and called for postwar foreign aid to rebuild Vietnam. At the same time, he was encouraged by the election in South Vietnam of Nguyen Van Thieu and Nguyen Cao Ky, warned against American isolationism, and upheld as an American responsibility the use of its resources, including the military, to aid the poor and oppressed. He also opposed an immediate U.S. withdrawal, and fearing a postwar bloodbath, urged that arrangements be made for refugees. [28]

CALCAV's moderate position in the wake of the March on the Pentagon was further underscored by the distance it kept from the national coalitions. With the introduction of resistance tactics, it became more difficult to build a national consensus, and some organizations began to loosen their ties with the umbrella coalitions. As Dave Dellinger of the National Mobilization Committee noted somewhat critically, "Groups such as the American Friends Service Committee and Clergy and Laity Concerned about Vietnam still attended meetings and entered into the agreements, but on several key occasions their participation was nominal at best, while their major energies and expenditures of money went into separatist actions." [29]

The public stand on civil disobedience makes clear the predominance of the national staff in CALCAV's operation. Although the people who signed the "Statement on Conscience and Conscription" represented a significant group, they were a distinct minority within the organization. Such forward positions were possible because the New York office generally initiated national actions which filtered down to the chapters. Local antiwar clergy were either inhibited by their more conservative congregations from taking strong liberal positions or faced occupational risks in doing so.[30]

The national debate over civil disobedience also reflected the diversity of CALCAV at the local level. The Anderson, Indiana chapter contained several members of the Church of God, a moderately conservative evangelical body headquartered in that industrial city. During the summer and fall of 1967, Anderson CALCAV launched a widespread distribution of war-related literature, hitting such disparate audiences as the Church of God's International Convention and secular groups such as the Lion's Club.[31]

CALCAV's Indianapolis affiliate, Hoosiers for Peace, provides another example of its attraction for evangelicals. A number of people from the national headquarters of the Christian Church (Disciples of Christ) worked with the Indianapolis group. As much as any CALCAV chapter, Hoosiers for Peace operated as a regional organization, working with small groups in several other Indiana cities. Activists in several of these communities were Mennonites or Brethren, two of the nation's historic peace churches.[32]

In contrast, other chapters reflected more liberal attitudes or less dependence on mainline churches for their constituency. Since early 1966, Madison, Wisconsin clergy had assisted CALCAV through telegrams, fund raising, and trying to stimulate greater concern within local congregations. A May 1967 visit by William Sloane Coffin aided their efforts by drawing 275 people to a dinner meeting and over 1,000 to a rally. By the end of the year, however, the local group dwindled to a core of less than a dozen, and a more radical attitude alienated prominent clergy in the area. As the Madison chapter's work in the churches declined and its emphasis shifted to Eugene McCarthy's presidential campaign, the links to CALCAV faded.[33]

As CALCAV entered the tactical transition to civil disobedience, it also prepared for a second national mobilization in Washington. The executive committee made preliminary plans to hold it in early February and built it around the release of a study on American war crimes, visits with Congress members coming up for reelection, and a strong appeal to the religious community to support conscientious draft resisters.[34]

Martin Luther King, Jr. announced the convocation at a January 12 news conference at the Belmont Plaza Hotel in New York City. He emphasized that while no protesters would be turned away, CAL-

CAV intended the mobilization primarily for church-related groups. King indirectly criticized the government's conspiracy charges and urged clergy and laity to go to Washington "lest persons in the federal government think that men of conscience can be cowed into silence by attack on dissenters or by blunderbuss indictments. . . . Either we will end the war in Vietnam or many of our most sensitive citizens must be sent to jail." Alluding to CALCAV's planned electoral activities, he vowed, "we will no longer vote for men who continue to see the killing of Vietnamese and Americans as the best way of advancing the goals of freedom and self-determination in Southeast Asia."[35] When asked to endorse a presidential candidate, King refused, but he welcomed Eugene McCarthy's candidacy and expressed his hope that Robert Kennedy would continue to oppose the war.

The press conference also served as a show of support for the recently indicted Boston Five. Both Coffin and King pledged to continue counseling young men to "follow their consciences" when faced with conscription.[36]

Coinciding with the beginning of the mobilization was the release of a new book that served as CALCAV's most blatant indictment of American actions in Vietnam. The executive committee had commissioned *In the Name of America,* a study of American military conduct in Vietnam, in October 1966, and asked Professor Seymour Melman of Columbia University to serve as Director of Research. For several months five Columbia graduate students collected published reports from a variety of reputable sources that judged the conduct of U.S. operations in Vietnam to violate the laws of war set forth in the Hague and Geneva conferences and in the Nuremberg principles. The nearly 1,000 exerpts filled over 400 pages and documented American and South Vietnamese violations of international law. The study concluded that "American conduct in Vietnam has been characterized by consistent violation of almost every international agreement relating to the rules of warfare." The researchers found that America's moral standards had eroded during the Vietnam War, and noted increasing instances of mistreatment of prisoners and indiscriminate killing. "What nation can so train its young without destroying its soul," the book asked. "What scars are left of the lives of those who are told that it is fitting and proper for them to do such things?"[37]

The expense of producing the book contributed to CALCAV's ongoing financial woes, but its publication produced some favorable publicity. To get the book out in time for the 1968 mobilization, Coffin and Brickner had to raise a $10,000 loan from Irving Fain, a Rhode Island businessman.[38] Each senator received a copy of the book during the mobilization. The State Department acknowledged that *In the Name of America* might lead people to draw moral conclusions about the war's conduct but called the allegations of war crimes by American forces "absolutely unsupportable."[39] Nevertheless, the release of the book received front-page coverage in two dozen newspapers, and in the next year and a half CALCAV sold nearly 30,000 copies.

The second mobilization got under way Monday morning, February 5, when over 2,000 people gathered in the New York Avenue Presbyterian Church for the opening plenary session. Coffin chaired the meeting, which featured speeches by Bennett, Father Robert Drinan, Dean of the Boston College Law School, and Seymour Melman. In his evaluation of *In the Name of America*, Drinan defended the right of the American people to know if the United States was violating the rules of warfare and to repudiate such a policy. Melman labeled violations of the laws of war as war crimes and questioned whether American officials must obey the law or whether they were above it.[40]

In the afternoon, participants met in state delegations, planned presentations, and visited with their representatives. Overlapping these congressional visits, CALCAV previewed fifteen war-related films for those attending the conference. That evening's ecumenical worship service preceded Rabbi Maurice Eisendrath's report on his recent trip to Vietnam and a showing of the film *Inside North Vietnam*, by British journalist Felix Greene.[41]

On Tuesday morning, February 6, participants chose from two topical conferences. Approximately 400 people attended the session chaired by Neuhaus on "The Religious Community and Politics 1968." Sanford Gottlieb, Executive Director of SANE, and Allard Lowenstein both urged support for McCarthy's campaign for the Democratic presidential nomination. Duff Reid, assistant to Senator Thruston Morton of Kentucky, advocated the election of a Republican who would de-escalate the war and indicated that the Republicans were "soul searching" for the best possible peace candidate.[42] Lowenstein used the opportunity to recruit a number of students from Union Theological Seminary to help in a letter-writing campaign. Two letters resulted, one to the President signed by 200 student body presidents who opposed U.S. policies in Vietnam, a second to Secretary of Defense McNamara signed by 1,000 antiwar seminarians.[43]

The second session, on "The Religious Community and the Draft," drew a crowd of nearly 1,200. Robert Price, Ron Young, National Youth Secretary of the Fellowship of Reconciliation, Flint Anderson, and Coffin led this gathering. When Carl McIntire interrupted, Coffin invited him to explain his viewpoint. The audience greeted with cheers and applause McIntire's comments that "conscience must be enlightened by the word of God" and that "I accept the Bible" and "believe in the Ten Commandments." When he said "Let every soul be subject to the higher powers," however, Coffin responded sharply, "First you're going to have to explain to me why St. Paul was in and out of the pokey with a regularity similar to Secretary McNamara's shuttling back and forth to Vietnam."[44]

This outburst was one of several counterprotests planned by the American Council of Christian Churches, a right-wing, fundamentalist group that came to Washington to oppose CALCAV and support U.S. policy in Vietnam. Between fifty and a hundred of its members picketed some of the convocation's activities over the two-day conference. McIntire condemned CALCAV as "the advance guard of Ho Chi Minh."[45]

Clergy and Laymen Concerned intended to highlight its second Washington gathering with a memorial service in the Arlington National Cemetery, but from the very beginning it encountered opposition from the Army. The Army denied its initial request to use the cemetery on grounds that the service would lack sensitivity. Fernandez called the refusal "an affront to the religious conscience of millions of Americans." CALCAV then sought an injunction from a federal court to force authorization for the service. On February 5, however, Federal Judge Mathew McQuire upheld the Army, ruling that the service would constitute "special pleading."[46]

After considering other possibilities, CALCAV finally received permission to hold a silent prayer vigil in the Arlington National Cemetery. Nearly 2,500 people gathered at the foot of the Tomb of the Unknowns and participated in a ceremony led by Martin Luther King, Jr. "In this period of absolute silence," King began, "let us pray." After several minutes, interrupted only by the changing military guard at the tomb, Rabbi Heschel repeated the words of Christ on the cross, "Eloi, Eloi, lama sabachthani?" ("My God, my God, why has thou forsaken me?"), and Roman Catholic Bishop James P. Shannon concluded, "Let us go in peace."[47] The worshipers moved quietly out of the cemetery in a half-mile procession, each holding a small American flag.

Back at the New York Avenue Presbyterian Church for the mobilization's final gathering, Dr. King again connected the war in Vietnam and domestic problems, reflecting, "Somewhere along the way we have allowed the means by which we live to outrun the ends for which we live." Coffin also spoke, encouraging young men to turn in their draft cards and resist the war.[48]

At the conclusion of the meeting, Thomas Hayes, Larry Friedman,

John Huhn, Vincent McGee, Jr., and Henry Bucher, Jr. met with Assistant Deputy Attorney General John R. McDonough and two other Department of Justice officials in the Justice Department Building. The delegation delivered a large scroll, several pages of petitions, and a bag full of envelopes signed by several hundred people who placed themselves in complicity with draft resisters. Hayes reasoned that since the war was immoral, resisters were justified in their actions. After the CALCAV delegation left, officials turned the documents over to special agents of the FBI.[49]

The 1968 mobilization produced the first real interest in CALCAV's activities by the Federal Bureau of Investigation. The FBI had been aware of CALCAV's existence at least as early as the beginning of 1967, but it made no effort to investigate until the following year. Apparently after reading about the upcoming mobilization in the New York *Times,* the FBI arranged to cover the proceedings, although the New York office balked at infiltrating CALCAV's national office for fear of possible public embarrassment if it were discovered. The FBI shared its information with the White House, the Secretaries of State and Defense, the Central Intelligence Agency, the Attorney General, Secret Service, the Washington Police Department, and several military agencies. Both the FBI and the 116th Army Military Intelligence Group carried out surveillance of the mobilization.[50]

The FBI found no evidence of communist affiliation or violent tendencies on the part of CALCAV. Reports on the organization described its activities as "dignified." Disregarding its own intelligence, however, the FBI placed CALCAV under Internal Security and Selective Service Act investigations in the fall of 1968.[51] That members of CALCAV might be guilty of violating the Selective Service Act was certainly no surprise given their public admissions to such violations. They had on numerous occasions even provided the government with evidence against themselves. The Internal Security investigation, however, seems to have been based on little more than J. Edgar Hoover's personal dislike and suspicion of the antiwar movement.[52]

Efforts by various intelligence agencies to undermine the peace forces did not affect the continued growth of Clergy and Laymen Concerned About Vietnam. By March 1968, CALCAV had ninety local affiliates and an extensive mailing list of 20,000 names.[53] Clergy still predominated on the national committee, but prominent lay leaders such as University of Chicago professor Hans Morgenthau and Philip Scharper, Vice-President of Sheed and Ward Publishers, had taken visible roles in the preceding months.

The antiwar arguments made by CALCAV and others received more credence in the wake of the Tet offensive in late January. This operation was a large-scale coordinated attack against South Vietnam's key cities. It proved to be a tactical defeat for the Viet Cong, but following as it did a series of optimistic reports by the Johnson administration, this impressive show of force was a political setback for the U.S. that added significantly to the public's increasing dissatisfaction with the war.

At the very least, CALCAV found itself increasingly favored by liberal politicians of both major parties. The office of Senator Mark Hatfield (R-Ore.), for example, solicited CALCAV's advice on generating public opposition to the draft to support Hatfield's bill that would replace the Selective Service System with a volunteer military.[54] A more generous assessment would credit it with influencing members of Congress to publicly oppose Johnson's Vietnam policies and helping to turn public opinion against the war. Even during times when success in altering the war's direction seemed a possibility, however, members of the religious antiwar movement struggled on through periods of doubt about their ability to influence administration policies. As Coffin observed, "Ultimately you have to do what's right, not what's effective."[55]

The arguments advanced by CALCAV found an expanding audience during 1968. The Roman Catholic monthly *U.S. Catholic* called the Vietnam War "wrong, unjust and immoral." The Disciples of Christ, reversing themselves for the second time in two years, matched the Lutheran Church in America's support for selective conscientious objection. American Baptists and the newly merged United Methodist Church upheld the rights of traditional COs who accepted the legal consequences. These resolutions did not necessarily imply the endorsement of that position over military service. Humanitarian concerns dominated the United Presbyterian assembly, which called for de-escalation, protection of civilians, postwar relief for war victims, and humane treatment for prisoners of war. The more conservative Presbyterian Church of the United States commended the President for his negotiating efforts while urging greater use of the United Nations. It too suggested postwar aid. United Methodists recommended negotiations by all South Vietnamese factions and the withdrawal of outside military forces.[56]

Whatever its ability to affect public opinion, CALCAV did not reflect the thinking of the majority of the churchgoing population at the beginning of 1968. In an admittedly unscientific poll, nine Protestant denominational magazines ran questionnaires prior to the Tet offensive. Out of a combined circulation of 3.6 million, 34,000 readers responded, 2,000 of them clergy. Of these readers 63 percent expressed dissatisfaction with President Johnson's handling of the war, but they disagreed on how to improve the situation. Of the clergy, 57 percent wanted to stop the bombing of North Vietnam, while 60 percent of the lay readers opposed a halt. On the statement "The United States should use all military strength necessary short of nuclear weapons to achieve victory in the war" two-thirds of the clergy disagreed, but over half of all respondents concurred. By an almost two-to-one margin, readers opposed sending U.S. troops should a Vietnam-like situation develop elsewhere, but by 55 percent to 40 percent they rejected the church's defending conscientious protest whatever the consequences. The United Church of Christ was the only American denomination that opposed a military solution and defended antiwar protest. "Officially the churches may coo like a dove but the majority of their members are flying with the hawks," the *Lutheran* observed.[57]

More reliable data confirms the more dovish sentiment among clergy than among the laity.[58] Studies of the Church of God (Anderson, Ind.) and the Southern Baptist Convention indicate that the majority of their adherents supported the Vietnam War for its duration and were highly critical of antiwar dissent.[59] The clergy ranked among the most active antiwar segments of the population despite the lack of an antiwar consensus within the nation's religious leadership. The opposition's willingness to publicly voice its criticisms added to the general impression of a dissenting clergy. While Protestant ministers divided fairly evenly in 1968 over various policy options, they were more dovish than the general population, and the doves' willingness to speak out probably gave them influence that exceeded their numbers.[60]

The impact upon public opinion enjoyed by mainline Protestants was limited but greater than that of the conservative evangelicals. The former had greater access to the media and control of most of the intellectually respectable journals, interdenominational bureaucracies, and prestigious seminaries. Conservative evangelicals, on the other hand, consistently supported the war in a variety of journals, but their denominations officially remained silently neutral, fearing involvement in politics.[61]

If the church constituency disagreed with CALCAV, however, the general public was openly hostile toward the antiwar movement. The public was undoubtedly influenced by the continuous attacks from the government and the media. A Louis Harris poll taken in mid-December 1967 revealed that 75 percent of the population believed the antiwar demonstrations only encouraged the communists to fight harder. Seventy percent viewed the demonstrations as acts of disloyalty, while 50 percent of those polled agreed that people who obstructed military or defense-industry recruiters should lose their draft deferments. Another Harris poll taken at Christmas showed that 58 percent favored increasing military pressure, and 63 percent were opposed to a bombing halt in North Vietnam.[62]

In the spring of 1968, the nation's attention was briefly diverted from the war by the latest senseless act in a bewildering decade. On April 4, Martin Luther King, Jr. was assassinated. CALCAV's national office had called for a nationwide fast during Passover and Holy Week but reoriented the fast as a memorial to the slain civil rights leader and peace activist. Local chapters held services in his honor during the week of April 8–12.[63]

King's murder opened a month of chaos and protest. Riots erupted in black ghettos across the country. Beginning on April 20, local SDS chapters began ten days of resistance to the war using a variety of tactics. On April 23, demonstrations began at Columbia University, and the ensuing violence grabbed national headlines. It very nearly eclipsed the events of April 26, when an estimated one million students took part in a national strike planned by the Student Mobilization Committee, the first such action since the 1930s. Students boycotted classes, held rallies and sit-ins, and passed out leaflets in an overwhelmingly peaceful display of their opposition to the war. The following day, hundreds of thousands attended demonstrations sponsored by the National Mobilization Committee. In New York City, Mayor John Lindsay joined 200,000 others for a rally in Central Park, where Coretta Scott King replaced her husband as the keynote speaker. Thirty thousand protested at the rally in San Francisco, and roughly 10,000 marched in Chicago, where an attack by police served as a prelude to the Democratic convention.[64]

Against this backdrop of tragedy and crisis, Clergy and Laymen Concerned About Vietnam made significant departures from its earlier practices. In the years since its inception, CALCAV had concentrated on educating public opinion about the war and lobbying government leaders to change the nation's Vietnam policy. Now for the first time it applied direct pressure to a defense contractor as a step toward ending the war. CALCAV targeted the Dow Chemical Company, producers of napalm. Several members of the national committee sent a letter to Carl Gerstacker, Chairman of Dow's Board of Directors, opposing the manufacture of napalm on moral, practical, and legal grounds, and asking that Dow terminate its contract with the Defense Department. The following week, at least 300 protesters arrived in Midland, Michigan for Dow's annual stockholder's meeting. In the days before the meeting, CALCAV people went door to door in Midland to express their views and later picketed as the stockholders met. A delegation of five CALCAV representatives participated in the meeting, and at one point Fernandez, in an angry exchange with Dow executives, explained, "This isn't a game for us. We are here because we love our country, not because we hate it." The group also informed the stockholders how napalm destroyed vegetation and burned the flesh of its victims. Chairman Gerstacker retorted that corporations could not end the war and suggested that CALCAV might accomplish more by talking with legislators. Dow Chemical was sufficiently concerned about the repercussions of these attacks, however, to issue a pamphlet denying many of CALCAV's allegations.[65]

Several CALCAV chapters built upon the national office's recent emphasis on the rights of conscience by mobilizing local sentiment against the military draft. The previous fall, Chicago CALCAV had held a day-long conference on the draft aimed at those uncommitted about the war, and the Medford, Oregon chapter had begun a draft information center as part of its Vietnam Summer project.[66] Denver CALCAV established a military counseling center, and director Duane Gall spoke with church groups on the draft and its options, ranging from voluntary enlistment and officer training to alternate service and resistance.[67]

With Oakland serving as a staging area for military personnel going to Vietnam, the Bay area was a natural location for both draft resistance and dissent within the military. As early as May 1968, Philip Farnham, director of San Francisco CALCAV, proposed an antidraft campaign that favored a return to a volunteer army, short-term noncooperation with the draft, and a long-term educational effort to block the renewal of the draft law. As a tool for the campaign, CALCAV compiled a question and answer pamphlet on the background of the draft in the United States, how the Selective Service system operated, the makeup and operation of local draft boards, and the option of noncooperative resistance to the draft.[68] In July, when nine soldiers who were AWOL wanted to publicize their opposition to the war, CALCAV found nine clerics willing to be chained to the men during a two-day service of liberation in an area church. They also handled the logistics, such as contacting lawyers and the press, arranging food, and planning the service. After 48 hours, military police moved in and arrested the soldiers, who were then imprisoned in five different locations within the state. CALCAV organized public and legal support and visited the men daily.[69]

CALCAV also instituted organizational changes. In the beginning, an industrious national staff had worked for subsistence wages and accepted direction from a steering committee. As early as spring 1967 Fernandez had discussed the idea of recruiting a corps of field workers to help sustain CALCAV's local work, but he received little support.[70] His participation in Vietnam Summer gave him the idea of having the national office fund staffs that would be hired by the local groups.[71] Some members of the steering committee felt the national subsidies would produce too much dependency upon the New York office. After debating the issue, however, the committee decided to proceed with the hiring of field staff to organize and work in major metropolitan areas. Problems arose in a few cities where entrenched leaders fought perceived intrusions upon their domain to the extent of threatening the vigor of their chapters. National officials urged them to resign and elect new officers who could revitalize antiwar activity.[72] The meager salaries, which CALCAV hoped to supplement from local and denominational sources, ranged from $750 to $4,000 per year. The chapters supplied room, board, and operating expenses. This change did not mark a shift in emphasis on the part of the organization, but it served as the beginning of a transition that by the early 1970s would give greater independence to the individual groups. By the end of 1968, over twenty field staffers worked in cities that included Boston, New Haven, Philadelphia, Chicago, St. Paul, Kansas City, Dallas, Seattle, Portland, San Francisco, Los Angeles, and San Jose.[73]

Field staff workers reflected different backgrounds and styles of leadership. Although Dallas CALCAV's operations began in early 1966, its first paid director was Richard Deats, on furlough from his position as missionary and teacher in the Philippines, who arrived in the summer of 1968. He found the city "progressive technologically but reactionary politically." The United Methodist Board of Missions paid his salary, while CALCAV paid his expenses and the chapter's programming. By early 1969 Dallas CALCAV operated with about fifty people drawn primarily from the middle-class religious community, both Christian and Jew, faculty and student. Deats's work combined the peace efforts of CALCAV and Southern Methodist University. CALCAV held most of its programs on the university campus, where it was actively supported by the United Campus Ministries and the Social Action Committee of the Perkins School of Theology. CALCAV sometimes worked cooperatively with other local antiwar groups, both secular and religious, helped with literature and fund raising for the Oleo Strut coffeehouse near Fort Hood, and sponsored occasional meetings in nearby Fort Worth. Deats found his efforts difficult but rewarding, and Dallas CALCAV remained active after his departure.[74]

Eric Robinson served Portland, Oregon as one of CALCAV's first full-time staff people in the fall of 1967, and his salary came from both CALCAV and the Portland Council of Churches. In the early 1970s, Portland CALCAV merged with the local Fellowship of Reconciliation into a tightly knit religious peace organization.[75]

Boston hired its first full-time staff member, John Cupples, in June 1968. Cupples had entered college in Stockton, California where he was involved in the local civil rights movement. From there he entered Harvard Divinity School and became active in peace issues while working toward his graduate degree. Among other things, he helped organize a national Seminarian's Conference on the Draft and the War in Vietnam, worked in Eugene McCarthy's Massachusetts primary campaign, and joined Boston CALCAV as a student assistant before taking the position as its executive director at age 24.[76]

Beginning in late 1967, CALCAV began to focus on the presidential campaign. Its continued faith in the electoral process reaffirmed its membership in the American political mainstream and differentiated it from the radicals. As antiwar activism increased, one of the more quixotic political campaigns of recent American history was building momentum. There had been talk in some circles of running a third party ticket of Martin Luther King, Jr. and Benjamin Spock, but King never consented, and the chances for success outside the major parties seemed highly unlikely. The Republican party was generally more hawkish on the war than Lyndon Johnson and almost certainly would not nominate an antiwar candidate. Thus, in September 1967, Allard Lowenstein and Curtis Gans formed the National Conference of Concerned Democrats and convinced a hesitant Senator Eugene McCarthy to make the effort to defeat Johnson for the Democratic presidential nomination. Ending the war in Vietnam was central to McCarthy's campaign. To reach that goal, he proposed a bombing halt, de-escalation of the fighting, and negotiations that included the National Liberation Front. He further hoped that his candidacy would alleviate the sense of political helplessness that many activists felt and would curb their willingness to take extralegal actions of protest.[77]

McCarthy's decision to run and his promise of a negotiated settlement in Vietnam won quick support from the leaders of liberal antiwar organizations such as SANE and Americans for Democratic Action. His stunning success in capturing 42 percent of the votes in the March 12 New Hampshire primary, however, was misleading.

Despite McCarthy's direct appeal to liberal doves, he drew a substantial number of votes from hawks who disapproved of Johnson's policy of gradual escalation or were unaware of his position on the war. Later studies revealed that McCarthy voters in New Hampshire were more likely to favor escalation of the war than withdrawal from Vietnam.[78]

Clergy and Laymen Concerned began early and pushed hard to make Vietnam a key campaign issue. In January 1968, the national committee developed a fourteen-page brochure called, "Who's Right, Who's Wrong on Vietnam?" Although McCarthy and New York Senator Robert Kennedy were the presidential favorites of most national CALCAV leaders, this paper did not endorse any particular candidate. It quoted a wide variety of politicians, military leaders, journalists, clergy, and others who represented both major political parties. "Who's Right, Who's Wrong on Vietnam?" refuted various arguments used to defend American involvement in Vietnam, portrayed U.S. officials as overly optimistic or deliberately misleading, and interpreted the war's opposition as patriotic, nonpartisan, and broadly representative of the American people.[79] The organization Business Executives Move for Vietnam Peace helped to defray the publishing and distribution costs. For $150,000, CALCAV sent out 4.2 million copies, one to every resident in New Hampshire, Wisconsin, Alaska, and Arkansas before those state's primaries, as well as everyone in Beverly Hills, California and 60,000 persons in Portland, Oregon. Delegates to the national nominating conventions also received them.[80]

Events in Vietnam like the Tet offensive and escalating antiwar sentiment at home began to erode support for the war within the administration. Newly appointed Secretary of Defense Clark Clifford developed grave reservations about America's chances of winning the war, while others suggested a bombing halt of North Vietnam, if for no other reason than to muffle public dissent. During the week of March 25, Johnson was stunned when the "wise men," a prestigious group of unofficial advisers, told him that the war could not be won and urged negotiation rather than military force as the only way to get out of Vietnam.[81] On the night of March 31, 1968, President Johnson appeared on national television to announce a new bombing halt and invite the North Vietnamese to begin negotiations. At the end of his speech, he shocked the nation when he declared that he would not run for reelection.

Reactions within CALCAV were generally favorable. The man who more than any other symbolized the tragedy of the war had removed himself from the presidential race, and now there was genuine hope that a peace candidate would be elected and finally end the war. Bennett believed that the President's decision presented a "real possibility that we can move to a different policy. . . . I think that he has seen that he himself has become a divisive factor. . . ." Heschel claimed that "it represents a victory for America. Period." Coffin was not convinced, however, and felt that like all previous bombing halts, this one could just as easily lead to further escalation.[82]

The hopes of CALCAV and other antiwar forces for a genuine peace candidate suffered a devastating blow early in the summer. In late April, Vice-President Hubert Humphrey had announced his candidacy, and his support within the party leadership made him the front-runner. Meanwhile Kennedy and McCarthy traded victories in the primaries. While McCarthy developed a loyal following among those who admired his courage for taking on the President, only Kennedy, with his organization and charismatic name, had a legitimate chance to keep Humphrey from the nomination. That challenge was extinguished on June 5, the evening of his victory in the California primary, when he became the latest victim of assassination.

Kennedy's death eliminated the possibility of a new president who was sympathetic to the aims of the antiwar movement. CALCAV immediately shifted to secure a peace plank in the Democratic party platform. Some members of the national committee traveled to Chicago as delegates to the Democratic Convention in August. Substituting for the ailing Reinhold Niebuhr, Neuhaus addressed the platform committee before the convention, asking it to endorse amnesty for both deserters and resisters. His testimony encouraged other groups to support CALCAV's position, but the platform committee was not persuaded.[83]

Individuals from CALCAV participated as both convention delegates and antiwar demonstrators, although most moderate and pacifist organizations chose not to attend. For months, various groups within the antiwar movement had looked forward to the Chicago nominating convention as a golden opportunity to demonstrate against President Johnson and his war policies. When he withdrew from the race, however, plans for the Chicago protest floundered. Radicals hoped to provoke the authorities into a violent response. The McCarthy campaign recognized that the Chicago activities lacked the organization of most mass demonstrations, and fearing possible violence, discouraged its supporters from coming. Only about 15,000 participants showed up for the convention protests. Neuhaus and several other convention delegates were among those peaceably arrested during the week's demonstrations, but others were less fortunate. The resulting war between Chicago police and protesters, later referred to as a "police riot" by the Walker Commission, ended with 660 arrests and over 1,000 people injured.[84]

The outcome of the Democratic convention disappointed those who had labored diligently to change the country's direction through the electoral process. Humphrey refused to break with Johnson's policies, and the leading Republican candidates were more hawkish than Humphrey. Those who hoped to cast their ballot for a negotiated peace in Vietnam were left without a major party candidate, which effectively removed the war as a critical campaign issue.[85] Public reaction to the events in Chicago was also discouraging. Fernandez, himself a victim of police tear gas, claimed that "tactics used by the Chicago police, openly and/or tacitly approved by millions of Americans, offer little indication of hope for a climate in which the Vietnam War can be ended by American withdrawal from that country."[86] The following day he reflected: "The fact that McCarthy fell short of the presidency and that the peace plank was never nailed boldly into the Democratic Party platform reminds us I think that miracles are not often granted, and that revolutions usually include many long marches, many defeats, many dry seasons, before they finally yield success."[87]

Since President Johnson's policy had failed to produce peace and Humphrey, Richard Nixon, and third-party candidate George Wallace offered little hope of ending the war, CALCAV tried to keep the issue alive by calling for an observance of Vietnam Sunday on November 3. This served as a time for the religious community to preach, discuss, and act on issues related to the war, both in denominational and in ecumenical situations. To support these activities, CALCAV provided speakers, films, literature, and other materials including 130,000 printed copies of "The Religious Community and American Politics." Many doors remained closed to them, however. Chaplain Captain Rubin Ascue turned down an attempt to arrange a prayer service for peace at Fort Dix, New Jersey, reasoning that such a service "was not in the best interest of the Army."[88]

Their options limited, some people within CALCAV and other antiwar liberals took encouragement from the President's last-minute bombing halt and supported Humphrey as the lesser of evils. Campaign polls indicated a late surge of support for the Democratic candidate, but he narrowly missed overcoming his initial disadvantage. On November 5, 1968, Richard Nixon was elected President of the United States.

CALCAV put aside the disappointment of the election results and concentrated on the issue of amnesty. The national steering committee believed that the personal conscientious witness of war resisters brought the political and moral issues of Vietnam to the forefront. As early as October 4, 1967, CALCAV cosponsored with the National Mobe a six-day trip to Paris and Stockholm. The delegation of about fifteen people, including Neuhaus, Harvey Cox, and Michael Novak, met with the U.S. exile communities there as part of a campaign for amnesty. CALCAV sought amnesty not only for Vietnam War draft resisters, but also for deserters. The inclusion of the deserters and exiles made it substantially more difficult to rally public support and attracted the attention of Hoover's FBI. Assuming that no amnesty would be granted before the end of hostilities, CALCAV de-emphasized its strategy of draft resistance through soliciting signatures on complicity statements. Instead it developed a campaign built upon the public's growing opposition to the war that was designed to increase the possibility of postwar amnesty. The campaign ran initially during the last four months of 1968. It focused on publicity through amnesty petitions and the establishment of a Committee of 100, which consisted of elected officials, academics, and religious and labor leaders, to draw attention to the issue and produce a ground swell for public acceptance.[89]

The defense of war resisters took a variety of forms. On August 15, a small group of southern California clergy held a vigil at the gates of Camp Pendleton to protest the court-martial of Marine private John Robinson, Jr. on charges of refusing to go to Vietnam. Heschel argued that rather than condemning such men, the country should praise them as "examples of great moral courage." The clergy also accused the Marines of forcing between 200 and 300 conscientious objectors aboard planes to Vietnam against their will.[90]

The testimony by Neuhaus to the Democratic platform committee was more conventional, but no idea was beyond the realm of possibility. Searching for any method that might aid conscientious opponents of the war, Fernandez even discussed a proposal to have the North Vietnamese release U.S. prisoners of war in exchange for an American release of its own draft resisters.[91]

At the end of December, CALCAV and the Fellowship of Reconciliation gambled that Johnson would be moved by the Christmas season and the approaching end of his term of office to make a magnanimous gesture toward war resisters. They held a joint news conference in Washington, D.C. on December 19. Two women, one a wife and the other a sister of men imprisoned for draft resistance, publicly requested that the President grant a Christmas amnesty to those who could not in good conscience bear arms in the Vietnam War. This appeal followed a similar request by the two organizations that encompassed those in prison, awaiting trial, or in voluntary exile because of their conscientious violations of the draft law. Both attempts were unsuccessful.[92]

In the last major action of its 1968 amnesty campaign, CALCAV joined with several other peace groups in holding a "celebration of conscience" at the Allenwood Federal Prison camp near Lewisburg, Pennsylvania. The steering committee had encouraged its members to visit imprisoned draft violators as a way of supporting and sharing the resisters' commitment against the war.[93] Allenwood was a minimum-security camp holding a number of war resisters for violating Selective Service laws. Over 1,000 volunteers, most of them young people from the Northeast, gathered at Bucknell University the day before the visit to Allenwood to attend workshops and share a communal meal. Ross Flanagan of the Society of Friends reaffirmed the purpose of the gathering, "to remind our society of the witnesses of these men of conscience." Of the more than 100 draft violators in Allenwood, most were Jehovah's Witnesses who did not participate in the service. Prison authorities bused in over twenty conscientious objectors from nearby Lewisburg Penitentiary so they could participate. Dr. Harvey Cox led the first groups of participants through the gates at 8:00 A.M., December 21. After 45 minutes the first of hundreds of others arrived for visits of fifteen minutes each. Over forty Allenwood prisoners attended the service, which included the baptism of the infant daughter of David Miller, the first convicted draft-card burner, songs by Joan Baez, readings from the Bible, communion, a period of silence, and a sermon by Harvey Cox, who referred to the men as "a light in a dark world." Only seventy of the visitors were able to get into the chapel at a time, and many never got past the prison gates.[94]

By the end of 1968, CALCAV and its allies in the antiwar movement had battled to a draw with Lyndon Johnson. To combat his critics, the President exaggerated the military's limited gains and ignited the domestic crisis that followed the Tet offensive. Alerted to Johnson's misleading claims by his political opposition, the American public was ready to accept a new direction.[95] LBJ stopped the war's escalation and stepped away from the presidency, but there was no end in sight to the Indochina conflict and no promise of amnesty for war resisters. CALCAV continued to expand its audience and attract active supporters across the country. Much of its success derived from its adherence to issues and tactics that appealed to its religious, middle-class constituency. During the previous eighteen months, however, the line between attraction and irritation had sometimes become blurred. Not all who participated in prayerful witness appreciated even a peaceful, orderly demonstration. Fewer still approved of civil disobedience. The sincere concern for the rights of draft resisters did not always transfer to acceptance of amnesty for military deserters. Not everyone who participated in electoral politics endorsed pressure against weapons producers, and many were troubled by accusations of American war crimes.

These differences reflected CALCAV's attempt to attract as broad a range of antiwar thought as possible without alienating any segment of the religious community. Its primary objectives of de-escalation and a negotiated peace settlement remained the same. With the election of the new President, few expected those goals to be easily reached, but many were willing to be proven wrong. Now they could only wait for Richard Nixon.

4

"HOW PATIENT MUST WE BE, MR. NIXON?"
(JANUARY 1969 to MAY 1970)

> We expected peace, but no peace came.
> —JEREMIAH 8:15 (LIVING BIBLE)

Two diverse observers debated the contemporary American political situation in a 1970 book entitled *Movement and Revolution*. Peter Berger, a conservative Boston College sociologist, and Richard Neuhaus, a self-described radical, were both leading members of CALCAV. Berger, who had overcome his suspicion of political change to participate in "the agony of one's time," accepted American power and global influence as a desirable fact. He opposed the Vietnam War largely because he believed the United States was pursuing an inhumane policy of indiscriminately killing civilians and devastating the countryside. He conceded the theoretical possibility of a morally just revolution in some areas of the Third World but argued that the situation in the United States neither demanded nor permitted it. Neuhaus felt that a revolution of American society was necessary to ensure justice for all. He opposed violence and hoped for a peaceful transformation but suspected that all nonviolent options had already been tried. Although he agreed that the conditions for a morally just, violent revolution in the United States did not presently exist, he could conceive of such conditions' existing in the future. The political analyses of Berger and Neuhaus were similar enough that they could work together in opposition to the Vietnam War, but on issues that were peripheral to that conflict, their positions were distinct and uncompromising. Both admitted that, "pushed far enough, our differences could put us on opposite sides of the barricades."[1]

These divergent outlooks mirrored the situation within CALCAV at the turn of the decade. The desire for a quick end to the war served as the primary rallying point for Clergy and Laymen Concerned About Vietnam. As American policy changed from escalation to gradual withdrawal and social issues proliferated at the end of the 1960s, however, new subjects found their way into CALCAV councils. The introduction of peripheral topics revealed an organization undergoing a transition from its relatively homogeneous origins to a greater ideological diversity that threatened its internal consensus.

The election of Richard Nixon did not inspire much hope among most antiwar activists for a quick and reasonable settlement of the war. The National Mobilization Committee sponsored a series of counterinaugural events, hampered by government provocateurs and FBI harassment. On Sunday, January 19, over 10,000 protesters marched down Pennsylvania Avenue, and about the same number attended a counterinaugural ball that evening. On Monday, inauguration day, several thousand antiwar activists lined the parade route, a few hundred of whom left to do some trashing on nearby streets.[2]

At its third Washington mobilization, Clergy and Laymen Concerned About Vietnam presented an interesting contrast. While they remained wary of Nixon's promise to "end the war and win the peace," activists in CALCAV allowed themselves a degree of cautious optimism. "We feel that in approximately a year the shooting in Vietnam might well cease," the mobilization call declared.[3] The group at the February 3–5 convocation was in high spirits. People spoke of being "encouraged," of seeing "signs of change," and of this being the last peace demonstration against the war. Even Richard Fernandez commented, "we're beginning to talk about things we wouldn't have talked about before October 31 [the latest bombing halt]."[4]

This uncharacteristic burst of hope in retrospect may seem unrealistic, but it reflected the continued faith of CALCAV's constituency in the ability of the American political system to recognize and correct its own mistakes. Over the next several months that faith would be severely tested.

Despite its optimism, CALCAV was not ready to declare the war over and close itself down. In fact, it was operating near its peak during 1969. It now claimed 100 local branches and a mailing list of 25,000. The national press recognized it as "one of the nation's largest and most influential peace groups" with "connections to middle-class America."[5]

The third Washington mobilization drew roughly 1,000 people. At Monday's opening session in the Metropolitan African Methodist Episcopal Church, Democratic Senator George McGovern of South Dakota criticized America's military machine for draining away needed money and personnel from industrial and social needs, and claimed that the conduct of offensive operations during the peace talks delayed an agreement and cost additional lives. He called for an immediate reduction of the U.S. troops in Vietnam by half, an end to all offensive missions, and the elimination of the draft. Following McGovern, Seymour Melman advocated cutting U.S. defense spending by leaving Vietnam.[6] At the conclusion of the session, the participants dispersed to other area churches for afternoon seminars.

At a Tuesday press conference, CALCAV released its 1969 position paper, "The Reconciliation We Seek," which contained several significant changes from the previous year. The 1968 statement had addressed almost exclusively the ongoing conflict in Vietnam. The newer version looked ahead to the war's conclusion and devoted half of its attention to other social and political issues. Both questioned America's underlying cold war beliefs as well as the U.S. policy in Vietnam, but the 1969 paper was more critical. The earlier position had contained a strong moral condemnation of the war but was restrained in presenting specific proposals. It endorsed that year's election campaigns as a valid political effort but lamented the law-and-order movement that relegated justice to a secondary importance. The most extreme recommendation in 1968 was for a new draft law that would recognize selective conscientious objection. "The Reconciliation We Seek" combined thoughtful suggestions with irritating assertions that probably hampered its potential effectiveness within the churches. Most of its proposals were not unreasonable, however. It urged ending all bombing of North and South Vietnam and proposed immediate steps toward disengaging U.S. troops without explicitly mentioning immediate withdrawal. The 1969 statement sought U.S. pressure against the Saigon regime to release South Vietnamese political prisoners while it also called for American protection, perhaps political sanctuary, for Vietnamese "whom we have encouraged to join in our misbegotten policies."

At times, the document lapsed into a tone similar to the radical indictment. The United States, it claimed, should abandon its support of oppressive governments in areas like Central America simply because they were anticommunist. Greater economic aid should go to the poorer nations without regard to cold war politics. Domestically, it declared that financial priorities that favored the militaristic system exploited all Americans. Among its most extreme proposals were amnesty for all draft resisters and deserters, aid for the reconstruction of postwar Vietnam, financial restitution to black citizens for past injustices, and the elimination of the draft.[7] Occasionally, even these points were tempered, however. On the question of amnesty, Fernandez recognized the political limitations on the President, noting, "our view is that Mr. Nixon, under the best of conditions, cannot even consider this until the shooting stops in Vietnam."[8]

Fernandez revealed further evidence of CALCAV's harder line when he vented some of his frustration at trying to rally support for war resisters. He voiced his displeasure that a number of religious bodies, including the National Conference of Catholic Bishops, the Lutheran Church in America, and the Union of American Hebrew Congregations, had endorsed the concept of selective conscientious objection but had failed to follow through with supporting actions. "There aren't very many high up in main line religious communities," he commented, "who after instigating statements in many cases will then be sensitive enough to stand with men who have demonstrated the sincere conviction that they're not pacifists, but that they can't kill Vietnamese either."[9]

The influence of radical tendencies is also evident in the topics discussed in small conferences during the mobilization. Participants dealt with revising the federal budget to reduce military expenditures and increase spending on the underprivileged. They also discussed issues such as apartheid in South Africa, the possibility of forming a new liberal political party, and housing cooperatives for the poor, as well as draft resistance, political trials such as those of the Milwaukee Fourteen and Catonsville Nine, and amnesty.[10] Congressional lobbying took place on Tuesday afternoon following the conferences.

Late Wednesday morning, CALCAV achieved a symbolic breakthrough. A delegation consisting of Coffin, Heschel, Neuhaus, Elston, Fernandez, and Coretta Scott King met with National Security Adviser Henry Kissinger for about forty minutes. This was the first conference in three years between any top government official and what the New York *Times* referred to as "militant pacifist leaders." They encouraged amnesty for draft resisters, probed the goals of Nixon's Paris peace talks, questioned his support of the antiballistic missile program, and argued the injustice of the Army's mutiny trials against prisoners who staged a sit-in at the Presidio military prison. CALCAV had originally sought to meet with President Nixon, and the plans to talk with Kissinger had only been completed late Tuesday evening. Nevertheless, this seemed a significant improvement over the past two years, when President Johnson had refused all meetings with the group.[11]

The mobilization's concluding service began early Wednesday afternoon, picketed by Carl McIntire and a group of about fifty. It served as a fitting conclusion to an impressive convocation. One observer was moved to write: "The three-day meeting retained the earnestness, the religiosity, the desire to influence the real world, which much of the Movement has lost along the way."[12] Even the worship service, however, illustrated the changes CALCAV was experiencing. As much as anyone, Richard Neuhaus exemplified the use of more strident rhetoric by some CALCAV veterans. At one point in his sermon he referred to the Vietnamese as "God's instrument for bringing the American empire to its knees."[13]

CALCAV's growing support of war resisters—draft evaders and deserters—highlighted the recent tendency among some of its members to consider Vietnamization the beginning of the war's end and to turn their attention to postwar problems. At the conclusion of the mobilization's final service on February 5, about 600 people filed out of the Metropolitan A.M.E. Church and marched the fifteen blocks to the Justice Department. Mrs. King, Heschel, Neuhaus, and Father Richard McSorley ceremoniously laid their hands on the head of Father Thomas Hayes, an Episcopal priest, to dedicate his ministerial role in CALCAV's commitment to the American deserters in Sweden.[14]

Clergy and Laymen Concerned first became involved with American exiles during a July 1968 meeting of the World Council of Churches in Uppsala, Sweden. Several delegates met with members of the American Deserter Committee, an organization of deserters that served as CALCAV's contact in Sweden, and upon returning to the United States suggested an initiative to publicize the existence and problems of the deserters there.[15] Fernandez and Dellinger organized a joint delegation to visit the American exile communities in both Paris and Stockholm and to check on the progress of the Paris negotiations. Neuhaus, Harvey Cox, and Michael Novak joined eleven others and traveled to France and Sweden from October 24 to October 30. The roughly twenty deserters in Paris seemed relatively happy and received good support from the community. William Bloom, an American Presbyterian minister working in France, made a special effort to work with them. While in Paris, the American delegation met with members of both the North Vietnamese and the National Liberation Front negotiating teams, but U.S. Ambassador W. Averell Harriman refused to see them.

In Stockholm, the delegation met with eighty to ninety men and found the situation there more difficult despite an enlightened, if inconsistent, program for political refugees.[16] Through speeches, articles, and public appearances, various members of the delegation explained that most of the problems facing the deserters in Sweden were related to the difficulties of assimilating into Swedish society. Learning the language, finding work, and fighting the red tape of a foreign bureaucracy all taxed the morale of the deserters. The delegates also reported attempts by the United States government to sow dissension among the deserters and between the exiles and the Swedish government. The Criminal Intelligence Division of the U.S. Army, for example, attempted to get the deserters to return to the United States, and the government sent a diplomatic signal from Sweden when it recalled Ambassador William Heath for five weeks in March 1968.[17] Despite their views on the Vietnam War, most deserters wanted to return to the United States. Neuhaus portrayed them not as men who had deserted America but as men who refused to be "agents of its deadly perversion in Vietnam."[18]

The delegation recommended that a staff member be placed in Stockholm to work with the deserters and that a communications channel be opened with their families back home.[19] CALCAV established the Sweden Project to undertake a ministry to those deserters and selected the Rev. Thomas Lee Hayes to head it. A graduate of Oberlin and the Episcopal Theological School, Hayes had served as Executive Director of the Episcopal Peace Fellowship for three years until contacted by CALCAV.[20] He, his wife, and their two daughters left for Sweden on March 20. His responsibilities included helping the American deserters adjust to Swedish life, counseling them on personal problems, and solidifying the tenuous status of political asylum, while also serving as an organizer and teacher and as a liaison between the exiles and the Swedish government.

One of his first objectives was persuading Swedish authorities to admit deserters as permanent refugees, a job he found ironic in light of America's historical role as a home for refugees.[21] The government required American deserters to register with the police upon entering the country. Before they could apply for political asylum, the war resisters had to present evidence that their immigration resulted from opposition to the Vietnam War. Hayes found, however, that the Swedish government would not recognize objectors to conscription from another country and therefore did not grant political asylum to Americans. Instead it gave them a "right to stay" that allowed immigrants to live and work in the country, and also required them to learn the language.[22]

By the time Hayes arrived in Sweden, the issue of political asylum was preeminent for the American Deserter Committee. A few months earlier, some of the deserters had been threatened with expulsion because of legal technicalities. Hayes held a press conference in Stockholm on April 21 to attack the Swedish bureaucracy's "psychological harassment" of the U.S. exiles. He also attacked a recent Pentagon study, based on files taken from the Swedish Aliens Commission, that explained most defections in terms of disciplinary problems and only a relatively small number as resulting from opposition to the Vietnam War.[23]

In an apparent attempt to limit the Americans' political activity,

Swedish authorities ordered some deserters to attend the language school at Osterbybruk or risk losing the minimal financial support provided until they could find jobs. When the Americans refused to move to this relatively isolated city, Hayes leased a farm in Vasterhaninge for a year as emergency housing and partial compensation for the loss of income. Hayes and the members of the deserter community contacted members of the Swedish government to counteract this and similar decisions. The American Deserter Committee initiated a political campaign that emphasized the contradiction between government policy and practice and demanded political asylum. It ended the threats regarding Osterbybruk.[24]

American deserters found it very difficult to acquire jobs, particularly in the fall and winter. The Swedish government did provide job training, placement, and housing assistance to some other nationalities, but it did not make these available to Americans. According to official policy, they were not obvious political refugees.[25] The threat of American sanctions against Sweden for harboring deserters and opposing American's Vietnam policies scared many potential employers away. Hayes urged CALCAV to utilize American business leaders to persuade the Swedish and Canadian business communities to do what they could to hire American deserters.

Hayes spent most of his time dealing with the problems of individuals. Acts of crime and drug use among the deserters taxed his energy and the patience of others in CALCAV, but the commitment to helping those who took a difficult stand made a difference.[26] By the summer of 1969, more of the deserters were in schools and universities, held jobs, or had found permanent housing. In general, their lives were beginning to stabilize.

During the summer, Bea Seitzman, a professor of social work at Columbia University, spent eight weeks in Stockholm working with Hayes. She returned in August and spoke to a CALCAV conference in Cambridge, Massachusetts. Her report corrected myths about the deserters and gave a generally favorable account of their progress. She praised CALCAV's Swedish ministry as a concrete expression of concern felt by one segment of the antiwar movement for one segment of the war's victims. The experience in Sweden exposed her to a common emotion among antiwar activists. "The overriding feeling that accompanied my work this summer, one that I fully expect will never leave me, is that of an acceleration of anger against our government!"[27]

After ten months, Hayes decided that his work in Sweden was finished. Conditions within the U.S. deserter community were much improved, and a new, more lenient Canadian policy toward deserters would probably reduce the future influx of men to Sweden. Hayes also believed that his continued presence would be a barrier to the development of some of the men, providing an illusion of security that made self-reliance more difficult.[28]

Hayes returned to the United States and spent three months traveling across the country speaking to community groups and on radio and television. The discovery that most Americans were unsympathetic to the plight of deserters and resisters shocked him.[29]

CALCAV's commitment to the exiles in Sweden did not end with Hayes's return, but the relationship was sometimes strained. Early in 1971, angry at the instability of the American Deserter Committee, Fernandez complained, "I really have a difficult time seeing why . . . we should continue support of a group that is so totally and continually in a state of disruption."[30] For as long as it could afford to, however, the national office provided $1,500 to $3,000 a year for the ministry in Sweden, dividing the money among the deserters and Swedish social worker Kristina Nystrom who worked with them.[31]

Other U.S. war resisters sought refuge to the north. From the mid-1960s to the early 1970s, thousands of Americans emigrated to Canada to avoid involvement in the Vietnam War. In late April and early May 1969, Fernandez visited U.S. exiles in Toronto and Montreal, while Phil Farnham visited Vancouver. Few of the exiles expressed a strong desire to return to the United States. Many had tried to fit into Canadian society by gaining landed immigrant status, which gave them the right to work and would eventually lead to citizenship. Draft resisters could obtain landed immigrant status fairly easily, but the larger number of deserters found it more difficult. Fernandez and Farnham discovered that the Canadian churches and synagogues played only a very minor role in assisting U.S. exiles. Toronto and Vancouver provided the most hospitable climates for American resisters, but there was little money in the antidraft programs of those cities.[32]

Fernandez recommended that CALCAV establish and maintain contacts with the major Canadian antidraft centers, send small, one-time financial donations to those centers, and urge American denominational bodies to contribute money for the antidraft project through the United Church of Canada. Clergy and Laymen Concerned intended to ask the Canadian government to grant landed immigrant status to U.S. military deserters, but this proved unnecessary when the Canadian Parliament did just that on May 22, 1969. Parliament's action gave American deserters who entered Canada the same rights as other immigrants. The fact that Canadian immigration policy no longer discriminated against military deserters and that its extradition treaties excluded resisters and deserters made Canada an inviting destination for American war resisters.[33] On May 29, CALCAV's national committee publicly thanked the Montreal resistance program. "Once our country was viewed as a haven of safety for refugees from injustice," the statement read. "To our sorrow and shame, the United States now has its own political prisoners and exiles. Your welcome to Americans who cannot in conscience take part in their country's military adventurism reveals Canada as a sanctuary of hope in North America."[34]

By the end of 1969, CALCAV raised over $5,000 from among its own membership to aid resisters and deserters. In mid-December, delegations from Boston, Buffalo, Detroit, and Seattle, took representative grants of $500 across the Canadian border and presented them to resisters and deserters from the antidraft centers in Montreal, Ottawa, Toronto, and Vancouver. The remaining funds went to the Canadian Council of Churches for distribution to other aid centers.[35]

Largely through the efforts of Richard Killmer, CALCAV initiated a meeting on December 2 between representatives of both the Canadian and National Council of Churches and a group of American draft resisters and deserters at Windsor, Ontario. This conference evaluated the needs of the American exiles and discussed potential efforts to build moral and financial support for them through the churches and synagogues. Its report to the General Assembly of the National Council of Churches resulted in the adoption of guidelines that led to the establishment in February 1970 of the NCC's Emergency Ministry Concerning U.S. Draft Age Emigrants in Canada. In the meantime, the Canadian Council of Churches raised money and presented grants to ten of the aid centers. Unfortunately for CALCAV, Killmer, a graduate of Princeton Theological Seminary, a former coordinator of Vietnam Summer, and the executive director of Minnesota CAL-CAV, moved on to the National Council of Churches to head the ministry to American deserters in Canada. By December 1970, the money raised by CALCAV in behalf of war resisters was exceeded only by the $100,000 raised by Killmer at the National Council of Churches from European church agencies.[36]

Underscoring CALCAV's drift to issues on the war's periphery was its role in attracting national attention to the Presidio trials. On October 11, 1968, a guard's shotgun blast killed a psychologically disturbed inmate as he walked away from a work detail at the Presidio Stockade near San Francisco. Three days later, 27 men took part in a sit-down strike to protest the killing of the prisoner and inhumane conditions at the prison. For this act, the Army accused the men of mutiny. Despite the recommendation by the official Army hearing officer that the facts did not support the charge of mutiny, the first six went before a court-martial early the next year.[37]

The San Francisco chapter of CALCAV in particular and the national organization in general played key roles in bringing this case into national prominence. To mobilize public opinion, CALCAV released a statement in San Francisco on January 27, 1969 that called the mutiny charges "inhumane" and "intolerable," and demanded that the Army drop them. Robert McAfee Brown was among the Bay area religious leaders responsible for the statement's national circulation. A significant number of the nearly forty church and synagogue leaders who signed it had direct ties to CALCAV. To support its position, CALCAV sponsored a campaign that produced over 3,000 letters to the Secretary of the Army and to members of Congress.[38]

During CALCAV's Washington mobilization, a group consisting of Phil Farnham, Sue Rowland, wife of one of the Presidio 27, and Catholic priests Mark Sullivan and Joseph Sonntag met with Secretary of the Army Stanley Resor to persuade him to call off the Presidio court-martials. They spent most of Monday dealing with the military bureaucracy before meeting with Robert Jordan, the Army's General Counsel. According to Washington correspondent Robert Kuttner, "Jordan all but admitted that the trials were unsupportable but that rather than lose face by peremptorily cancelling them, the Army civilian hierarchy would prefer to have any verdicts of guilty over-turned by the normal appeals process."[39] The group decided to remain at the Pentagon until Resor agreed to meet with them, but that evening they were removed from the building in wheelchairs and taken back to mobilization headquarters. They finally met with Resor on Wednesday, but he was less candid than Jordan had been.

These efforts failed to prevent the Presidio trials. The Sixth Army court-martial boards convicted four of the first nine men tried, handing out sentences of up to sixteen years. Still hoping to have the charges and convictions thrown out, CALCAV declared March 18, the date when the remaining sixteen men went on trial, as a Day of Conscience. Peaceful demonstrations of various sizes occurred in cities across the country, and CALCAV monitored the cases as they progressed.[40]

CALCAV wasted little time in displaying its lack of patience with Nixon's efforts to end the war. At a news conference at the Belmont Plaza Hotel in New York City on February 21, 1969, CALCAV made public a letter sent to Nixon demanding to know his plans for ending the Vietnam War. It credited his election to the "overwhelming disillusionment" with America's Indochina policy and warned of the risks that a continuation of that policy would entail. "We fear the time is approaching, Mr. President, when we must declare your administration accountable for the continued suffering and death in Vietnam."[41]

Nixon's secret plan to end the war was quickly exposed as hollow campaign rhetoric, and CALCAV resumed its attacks. That the moratorium on criticism of the new administration had ended was evident in March when CALCAV places ads in four major religious periodicals and the New York *Times* headlined, "How Patient Must We Be, Mr. Nixon?" Addressing the public, the ad stated: "Exactly one year ago . . . the bombing of North Vietnam was curtailed. At the same time President Johnson announced he would not seek another term in office, declaring his desire to achieve a peaceful settlement of the war. You thought the corner had been turned. You were wrong. A year later our country is on the same bloodied and blundering course in Vietnam." Blaming Nixon's support of the "corrupt Thieu-Ky regime" for the absence of a peace settlement, CALCAV urged the withdrawal of American power so that "new forms of leadership" could emerge to replace the current South Vietnamese government.[42]

The Nixon administration reacted to such criticism by trying to minimize any effectiveness the antiwar movement might have with the general public. As part of this strategy, Attorney General John Mitchell used grand juries to harass the movement. This practice differed little from the indictment of Coffin and the Boston Five in 1968. The most notable example of this harassment came in March 1969 when a Chicago federal grand jury indicted eight men on charges of conspiracy to incite rioting at the Chicago Democratic National Convention.

These government counterattacks had little immediate impact as protests against the war continued throughout the spring. Although the National Mobilization Committee did not coordinate a major spring action, groups such as the Chicago Peace Council, Fifth Avenue Peace Parade Committee, A Quaker Action Group, and the Student Mobilization Committee sponsored a number of demonstrations around the country on April 5. In New York 100,000 people turned out, with other sizable crowds in Chicago, San Francisco, Atlanta, Los Angeles, and Austin.[43]

Over the next several months, CALCAV's activities reflected both the conflict within its own membership and the dichotomy that increasingly characterized the larger antiwar movement. On May 7, for the second year CALCAV targeted Dow Chemical's annual stockholder's meeting for a demonstration. About 300 protesters, many from Michigan CALCAV chapters, gathered earlier to discuss Dow's involvement in chemical warfare and to distribute leaflets throughout the town. The company denied rumors that it would not bid on a new government napalm contract or would deliberately allow itself to be underbid. In case the rumors were true, however, about 150 people gathered near the entrance of the Dow building on the day of the stockholder's meeting singing and passing out flowers to those going inside as a show of their appreciation.[44]

Seven of the protesters held a teach-in inside the stockholder's meeting, but they were not well received. Carl Gerstacker, the Chairman of the Board of Dow Chemical, answered them, saying: "Gentlemen, I think you should be ashamed of yourselves. You people who are ministers or priests—you talk to us of peace, or moral decisions, of our nation's heritage, but you're asking us, Dow Chemical Company, to make a decision that would take away from our government, which is elected by the majority of our people. . . ." The majority of the stockholders applauded enthusiastically. Gerstacker went on to accuse CALCAV of lying about Dow Chemical, the "Goebbels-Hitler technique," and directed them to try to have napalm declared illegal if they were really concerned about the issue.[45]

Daniel Bernstein, a wealthy New York stockbroker and financial backer of CALCAV, had a more significant impact. Bernstein, who sat apart from the CALCAV delegation, discussed the foolishness of holding on to a nonessential napalm contract that had brought such bad publicity to the company. "I have friends that are in the same position as stockbrokers," Fernandez recalls him saying. "We don't even talk about your company anymore."[46]

Despite its denial of the earlier rumors and its denunciation of CALCAV's efforts, Dow evidently feared the impact of these protests on its public image, sales, or both. Shortly after, it lost the napalm contract. Certain that the company had intentionally overbid to lose the contract, Fernandez wrote a letter of thanks to its president.[47]

This incident emphasizes the problems CALCAV faced in presenting its message to the public. Its view that each individual should accept responsibility for involvement in the war effort ran counter to attitudes like Gerstacker's that trusted the government to make its moral evaluations. Although CALCAV's action was legal and based on rational persuasion, it drew criticism. Stockholders opposed disturbing their investments, and to many moderates and conservatives, economic pressure seemed an inappropriate method to encourage political change.

Other events drew mixed reactions as well. On May 23, the Fellowship of Reconciliation and CALCAV cosponsored a series of news conferences that focused on political and religious repression by the Saigon regime. Perhaps the most widely reported of the more than thirty press conferences was the one in Washington, D.C., where Louise Ransom returned to the South Vietnamese Embassy the medals that the Saigon government had posthumously awarded her son Mike, killed in Vietnam over a year earlier. Ransom explained that she could not keep medals from a government that was so intolerant of dissent, citing the closing of over thirty Saigon newspapers as evidence. An embassy official claimed that the newspapers were shut down because they did not serve the national interest.[48]

The same day, a delegation including Robert Ransom, Robert Drinan, Don Luce, Ann Bennett, and Fernandez met at the White House with Richard Sneider of Kissinger's staff. Sneider assured the group that there was less political repression in Vietnam than had existed a few years earlier, but he could not provide any specific evidence to support this claim. Later at the Lafayette Hotel, representatives announced that CALCAV and several other religious organizations planned to send a delegation to South Vietnam to study further the issue of political repression. Scheduled to travel from May 25 to June 10, the group included Drinan, Ann Bennett, John Pemberton of the American Civil Liberties Union, Representative John Conyers of Michigan, Retired Admiral Arnold True, Rabbi Seymour Siegel, and Bishop James Armstrong of the United Methodist Church.[49]

Antiwar criticisms of the Saigon regime were not examples of exaggerated radical rhetoric. South Vietnam's brand of selective democracy was persuasively documented, a situation that seriously blurred the distinction between the communist-led Viet Cong and the "free" forces of the South. Despite the accuracy of these charges and growing sentiment against the war, antiwar activists faced continued disapproval. In the tradition of blaming the messenger who bears bad news, much of the public vented its frustration against the peace movement for pointing out the discrepancy between U.S. goals and reality. Some even viewed the criticism of Saigon or the antidraft position as a repudiation rather than a reaffirmation of American values.

In early May, CALCAV joined several organizations in forming the National Council to Repeal the Draft.[50] On May 30, local groups held solemn Memorial Day actions in various parts of the country as a response to the more typical military observances and to highlight the mounting death toll in Vietnam. CALCAV and several other antiwar groups sponsored a June 17 and 18 demonstration in Washington that focused on the concern for American soldiers who were asked to die for a repressive South Vietnamese government while their rights were curtailed inside the military system.[51]

During that summer, CALCAV became more actively involved in pushing religious denominations to take positions on the war and related issues such as amnesty and draft resistance. Workers at various conventions staffed information tables, spoke with delegates, and distributed literature in order to reach as many people as possible. CALCAV personnel, as outside observers or as members of the respective denominations, also pressed for statements of church opinion. Working with a progressive group, usually a social action committee, they might suggest a particular issue or specific wording. The committee would then present a resolution to the entire gathering for debate and a floor vote. What critics may have seen as intrusive or coercive, supporters viewed as educational. The national committee sent representatives to the conventions of the United Church of Christ in Boston, the Lutheran Church—Missouri Synod in Denver, and the Episcopal Church in South Bend, Indiana.[52]

At the 1969 Episcopal convention, a special meeting called to consider racial questions, CALCAV brought in two AWOL soldiers from Hawaii and hid them for a few days in the suite of the Assistant Bishop of Washington. When they arrived at the convention floor, according to Fernandez, "These two guys got up and told their story —one was a South Carolinian Episcopalian. . . . He went to a church in Pee Dee, South Carolina, man, and he had been taught that he was always to obey his conscience. I mean it was unbelievable testimony."[53] Nearly half of the convention's participants stood in support of the soldiers' right not to go to war.[54] Fernandez compared the mood to a Billy Graham crusade and recalled the conversion of one man who announced: "If you had told me a week ago when I got on a plane from Kansas City that I would stand up today for two deserters of the United States of America. . . . I would have laughed in your face."[55]

Despite CALCAV's more visible presence, in 1969 the churches seemed less concerned with Vietnam than with racial matters. James Forman and the Black Economic Development Conference had issued a Black Manifesto demanding financial payments from white churches as compensation for the historical exploitation of American blacks.[56] Nixon was bringing U.S. troops home, and with de-escalation, the war appeared to be coming to an end. Nevertheless, several conventions dealt with the questions of war resistance. The acceptance of selective conscientious objection grew with the endorsement of the United Presbyterian Church, the Presbyterian Church in the

United States, and the National Conference of Catholic Bishops. American Baptists and the United Church of Christ supported amnesty for war resisters, while United Presbyterians favored draft counseling centers. The Disciples of Christ and the United Church of Christ recommended an end to the draft altogether.[57]

The changes in American policy tempted CALCAV to look ahead. At an April meeting, its steering committee decided to continue the organization beyond the end of the Vietnam War. The national committee planned a conference in the Boston-Cambridge area for late August to discuss this new commitment and begin preparing for the future. At a preconference planning meeting in July, discussion centered around four main points: getting a sense of the variety of values within the organization; locating its proper constituency; choosing the issues it should focus on; and setting up the proper organizational structure. In discussing future issues, the planning committee concluded that CALCAV was presently viable because people could identify with its opposition to the war. Some wondered, however, whether they could mobilize the religious community around future issues that were not constantly in front of the public. The participants discussed as possible conference topics developing a branch for research, strengthening their ties to the seminaries, building a relationship with an existing organization such as Dispatch News Service, and focusing on development at the local level.[58]

Neuhaus chaired the Cambridge Conference held at the Episcopal Theological School August 27 and 28. Recognizing that CALCAV's primary constituency constituted the committed and potentially committed in the churches, he believed that it should bring a religious witness and influence to the issues of social change by making the religious community a stronger agent of that change. Fernandez raised the possibility that CALCAV publish its own journal, and felt that it should do more in the field of theological education. Others discussed the upcoming national antiwar actions.[59]

The Cambridge conference produced no significant policy decisions, only agreement to continue as an interfaith movement.[60] It did, however, generate regional meetings in October to encourage new efforts where peace activity had been minimal. Richard Killmer joined Fernandez to meet with thirty people in Dallas, then moved on to Augusta, Maine and Rapid City, South Dakota. The conferees at each stop expressed their frustration and isolation at working in areas generally hostile to their message. Those in Dallas established a newsletter and speaker's bureau to link their programs in the southwest. The 35 people at the Maine conference formed a statewide CALCAV chapter to initiate and coordinate local efforts, and while representatives from the northern plains area decided not to organize regionally, various state groups renewed their efforts to end the war.[61]

CALCAV's activity throughout 1969, especially its support of draft resisters and deserters, intensified the FBI's interest. An item that appeared in the May *Issues and Actions* newsletter attracted particular attention. Having been approached several times to aid military deserters desiring to remain in the United States "underground" and having assisted these men in finding housing and work so they would not be detected, the national office asked for people willing to help future deserters.[62] These actions would violate federal laws, and before the month was out, J. Edgar Hoover ordered an investigation of CALCAV for sedition. By the late fall, the FBI, assisted by military intelligence agencies, had failed to uncover any evidence of CALCAV's harboring or assisting military deserters. Although greatly agitated by CALCAV's resistance activities, Hoover himself admitted its members were "not known to be violent and would not resort to acts of destruction or terrorism." Still the internal security and sedition investigations continued.[63]

CALCAV leaders assumed that their phones were tapped and that most of their activities were being observed. They occasionally took the precaution of making sensitive calls on pay telephones but generally did not spend much time guarding against FBI and other intelligence activity.[64]

The expansion of both CALCAV and FBI activities occurred as the national antiwar coalitions experienced another period of readjustment. Students for a Democratic Society openly split into two opposing factions at its annual convention in June. With the National Mobe unable to put together an effective program, the Cleveland Area Peace Action Coalition sponsored a national antiwar conference by invitation only at Case Western Reserve University the first week of July. The participants formed the New Mobilization Committee to End the War in Vietnam, and agreed upon a mass demonstration in Washington, D.C. in the fall.[65]

A second organization, the Vietnam Moratorium, developed independently of the New Mobe. Organizers Sam Brown and David Hawk proposed that on October 15, there would be a moratorium on business as usual across the country while people demonstrated their views on the war in their own communities. In each succeeding month, the moratorium would expand by one day until the United States withdrew from South Vietnam or negotiated a settlement. To moderates within the coalition, the moratorium presented the opportunity to attract the large middle group of Americans who strongly opposed the war but were fearful and uncertain about being allied with radicals who participated in the national coalitions. The organized antiwar movement, which had been moving progressively to the left and had been damaged by events such as the Chicago Democratic Convention, now had the possibility of reaching back and capturing the center of the American public.[66]

In the fall of 1969 national antiwar activity peaked. The Vietnam Moratorium on October 15 was indicative of the grassroots antiwar movement. This decentralized protest built around local actions was an impressive success and drew 100,000 participants in both New York and Boston, 50,000 in Washington, 25,000 each in Ann Arbor and Madison, and 20,000 in Minneapolis, Philadelphia, and Detroit. Hundreds of thousands more met in cities and towns all over the country. The programs had a moderate to liberal tone and attracted a great deal of establishment political support.[67]

The New Mobe's massive demonstration in Washington followed in mid-November. A major part of the November Mobilization was the March Against Death, originally suggested by Stewart Meacham of the AFSC and adopted by the Quakers and other religious groups. Susan Miller of the Episcopal Peace Fellowship directed the project with assistance from Trudi Young, later to be a key figure in CALCAV. The March Against Death began at 6:00 P.M., November 13 as the first of 43,000 people carried a placard bearing the name of an American soldier killed in Vietnam from the Arlington National Cemetery, across the Memorial Bridge, past the White House where the name was called out, and on to the Capitol where they placed the placards in caskets to be carried in the rally on November 15. Of the march, Fred Halstead observed, "The mood was solemn and determined, and for many of the participants it was obviously a deeply felt spiritual experience."[68]

Among the marchers was a group of students from Ann Arbor. Typical of the young people who worked with the local religious community, they came from middle-class homes and held moderate political perspectives. CALCAV workers had helped prepare them for the demonstration, but experience proved to be the most enlightening teacher. "I remember the first meeting when they came back," observed Barbara Fuller. "They were so totally amazed . . . by the fact that when they walked by the White House, they saw soldiers with machine guns."[69]

On November 15, a crowd estimated as high as 750,000 gathered at the Washington Monument for a rally chaired by Dr. Spock and Coffin. Not everyone was pleased with the results. Sam Brown believed the New Mobe directed its efforts too far to the political left and ignored the center. Hawk felt that the day's speeches should have been coordinated to refute President Nixon's "silent majority" speech and was disappointed that they were instead, "largely rhetoric designed to 'heighten the consciousness' of the marchers. . . ." Coffin himself noted that "There were precious few good speeches, and those who tried to make one—like George McGovern—were hooted down by the SDS, many of whom may well have been provocateurs."[70]

While this tenuous cooperation between liberals and radicals continued on the surface, the internal tensions remained. Liberals who continued to believe that the war could be ended through the existing political system recognized that alignment with radicals would repel moderate voters. Many people within CALCAV's natural constituency, the religious community, feared association with the Mobe because of the left's involvement. Even planning sessions became strained when questions of ideology emerged. Elston remembered the Socialist Worker's Party as

> the ones who created this incredible confrontation at every damned planning meeting. Ah, the Trots [kyites]. The Trots are so irrelevant to everything. They were a blessing to the Mobe, however, because they were not large but they were extremely well-disciplined. They were not crazies, they didn't want violence. They were the best of the security contingent. The Mobe meetings were dreadful because of them, but the actual planning was blessed by having those folk keep an iron hand on security.[71]

Moderates and liberals recognized that participation in coalition movements exposed them to possible manipulation by the radical left, but fearing the danger of becoming too timid, they frequently remained in the coalitions. As Robert McAfee Brown admitted, however, "Every now and then you get burned."[72]

CALCAV served as a bridge between the cautious and the radical, and it maintained a good relationship with all the major factions within the antiwar movement. Fernandez managed to soothe some of the nervousness over vandalism by fringe elements, pointing out that those crimes would be handled by the police and that the movement's work was to stop the bombs from falling on Vietnam.[73]

The national office of CALCAV urged its members to participate in these events, especially the March Against Death. Fernandez served on the New Mobe's steering committee and CALCAV sponsored an antiwar worship service at the Washington National Cathedral on November 14 as part of the demonstration. Eugene Carson Blake, Executive Secretary of the World Council of Churches, delivered the sermon, with Coffin and Louise Ransom among the others who took part. At the end, folksinger Pete Seeger led the entire congregation in singing "We Shall Overcome." "When the service was over no one moved," Coffin recalled. "Like the giant columns around us the more than five thousand people stood motionless, their fingers raised in the V sign of the peace movement. The silence was awesome."[74]

The mood of the mobilization was broken only once. Later in the day a small group of ultra leftists broke away from the main demonstration and moved toward the Justice Department to show their support for the Chicago Eight defendants, but this protest was broken up by police. These events disturbed Coffin, who later recalled:

> I had to admit that the peace movement was no longer peaceful. Although the great majority, and in particular the newer converts, were committed to nonviolence, a minority of the younger veterans of the movement were not. Frustrated in a way that was understandable if not excusable, they were taking on the worst features of the very people we were opposing. In doing so they were alienating others whose support we needed. Even more than Nixon, they were isolating themselves from the American public.[75]

After November public dissent against the war slowed somewhat, largely because of Nixon's policy of Vietnamization. The President borrowed the strategy from the last months of the Johnson administration, and made it public during a televised speech on November 3. Nixon's version of the policy advocated a phased withdrawal of American ground troops, a reduction in draft calls, expansion and improvement of the South Vietnamese Army (ARVN) with a corresponding increase in U.S. air power, the eventual invasion of Cambodia and Laos, and identification of the antiwar movement as the main barrier to an honorable settlement of the war. With this speech, Nixon placed the antiwar movement on the defensive and weakened one of its most appealing issues, withdrawal of U.S. combat troops from Indochina.[76]

The lower level of public protest resulted from other factors as well. Some within the movement grew increasingly discouraged by their apparent inability to influence Nixon's policies, or paradoxically, believed that the war was now winding down, if not ending. Tired of internal debates or preoccupied with new issues, a significant number of activists dropped out of the organized movement, a trend that was obscured by a constant flow of new demonstrators.[77]

In the wake of some of its greatest successes, the fragile antiwar coalition neared collapse. At a Cleveland meeting of the New Mobilization Committee leadership in December 1969, radicals criticized many of the principal leaders of the November 15 actions as elitist. Frustrated by these attacks, moderates grew discouraged and reassessed their roles within the coalition while radicals stressing the "correct" ideology and confrontational tactics came to dominate the conference. The Moratorium Committee lost much of its energy and effort after its October actions and abandoned its idea of expanding its activities by one day each month. The public's view of the antiwar movement remained one of hostility, a perception Sam Brown credited to Nixon's ability "to identify himself with the cause of peace."[78]

Balfour Brickner noted a decline of Jewish opposition to American policy in Vietnam because of fears that it might jeopardize U.S. support for Israel. He laid the blame for such perceptions on subtle messages from the Nixon administration and admitted that Nixon's tactics had slowed the momentum not only of Jewish dissent but also of the antiwar movement in general. Brickner reassured his fellow believers that the government would not connect the issues of Vietnam and Israel and urged them to keep speaking out on the wrongness of the war.[79]

CALCAV reflected the ideological diversity of the larger antiwar movement without falling victim to the paralyzing inability to act cooperatively toward common goals. By the end of President Nixon's first year in office, CALCAV leaders agreed that his policy in Vietnam was unacceptable. It was evident, however, that by the winter and spring of 1969–1970, the different positions were clearly delineated.

The moderate liberal viewpoint continued to dominate the organization's public pronouncements. Several voices criticized the Vietnamization strategy as an attempt to appease the public and quiet the peace forces with token troop withdrawals while continuing the war. Bennett warned that if Nixon continued the war into the seventies, "those who regard it as an awkward war may be satisfied by the avoidance of American casualties; but those who regard it as an immoral war . . . will continue to protest and protest. They will try to bring down another president."[80] Novak also urged the peace movement to eliminate any self-doubts it might have and maintain pressure on the President.[81]

While these arguments focused on U.S. policy, many moderates concentrated on the situation in Vietnam. Some, including former supporters of Thieu like John Sheerin, believed that American support for the corrupt Thieu-Ky regime was the major barrier to a peaceful settlement of the war. Nevertheless they continued to be concerned about the fate of a postwar Vietnam and refused to advocate an immediate American withdrawal. Bennett believed that the various Vietnamese factions would balance each other and indigenous controls would prevent "the slaughter that otherwise might accompany transitional anarchy." If necessary, however, the U.S. should provide for the safety of those who were compromised by fighting on the American side. Sheerin was certain that pro-American Vietnamese would be killed if the Viet Cong gained political control, and suggested they be moved to defensible enclaves before negotiation of a cease-fire that recognized the status quo. Novak in particular was convinced that an immediate U.S. withdrawal was neither morally nor politically correct. He concluded from a recent trip to Vietnam that the NLF's major source of political strength was the hatred of the American presence. Many of the South Vietnamese were nearly as opposed to the NLF. Novak accepted the reunification of North and South Vietnam. He also recognized that as the best-organized political structure, the NLF would probably emerge as the dominant faction in the south, and the resulting economy would be at least partially state controlled. He urged the United States to immediately de-escalate the level of destruction and predicted that following the end of hostilities, an uneasy period of three to five years would occur when there would be a danger of reprisals from both sides. To help Vietnam in this adjustment period, an American force of 50,000 should remain for those years while the other forces should be withdrawn quickly.[82]

Neuhaus continued to argue for a general amnesty for those who violated the Selective Service Act. Calling for compassion over revenge, he noted: "these young men took a position which most of us shared, but are in a situation where faithfulness to that position makes them subject to legal reprisal." He reported that U.S. exiles in Sweden were growing discouraged about the prospects for amnesty but pointed out that over 3,700 individuals had subjected themselves to prosecution by signing CALCAV's Conscience and Conscription statement released two years earlier.[83]

CALCAV and the Fellowship of Reconciliation joined forces to sponsor a 75-day Lenten-Passover Fast Action Project to maintain public focus on the war. The project consisted of a daily fast in front of the White House from Ash Wednesday, the beginning of Lent, through Passover—February 11 through April 28. The national office encouraged local groups to plan supporting activities during this same period.[84]

At the project's opening press conference, Fernandez was careful to mention that there was no connection between the Fast Project and the New Mobe. When asked what the clergy would do to aid American prisoners of war in North Vietnam, he discussed the Committee of

Liaison, a newly formed organization intended to improve communication between U.S. POWs and their families. The Committee of Liaison, which counted Dellinger, Cora Weiss, Ann Bennett, Stewart Meacham, and Fernandez among its founders, used its direct contact with the North Vietnamese over the preceding two months to help over 380 families receive letters from American prisoners, some for the very first time. Fernandez also charged the U.S. government with discouraging the relatives of prisoners from dealing with the committee.[85]

FOR and CALCAV designed the fast to tie the traditional renewal periods of the Christian and Jewish faiths to the need for an immediate withdrawal of U.S. troops from Vietnam. Participants held the hope, but not the illusion, that the President would respond to it positively, but its primary purpose was to witness to the injustice of the war. "While it is debatable whether this action will produce a new world, without war," the official announcement read, "it is nevertheless true that it has the potential of producing new people, who will work harder for peace. . . . Good men dying for an unjust cause does not make that cause any more just."[86]

To open the period of fasting, the two groups held a worship service on Ash Wednesday at the Metropolitan A.M.E. Church in Washington. About 100 people attended the service, which included the burning of what were described as "documents of repression," such as dollar bills, copies of records from a Dow Chemical office, an Army identification card, income tax forms, a driver's license, a military recruitment poster, and copies of campaign speeches. When it ended just before noon, about fifty people, some with foreheads marked by the ashes from the documents of repression, walked to the White House accompanied by the slow beat of a drum. For the next 75 days, small groups from around the country, usually of five to twenty people, marched and fasted in front of the White House. Following the demands of their permit, protesters remained in constant motion, walking in a circle for six hours a day. During the early weeks they bundled up against the brisk weather, warmed only by juice or tea. Fernandez, Sharon Rose, and John Harmon fasted for ten consecutive days. The project sponsored a special Good Friday action on March 27, when about 130 people carried a large cross and antiwar signs to the Selective Service headquarters and the Departments of the Interior and State and held a service across from the Watergate East apartments.[87]

The fast reflected the moderate to liberal outlook that dominated CALCAV, but individuals frequently advocated radical measures with inflammatory rhetoric. Reflecting the discouragement caused by years of antiwar dissent, the writer of one *Issues and Actions* editorial viewed the war in the context of the larger evil of "American imperialism and economic exploitation." The solution then was to "join those who are angry and who hate the corporate power which the United States presently represents. . . . to help liberate our own nation from its reactionary and exploitative policies."[88]

Acts of civil disobedience also escalated beyond previously accepted limits. At its February 1970 meeting, the steering committee decided to promote a tax resistance campaign. They agreed that a boycott of the 10 percent federal tax on telephone service would be most effective. It would be less threatening to people than withholding their income tax and would therefore attract much greater support, and it would cost the Internal Revenue Service just as much effort to investigate small amounts as it would large amounts. Several steering committee members were already refusing to pay the tax.[89]

In the spring, CALCAV returned to an earlier unpopular topic, working on a new war crimes project entitled "In the Name of America II." It intended to commission the Law Center for Constitutional Rights and the American Civil Liberties Union to make a legal investigation of American war crimes in Vietnam, and at the same time have the Institute of Political Studies look at the development and implementation of those policies. Richard Falk, writing in the *Nation,* went further when he called for an official inquiry on war crimes, not just the My Lai Massacre of March 1968. Falk noted that official U.S. policies appeared to violate international treaties ratified by the government and placed responsibility for rank-and-file behavior on those in command and in policymaking positions.[90] J. Edgar Hoover viewed this project as an attempt to weaken the American position and as another propaganda tool for the North Vietnamese. He disapprovingly noted that CALCAV operated "in a manner whereby deserters, draft evaders and anti-Vietnam war groups receive a favorable image in the press."[91]

This escalation of protest alienated some of CALCAV's supporters who felt that the radical influence was taking over. Peter Berger, for example, detected this shift in late 1969. When Michael Novak returned from his trip to Vietnam and reported to the national committee that the Viet Cong were feared and hated in the countryside, Berger remembered that, "Except for me, hardly anyone at the meeting was willing to give credence to this."[92]

President Nixon's announcement on April 30 of an American invasion of Cambodia brought renewed vigor to the slumping antiwar movement. CALCAV cosponsored a religious service protesting the Cambodian invasion on the sidewalk across from the White House on May 3, which drew slightly more than 100 people. Police arrested 74 persons when they refused to leave the area because they lacked a permit. The charges were later dismissed on a technicality.[93]

In its own immediate response, the New Mobilization Committee called an emergency demonstration in Washington, D.C. for May 9, but before it could take place, another tragedy intervened. On May 4, National Guardsmen on the campus of Kent State University in Ohio fired into a crowd of students, killing four and wounding nine others. Various groups called for a national student strike, although no single organization gave direction or controlled it. Almost spontaneously, over 500 colleges and universities were closed down either because of student actions or by their administrations. An estimated 60 percent of the nation's campuses experienced antiwar activities of one type or another.[94] The Kent State massacre undoubtedly swelled the May 9 demonstrations, which attracted roughly 130,000 people to Washington and tens of thousands more in cities like Minneapolis, Chicago, Denver, and Austin.

The size and intensity of the turnouts impressed even the White House. "Washington took on the character of a besieged city," Henry Kissinger recalled. "The very fabric of government was falling apart. The Executive Branch was shell-shocked."[95] Some within the movement, however, were disappointed that no civil disobedience was planned and viewed the protest as simply another nonthreatening witness of the antiwar spirit. Norma Becker remembered it as "such a letdown. . . . The demonstration was like a picnic, which did not correspond to the mood or psychology. . . . What happened in Washington on May 9 was not commensurate either to the invasion of Cambodia or to Kent State. . . . There was a deep and pervasive feeling of sellout."[96]

In response to the American invasion of Cambodia and the deaths at Kent State, CALCAV joined with the social action boards of some major religious denominations to sponsor a Washington mobilization of clergy and laity May 26 and 27. Held at the New York Avenue Presbyterian church, the convocation drew close to 1,000 people and focused on supporting congressional doves who hoped to de-escalate the war by curtailing federal funds for military purposes in Indochina. For its part, CALCAV prepared and distributed by mid-June over 20,000 copies of a paper entitled "The Widening War."[97]

Individual chapters sometimes acted separately. Following the Cambodian invasion, Iowa CALCAV planned a trip to Washington to lobby in support of the Hatfield-McGovern amendment, which called for a definite time limit for American aid to the war. Iowa leaders were concerned that their group would be overwhelmingly college-age and not taken as seriously as they should be. To offset this, they recruited concerned, middle-aged Iowans, including Peg Mullen, whose efforts to find out the cause of her son's death in Vietnam were later recounted in C.D.B. Bryan's book *Friendly Fire*. The group drove to Washington on two chartered buses and slept in the Episcopal Church of St. Stephen and the Incarnation. Mullen recalled that they were the "worst looking bunch" she had ever seen, but the next morning they put on suits and ties for their lobbying efforts.[98]

On June 2, after representatives from the Moratorium Committee instructed them in lobbying procedures, the Iowans met with their senators. Senator Harold Hughes (D-Iowa) supported the amendment and spent over an hour with them, but Senator Jack Miller (R-Iowa) supported the war and became furious with the group. The following day they met with Illinois Senator Charles Percy and with an aide to Senator Hugh Scott of Pennsylvania, and watched debate on the Cooper-Church amendment to cut off funds for U.S. military actions in Cambodia. On June 4, they were briefed by officials at the Pentagon and asked numerous questions about secret operations on countries that bordered Vietnam. Although the Hatfield-McGovern amendment did not pass, on June 24, the Senate overwhelmingly repealed the Gulf of Tonkin resolution.[99]

Eliot United Church of Christ, CALCAV's Boston-area headquarters, held a peace vigil during the American invasion of Cambodia. Over 25 percent of its membership signed a petition against using church property for a demonstration which would "offend" much of the community. The congregation maintained a tenuous coexistence between those who supported an activist church and those who did not, a balancing act that one observer called "a delicate battle, at best."[100]

These sentiments reveal important aspects of CALCAV's grass-roots network. Local groups did not necessarily accept the strategies and programs of the national office, and they faced significant challenges to their work within the religious community. Diversity characterized the various chapters that emerged at different times and pursued common goals in distinctive ways. Nevertheless, certain common threads held them together. Each pursued a religious constituency that was generally moderate and middle class, opening the antiwar movement to people who would otherwise have had no outlet. They maintained effective links to the national office through mobilizations, correspondence, programs, staff, and funding. Perhaps most important, despite their emphasis on different specific issues, their attention remained focused on ending the war.

Nixon's escalation in Southeast Asia sparked sharp responses from a few denominations in a year that otherwise produced relatively little debate within the churches. The heads of the United Presbyterians, United Methodists, National Council of Churches, and United Church of Christ released a statement that affirmed the right of dissent, urged nonviolence on all sides of the war, and claimed that Nixon's action in Cambodia was tearing American society apart. The Episcopal Church's Executive Council overwhelmingly called for the total withdrawal of all American forces and an end to the war. Later that year, however, the Episcopal convention divided, with the House of Bishops supporting and the House of Deputies rejecting a resolution on Vietnam.[101]

The most heated reaction came from the General Assembly of the United Presbyterian Church. The report initially presented to the assembly "strongly condemns the invasion of Cambodia as an unjustified and dangerous extension of the already illegal, inhumane, and unpopular war." President Nixon responded to the convention's request for a representative to present the administration's views and sent Housing and Urban Development Secretary George Romney the following day. Romney declared the war a mistake, but claimed Nixon was turning things around and asked for more time to make the Cambodian policy work. The assembly's final resolution removed the harsh condemnation but called for the withdrawal of all U.S. troops by June 30, 1971 and upheld the right of nonviolent dissent.[102]

Even Cambodia and Kent State, however, proved incapable of keeping the larger antiwar coalition together for long. By June 1970, the New Mobe divided into two smaller coalitions, which never reunited and only occasionally cooperated with each other. As Becker recalled, "that was the worst period in the movement — after May 1970."[103]

In the months before May 1970, Clergy and Laymen Concerned About Vietnam maintained its intense opposition to the war. It emphasized support for war resisters, pressured war-related corporations, motivated religious denominations, and continued its public demonstrations. At the same time it reflected the ideological diversity that threatened to incapacitate the antiwar movement. The prolonged stay of Americans in Vietnam, now Nixon's war, accommodated the infiltration of radical ideas and rhetoric into CALCAV. Despite the resulting tensions, it continued to function as a religiously based, slightly left of center organization that focused on ending the war in Vietnam. Changes in the next few years, however, would challenge both the creativity and stability of the nation's largest religious anti-war group.

5

FROM MOVEMENT TO ORGANIZATION
(JUNE 1970 to DECEMBER 1971)

> Let us therefore follow after the things which
> make for peace.
>
> — ROMANS 14:19 (KING JAMES)

In August 1970, long-time CALCAV supporter Daniel Bernstein died of leukemia. He left one-eighth of his estate to the National Council of Churches with the stipulation that Richard Fernandez knew his intentions. The Bernstein money proved to be CALCAV's financial watershed; its share of the estate was estimated in excess of one million dollars. Over the next several months this unexpected influx of money allowed CALCAV to expand the scope of its activities. It also initiated a transition from a loose, movement-style operation to a more highly structured organization.

From its inception, CALCAV had struggled financially. Fernandez and Coffin had raised most of the large donations during the first several months. Some contributed generously, such as the young Boston couple who donated $25,000.[1] Thousands of people made small contributions. The organization's growth throughout 1966, however, had produced a mounting financial problem. By October, CALCAV was $5,000 in debt and the executive committee could not decide how to open new channels of funding, a situation that left Fernandez "a little disturbed."[2] The National Council of Churches was also concerned, since bookkeeping arrangements with CALCAV made it responsible for underwriting the loss. Elston had been sitting in for David Hunter as the NCC's liaison on CALCAV's steering committee and was called in to explain the debts to his supervisor. Painfully aware of the difficulty of trying to move anything quickly through the various channels and church organizations, Elston pleaded for continued NCC support, arguing that, "this is the most important thing that is happening in the churches. . . . If we didn't have

104

CALC, we'd have to invent it. For God's sake don't let it go under. You can afford $5,000 even if they don't pay it back."[3]

Although he succeeded in maintaining support for CALCAV, financial uncertainty remained. By the fall of 1967, the organization had built up an $18,000 deficit and had to curtail all expenditures except its meager salaries and a few telephones. Travel, large mailings, and literature distribution were temporarily eliminated. Financially, CALCAV was in the red for 24 of its first 27 months. To extricate itself from this situation, the executive committee in November 1967 conducted a direct mail appeal. Letters went to all 17,000 current members, to 3,000 known contributors to liberal causes, and to 15,000 clergy not on the CALCAV mailing list. The mailing cost $7,500 but was expected to return between $25,000 and $50,000. CALCAV sought additional funds from private foundations.[4]

Controlling its financial situation was one of CALCAV's most difficult problems. Until 1970, there was never a cost accounting of its funding. According to Fernandez, "the first two years there was no budget, we just spent money."[5] Operating expenses steadily escalated. In 1969, for example, CALCAV spent about $450,000, primarily on national office and field staff salaries ($126,000), its ministry to deserters in Sweden and Canada ($34,000), a monthly newsletter ($33,000), promotion ($44,000), and fund raising ($52,000). It raised money primarily through personal solicitation of donations and direct mail appeal. Solicitation drew well over $100,000 in 1969, with Fernandez responsible for nearly all gifts in excess of $1,000 (there were 36 individual contributions over that amount). The direct mail campaign that year collected $165,000.[6]

Income from the Bernstein estate made new programs possible, but did not end CALCAV's financial struggles. For tax purposes, the NCC had to establish a formal procedure for distributing the funds, and CALCAV received the money in smaller amounts only after submitting grant applications for various projects. Investments during the long, drawn-out legal procedures eventually boosted the value of the bequest to $1.8 million. Fearing that the Internal Revenue Service would be attracted to such a large donation to an antiwar organization, which indeed it was, the NCC also distributed about $150,000 of the Bernstein money to other groups. It rebuffed IRS attempts to conduct an open-ended investigation of the funds. Had it been allowed to do so, CALCAV's filtering of loans to antiwar coalitions may have endangered its tax-exempt status.[7] The line between religious and political advocacy could become so blurred it was sometimes invisible.

With the Bernstein bequest unavailable for several months, financial burdens mounted and CALCAV remained deeply in debt. By November 1970, it owed $85,000 in bills, including $50,000 to the National Council of Churches. In March 1971, Robert Ransom submitted CALCAV's first financial report in five years. It revealed that 90 percent of the money spent went to field expenses with very little left for programming. The growing debt had reached $152,000 and could be paid off only if the Bernstein money became available soon. Despite public perception that the war was winding down, however, income was increasing. Direct mailings or local funding sources accounted for more than large donors.[8]

Financial troubles continued into 1972, largely because of the inaccessibility of the Bernstein estate. The Internal Revenue Service had to clear the money before the NCC could distribute it, and the IRS moved very deliberately. Without this income, CALCAV was unable to pay its bills or maintain adequate salaries. To deal with the crisis, Bennett tried to speed up the NCC's release of the Bernstein money while Richard Van Voorhis began negotiating a $200,000 loan from the Amalgamated Bank of New York City.[9]

The steering committee made sharp budget cuts in August 1972, but by January 1973 CALCAV's debt had increased to $414,000. At an emergency meeting on December 16, 1972, the committee took the radical step of raising $200,000 from among its members to keep CALCAV alive. By mid-February it had raised $170,000. Any available funds went first to avoid legal action or prevent the removal of vital equipment. Most of the national staff took voluntary pay cuts so that some money could go to the field staff, which had not been paid for six months. Even so, salaries for the field staff remained months in arrears. The 1973 budget of $601,590 assumed that the Bernstein money would come in. In fact, it did yield $175,000 during February and March, but expenditures continued to outrun payments, and the debt fell only to $391,000 by the end of June.[10]

CALCAV's national leadership chose to spend the Bernstein bequest immediately to try to end the war, but looking back, Fernandez had second thoughts:

> I could have taken the other position, our job is to bank it [the Bernstein money] so this organization, for a lifetime, would have a base budget of $200,000. If I had it to do over again, that's what I would have done. . . . I would have done something other than just spend it, and the way it came through the probate process was we were always spending it before we had it.[11]

CALCAV's office manager fought a constant battle trying to keep the creditors at bay.[12]

Financial considerations and the availability of the Bernstein money played a key role in CALCAV's national programs during the early 1970s. Edward Richter, editor of *New Approach,* met with some of CALCAV's leaders early in 1970 to find out if they would consider taking control of the journal. Several members expressed an interest, and when further research indicated that it would be less expensive than publishing their own newsletter, they placed the proposal on the agenda of the upcoming staff meeting in Clinton, Michigan. By June, however, CALCAV decided not to acquire *New Approach,* choosing instead to build its own publication from scratch. The high cost of the newsletter *Issues and Actions* encouraged trying a different approach.[13]

The new paper, called *American Report,* made its debut on October 2, 1970. Brickner, Neuhaus, Novak, Sheerin, and James Finn made up the editorial committee, and Robert Lecky served as the paper's first editor. Initial plans called for a weekly, eight-page newspaper to cover the efforts for peace by religious institutions and to communicate with the adult peace movement. Its first issues typically addressed topics ranging from CIA operations in Southeast Asia and Nixon's new peace proposals to Jewish radicalism, corporate reform, abortion, and American Indians. To help build up its circulation, CALCAV sent copies to its entire mailing list for three months, then to contributors and subscribers.[14] *American Report* generally reflected the thinking of CALCAV's national office, but it also sought to maintain a certain independence. That independence sometimes exposed the differences among CALCAV's membership. In a brief evaluation of the paper only five weeks after it began, Heschel and others complained that it was oriented a little too far to the left.[15]

Over the next several months, the paper improved in quality and appearance and gained wide circulation within the antiwar movement. Under managing editor Ron Henderson, writing quality improved, advertising increased, and subscription renewals climbed from 30 to 80 percent. On the negative side, sales promotion was poor and the annual budget grew to $165,000 by September 1971, forcing staff cuts by attrition.[16]

Over the next two years, *American Report* was paradoxically both a blessing and a problem. Circulation grew to 24,000 by September 1972, when the paper shifted to a 24-page biweekly format, and continued to rise as CALCAV began a serious drive to recruit student subscribers. Problems continually plagued the paper, however. Lecky cut back his work on the paper to half-time on November 1, 1972, and resigned entirely at the end of the year to take a position with the Fund for Peace. Budget problems also threatened the jobs of other staff members. It was not until June that the steering committee selected Robert Hoyt to replace Lecky as editor. By the summer of 1973, subscriptions began to fall, and the resulting difficulties in paying writers and news agencies caused staff morale to suffer accordingly.[17]

Perhaps the biggest problem was the disagreement among national leaders over some of the positions taken by the paper. Neuhaus called it "depressingly, tediously predictable," and accused it of failing to fulfill a major part of its role, which he felt was to "raise the level of moral, political discourse about U.S. foreign policy in general, Viet Nam in particular."[18] Lecky seemed to acknowledge some of these criticisms in a resignation article that recognized a need to work with CALCAV's constituency rather than at it. "There have been times when the movement has dumped very heavily on middle-class hopes and values, he commented, "and other times when we have desperately sought their aid in ending the war."[19]

The Middle East was the most troublesome issue. Plans to publish a special supplement on that region in February 1973 threatened to offend the Jewish community and weaken CALCAV's ability to maintain Jewish support against the war. A specially appointed committee placed temporary restrictions on *American Report*'s handling of the Middle East, but those restrictions were removed in July 1973. By November, after the start of the Yom Kippur War, Brickner accused the paper of having a one-sided, pro-Arab bias. Readers who wrote to cancel their subscriptions generally cited the newspaper as being too radical or disapproved of its anti-Israeli position.[20] At one point the dispute became so heated that Neuhaus attempted to end publication of the paper and convinced Coffin to support him. Fernandez and Elston thwarted the effort.[21]

American Report attracted an interesting readership. A survey compiled in November 1973 indicated that the majority worked in education, as clergy, or in some other professional occupation. Half claimed at least one post-graduate degree. Two-thirds were men, with a similar percentage over forty years of age. Fifty percent were Protestant, 15 percent Catholic and 6 percent Jewish. One out of four claimed no religious affiliation. Politically, two-thirds were Democrats, one-fourth Independents, and only 3.5 percent Republicans. The respondents supported a wide variety of liberal organizations, led by the American Civil Liberties Union, Common Cause, AFSC, CALCAV, and other civil rights and peace groups.[22]

CALCAV continued to agitate against the war in a number of other ways. It aided a group called the GI Office which set up coffeehouses near military bases to support war resistance within the military.[23] An incident occurred at Fort Jackson, South Carolina when some of the local GIs were refused permission to hold a silent prayer service for peace in Vietnam in the base chapel. Fernandez went to Fort Jackson with Nicholas Von Hoffman of the New York *Post,* where he failed to convince the military authorities to allow the service. The commanding officer explained to him, "Reverend . . . you should understand this . . . Ford would not let Chevrolet advertise in its windows, we're not going to let people pray for peace in our chapel."[24]

Writing in the fall, but responding to several months of Vice-President Spiro Agnew's invective against public protest, Robert McAfee Brown again defended the right of dissent. He viewed Agnew's harsh rhetoric as a deliberate attempt to divide the nation against itself, thus abandoning the moral leadership that elected officials should provide. The Vice-President's token references to the right of dissent remained unconvincing. Brown pointed to the massacre at Kent State as the logical culmination of Agnew's verbal assaults: "there must be some moment when, deep in the inner recesses of a decency all men share, you have to confront the fact that rhetoric such as yours—the rhetoric not of an ordinary citizen but of the Vice-President of the nation—helped cause those bullets to fly."[25]

The massive demonstrations that followed the Cambodian invasion and Kent State were among the last successful actions by the national antiwar coalition. While large turnouts did occur in April 1971 and January 1972, the competing tendencies within the movement had already created an open split that rendered cooperation extremely difficult. Those organizations wanting to focus strictly on ending the war formed the National Peace Action Coalition (NPAC) at a mid-June conference in Cleveland. NPAC, increasingly influenced by the Socialist Worker's Party, called for the immediate and unconditional withdrawal of American forces from Indochina and stressed mass public demonstrations. Other groups favored a broader, multi-issue organization and, in a series of conferences over the next several months, ultimately formed the People's Coalition for Peace and Justice (PCPJ) early in 1971. With the Fifth Avenue Peace Parade Committee providing much of its direction, PCPJ encompassed issues such as civil rights and economics in its critique of American society and included civil disobedience among its tactics. Although the war continued to receive primary emphasis, the inclusion of additional issues made it more difficult to build a consensus within the PCPJ coalition.[26]

CALCAV continued to participate in cooperative ventures. It joined with the Fellowship of Reconciliation and American Friends Service

Committee to send a delegation to the Citizen's Conference on Ending the War in Indochina. About 170 Americans flew to Paris in early March, where they met with representatives of the NLF, North Vietnam, South Vietnam, and the United States.[27] In January CALCAV allied itself with an antiwar medical group that collected medical books for use at the University of Hanoi medical school. Fernandez served as a liaison between the steering committee and the People's Coalition for Peace and Justice. Having been part of the PCPJ organizational meeting, he was encouraged to continue his work in the coalition, but the steering committee refused to endorse it as an organization because they disapproved of some of the rhetoric and leadership.[28]

Just as the Cambodian invasion had rejuvenated the antiwar coalitions the previous year, a new American initiative provided another rallying point. On February 8, 1971 South Vietnamese forces invaded Laos with U.S. air support. Antiwar leaders immediately called national protests, and two days later an estimated 50,000 people gathered in Washington to demonstrate against this new expansion of hostilities.[29]

With this blatant evidence that the war was not, in fact, winding down, Brown, Coffin, Neuhaus, Brickner, and Philip Wheaton called a Washington mobilization for Tuesday, February 16. Activities began at 10 A.M. in the Church of St. Stephen and the Incarnation, with nonviolent civil disobedience planned later in the day. "Effectiveness . . . in this instance is not whether the government will change its policy," they rationalized, "but whether or not we are going to be individually and corporately incapacitated by this new military adventurism of the Nixon administration."[30]

The issue of civil disobedience remained a topic of debate within the antiwar movement. As an organization, CALCAV accepted civil disobedience as one tactic among many. If used selectively and carried out properly, it could make a positive impression on much of the American public. Not everyone in CALCAV was willing to participate in civil disobedience, but most accepted it as a legitimate tactic for those who chose to use it. Some felt that it produced the added benefit of giving younger activists a physical outlet for their frustrations and thereby reduced instances of trashing or other destructive acts.[31]

The invasion of Laos also temporarily reunited the divided antiwar coalitions. Several weeks earlier, NPAC had planned a week of actions culminating in mass demonstrations in Washington and San Francisco on April 24. PCPJ called for activities May 1–8, and until Laos the two groups had been unwilling to cooperate. PCPJ finally agreed to endorse the April 24 demonstrations and set up a series of civil disobedience actions built around May 3 when several thousand would actually try to block the streets of the capital. With additional support from the Student Mobilization Committee and Vietnam Veterans Against the War, the April 24 demonstrations drew 500,000 to Washington and an estimated 200,000 to San Francisco.[32]

From Sunday, May 2 to Wednesday, May 5, the civil disobedience forces conducted their own series of actions. The largest occurred on May 3 in Washington, when roughly 15,000 people tried to close down the city streets and stop government activity. Though these efforts failed, the indiscriminate mass arrest of 12,000 people resulted in successful legal actions against the police.[33]

The early months of 1971 also included renewed concerns over an issue that the American public preferred not to think about. From January 31 to February 2, CALCAV joined with other organizations in a project sponsored by the Vietnam Veterans Against the War. The Winter Soldier Investigation brought over 100 GIs to Detroit to give testimony on war crimes that they had committed or observed. This project was the latest in a line of formal and informal studies of American war crimes in Vietnam.

As early as 1967, the Bertrand Russell Peace Foundation had sponsored the International War Crimes Tribunal in Stockholm (May) and Copenhagen (November) and accused the United States of violating numerous treaty agreements, condemned its use of napalm and cluster bombs, and pronounced it guilty of genocide. These proceedings, published in 1969 as *Against the Crime of Silence,* were generally ignored in the United States.[34] In January 1968, CALCAV released its own study of war crimes entitled *In the Name of America,* 400 pages of reports taken from reputable newspapers around the world. Though widely publicized, this study too failed to arouse the public.

The Winter Soldier Investigation had something the others lacked. The revelations of the My Lai massacre and subsequent trial of William Calley shocked the public into acknowledging the issue. The testimony from over 100 veterans revealed acts of brutality which indicated that the My Lai incident was not unique. The Winter Soldier Investigation succeeded in drawing attention to these atrocities in its attempt to prevent similar acts in the future. In the March 28 *New York Times Book Review,* Neil Sheehan called for a national inquiry into war crimes. In government circles, however, this effort too was largely ignored, and no inquiry followed. The issue of U.S. war crimes never aroused much enthusiasm among the general population.[35]

CALCAV's steering committee initiated its own two-day conference on war crimes in late May. In New York City 25 to 30 religious leaders met to discuss what churches and synagogues might do to prevent future atrocities. The consensus on the My Lai trial was that, although Lt. William Calley deserved punishment for his role in the massacre, criminal activity in Vietnam existed on a more massive scale. The group discussed educational and symbolic ways in which it might bring public attention to bear on the issue and gave Brown the responsibility of writing a position paper.[36] In his last Vietnam-related editorial before his retirement in December 1971, Sheerin reiterated the call for a congressional investigation into the responsibility of the government and the high command for war crimes committed in Vietnam.[37]

CALCAV's concern did not easily translate into concrete achievements. Despite years of lobbying, demonstrating, and even civil disobedience, the war in Vietnam continued. The Vietnamization policy was responsible for much of the difficulty, though certainly not all. The substantial decrease in the number of American ground troops and the accompanying reduction of U.S. casualties camouflaged the escalating air war. This convinced much of the American public that the war was winding down significantly, thus eliminating the need for further pressure to end it.

CALCAV now faced the arduous task of convincing an increasingly apathetic public that the war still demanded its attention. It knew that most of America's 370,000 local religious congregations had no programs dealing with the war and that the vast majority of the nation's 150,000,000 church and synagogue members had taken no action against it. Even though public demonstrations were subsiding, CALCAV's national leadership believed that the persistence of the massive antiwar movement had paid off. Gallup polls indicated that 73 percent of the public opposed the war, and CALCAV sensed an opportune time to broaden its support and stimulate greater action on the local level. Recalling the church's role in the abolition of slavery and in the civil rights movement, many believed that the nation's religious community could make a difference in ending the war.[38]

As if to prove them right, CALCAV and 23 other religious groups designed an ambitious program to pressure Congress and the President to withdraw all U.S. troops from Southeast Asia by December 31, 1971. This "Set the Date" campaign began in March 1971 to stimulate church and synagogue peace activities and lobby elected officials to back the concept and target date of the campaign.[39]

The idea of a timetable for U.S. military withdrawal attracted support from individual denominations. National conventions of the

United Presbyterians and American Baptists advocated withdrawal by the end of 1971, while the United Church of Christ favored a more flexible deadline tied to a cease-fire, release of prisoners, and supervised elections.[40]

In one of the program's more unusual actions, Minnesota CALCAV organized a peace walk in June through southern and western Minnesota that covered 53 towns and 440 miles in thirty days. Many of the participants walked the entire distance, others joined for shorter stretches. Local organizers, usually but not exclusively clergy, turned out substantial crowds in communities with little previous history of peace activism. Most of the newspapers along the route gave advance notice of the approaching Peace Walkers and provided generally favorable editorial comments. A few of the towns organized a brief welcome; a boys' choir in Northfield, folksingers in Rosemount, an accordion and drum duo in Lamberton. People turned out for dinners, rallies, and meetings, or joined the Peace Walkers as they distributed leaflets to private homes and businesses and visited local draft boards or military recruiters. At Litchfield, 40 residents joined the march at the city limits, and 150 attended the rally. Of Taunton's 200 residents 30 turned out at the local Catholic church for an evening discussion. In each community, interested people showed up to discuss the war, setting a date for American withdrawal from Vietnam, and organizing in their own area.[41]

Townspeople provided some of the march's most poignant moments. At the rally in Marshall, a woman listened quietly before explaining that a year earlier her son had refused induction into the Army because he felt the war was wrong. The experience had so confused and upset her that she had thrown him out of the house. The rally filled her need to talk with people who understood her son's feelings. In Litchfield, a recently returned veteran told how his opposition to the war had made him feel alone in his own town until the rally. He showed his own slides of Vietnam in a presentation that touched the emotions of visitors and friends alike.[42]

The marchers faced only minimal opposition during their journey. Though forced to endure occasional harassment from passing cars, they encountered no physical threats. Local organizers faced some pressure from within their own communities, however. Trustees at a couple of churches refused to allow Peace Walkers to hold rallies or sleep in their buildings. Several women who prepared food for the visitors were accused of being communists. A Catholic priest who planned to house the Peace Walkers had financial support for his program for migrant workers threatened by several parishoners.[43]

For the most part, however, Peace Walkers found receptive audiences who walked with them, offered them food along the road, and seemed surprised that so many were not students. What they also found was a great deal of discouragement and frustration growing out of the deception of politicians and their own inability to do anything to end the war. The arrival of visible support from CALCAV brought together people who discovered, often for the first time, that there were others in their own town who felt as they did. In some areas, they organized themselves to fight against that feeling of powerlessness and joined with those in the Twin Cities to apply pressure to end the war.[44]

Despite efforts like this, CALCAV's national office had reservations about its ability to stimulate an effective national movement. Fernandez believed that the field staff, while very involved in local antiwar coalitions, was only adequate in working with antiwar activists in the churches and fell short in educating and encouraging additional antiwar sentiment within the churches.[45] In April 1971, the steering committee adopted a Neuhaus proposal for an intensive campaign within the churches and synagogues to increase and solidify CALCAV's constituency. The campaign would focus primarily on the war but would also raise fundamental questions about the nature of what some referred to as the "American Empire." Preparations for this operation would culminate at an August organizing conference in Ann Arbor, Michigan.

The Ann Arbor conference would allow CALCAV to examine the changes it had experienced in its more than five years of existence. In the beginning, decisions at the national office were made by a small executive committee that met on an irregular basis. The prominent names that comprised the national committee attracted attention and provided credibility for CALCAV, but they played no role in making policy. With the appointment of Fernandez, the executive director coordinated activities on a daily basis and was advised and directed by a steering committee of varying size. A small office staff assisted Fernandez, but the operation was highly informal. As one working paper accurately commented in 1970, "most institutional churches . . . err on the side of order; we have erred on the side of anarchy." Until that year, CALCAV had operated without a constitution or bylaws. The new bylaws established permanent subcommittees to oversee personnel, finance, programming, and editorial policy. In May 1971, the steering committee appointed a new executive committee to provide direction between its own bimonthly meetings. The unexpected Bernstein money induced the national office to abandon the movement style for a more structured approach that included personnel policies, salary levels, and sabbaticals.[46]

On the national level CALCAV still bore a strong resemblance to its early days, though noticeable changes had occurred. The national committee had grown in size from 40 in 1966 to 74 in late 1970. Of the original group 29 remained on the committee, which now included a few laypeople among its members. The most obvious difference was that the earlier males-only committee now contained 13 women. The steering committee, cochairs, and chief staff members who provided CALCAV's leadership reflected the same combination of similarity and change. In late summer 1971, this group was still composed primarily of educators, denominational or ecumenical officials, journalists, and ministers. Approximately two-thirds were Protestants, and 75 percent were men. By design, nearly all lived in the New York area or the eastern corridor, which enabled them to attend the regular meetings. In addition to the inclusion of women, the most significant change was the proportional decline of Jews and an increase in Catholic participation. Jewish reluctance to criticize the war grew partly from a fear of upsetting President Nixon, a strong supporter of Israel.[47]

National CALCAV dominated the local chapters. The New York office focused on attracting prominent religious figures while the chapters served as a local outlet for mainstream denominations. CALCAV's traditionally loose organization hindered adequate communication between its national and local units. The relationship between New York and the field rested primarily upon national funding of local field staff and providing resources such as literature and speakers. Local chapters hired field staff, with virtually no nationally established criteria or coordination. They also raised their own operating funds and ran their own programs, while the New York office planned national projects such as *American Report* and the Washington mobilizations with little consultation of local groups. The national organization and most of the local chapters developed from within the religious community, but local groups operated in a variety of styles. Some developed a countercultural orientation and contained members who felt alienated from the major churches. When the Bernstein money allowed the national office to operate at a higher financial level, a certain amount of friction emerged among the chapters that maintained their movement style and minimal salaries.[48]

One manifestation of this tension was growing debate over whether CALCAV should continue to focus on Vietnam or become a permanent multi-issue organization. The years of activism and a shift in the direction of the war diverted the attention of many to other issues. "At the beginning we were very unified, because the board was made up of people who really saw eye to eye," Coffin explained. "It was pretty much a single religious voice concentrating on one issue." CALCAV's national mobilizations in the late 1960s epitomized its cohesive religious thrust. As the movement grew and permanent chapters sprang up around the country, however, the organization became more heterogeneous. Individuals in local chapters were not always guided by the same religious urgency or sometimes failed to get that point of view across. By the early 1970s, many people also adopted the view that Vietnam was not an aberration but one of a multitude of problems with American society, including racism, poverty, and corporate power. Clergy and Laymen Concerned About Vietnam was not immune to the influence of these ideas, and as time went on, Vietnam began to share CALCAV's attention with several other important issues. "The combination of there being a splintering of the religious voice and a splintering of the issues," Coffin remembered, "did dissipate a lot of energy."[49]

These internal deliberations even affected the name of the organization itself. Although no official action had been taken, within the past year various local chapters had dropped the words "About Vietnam" from the name, and the national office eventually followed. Clergy and Laymen Concerned (CALC) reflected the movement toward a broader analysis of American life that would extend beyond the Vietnam War.[50]

During this period of introspection and transition, CALC held its most significant meeting since a handful of people met in John Bennett's apartment in 1966. The week-long national organizing conference in Ann Arbor would allow CALC to evaluate its effectiveness in reaching the religious community, establish program priorities on both national and local levels, and develop a long-range strategy for pursuing social change.[51]

CALC hired Carl Rogers and Trudi Young as new additions to the national staff to help with the preparations. Rogers, a Presbyterian, had helped organize Vietnam Veterans Against the War in 1968 and had worked on the Presidio case and the senatorial campaigns of Eugene McCarthy and Charles Goodell. Young, a Quaker, had worked with the American Friends Service Committee and New Mobilization Committee and was the National Coordinator of Women Strike for Peace.[52] In June, CALC appointed Young as a codirector primarily responsible for field staff, local chapters, office administration, and programs.[53]

Fernandez, Rogers, and Young joined members of the steering committee, national office, and field staff to make up the Ann Arbor Conference Committee. In May they gathered in New York to begin planning.[54] CALC hired two consultants to work with the planning committee in developing an agenda and format for the conference. Paul Kittlaus, a United Church of Christ minister, had cofounded an action training center in Los Angeles that helped churches resolve internal conflicts. Bob Bonthius worked at an urban training center in Cleveland.[55]

In early June, ten members of CALC's national and field staffs publicized the conference in visits to 42 cities in 32 states. Advertisements in religious periodicals, mailings to religious peace organizations, and *American Report* further spread the word. The planning committee set two goals: to project a program that CALC chapters could work on together across the country and to achieve greater coordination within the organization.[56]

Preparations for the conference did not always proceed smoothly. Some of the mailings were fouled up, registrations were slow, and staff morale suffered accordingly. Conflicts with Muhammad Kenyatta and the Black Economic Development Conference (BEDC) in 1970 made some Ann Arbor churches the targets of sit-ins. The local religious community answered the BEDC demand for funds by securing injunctions against the sit-ins. When it became known in 1971 that CALC planned to meet in some of the Ann Arbor churches, local black leaders threatened to picket the conference, an action CALC sidestepped by shifting its conference to the University of Michigan campus.[57]

The Ann Arbor conference of August 17–22 attracted over 400 people from more than forty states, the District of Columbia, and Canada, half of them unaffiliated with CALC. There were roughly equal numbers of men and women, most of them young, and a number of staff people from various denominational boards and agencies. Eighty-four percent claimed some religious affiliation, with the same percentage active in at least one peace organization. The largest represented religious groups were Catholic, 21 percent; Methodist, 14 percent; Episcopal, 9 percent; United Church of Christ, 9 percent; Presbyterian, 8 percent; and Quaker, 7 percent. Only 2 percent were Jewish. This strong Catholic participation contrasted with hesitation to join the antiwar forces in the mid-1960s. Jewish representation had declined, however. Those who belonged to other antiwar organizations most frequently joined coalition groups, 27 percent; Fellowship of Reconciliation, 18 percent; American Friends Service Committee, 10 percent; and various denominational peace fellowships, 20 percent, which emphasized the religious roots of CALC's peace witness. The majority participated in electoral politics, marched in rallies, or contributed money or petitions to the antiwar cause. About a third withheld part of their taxes or had committed some form of civil disobedience.[58]

The actual conference consisted of small discussion groups on issues ranging from war crimes to electoral politics to amnesty, action training sessions that dealt with organizing techniques and tools, and evening services of worship and celebration. Participants had the opportunity to evaluate films, tapes, and literature prepared by CALC as organizing tools. Speakers such as Harvey Cox, Dave Dellinger of PCPJ, and Fred Branfman of Project Air War addressed perceptions that the war was ending as well as the topics of U.S. covert wars and economic justice, among others. Some of the plenary session speakers openly criticized the conference's lack of significant black participation, but the harsh comments by Muhammad Kenyatta, who spoke during one of the sessions, did little to win supporters to his cause.[59]

Despite CALC's preparations, the Ann Arbor conference took an unexpected turn. The conference planning committee had suggested four campaign ideas under the assumption that the conferees would adopt one or two as a national long-term campaign. The participants, however, developed eight additional ideas, and the planning committee showed remarkable flexibility in allowing the conference to seek its own direction. Each day the campaign groups met to hammer out the goals, strategies, staff, and funding for a dozen potential programs equally divided between short-term and long-term commitments. Some suggested organizing peace actions within a single parish or around specific events such as the PCPJ fall offensive or during upcoming holidays. Specific campaigns included a Daily Death Toll vigil and "die-in" at the White House symbolizing the war's Indochinese victims, antiwar advertisements to "unsell" the war, working for repeal of the draft, and focusing on political prisoners and war crimes. Others designed educational programs to expose the invisible and arbitrary wars conducted by the executive branch, or to prevent the rebellion in Bangladesh from becoming another Vietnam. The campaign on corporate involvement in the war recommended divestment and proxy fights against corporate exploitation of the war for greater profit, while a program for economic responsibility urged boycotts of industries with war contracts and challenged consumers to alter their lifestyles toward sharing and simplicity. The campaign for social justice linked the domestic issues of racism, sexism, poverty, and police repression to foreign policy, and proposed restructuring CALC and the churches to give greater economic and political power to the dispossessed. Using provocative phrases like the "inherent system of racism" and "the ruling powers," it advocated at least one-third representation on national and regional staff and steering committees of what was vaguely called the "poor and most oppressed."[60]

The conference worked out a ratification procedure to determine which campaigns would receive national attention. The participants would select certain proposals and try to convince their local group to support them. Local chapters would then develop the campaigns for their area and report to the national office by October 10. CALC pledged to support each campaign supported by at least one-third of its chapters; so programs depended upon how much work they could generate at the local level.[61]

None of the campaigns received the minimum fifteen committed chapters by the October deadline. Those receiving the most support were Economic Responsibility (12), Single Parish (10), Daily Death Toll (8), Corporate Involvement (8), Unsell (6), and the Invisible War (6). Only four chapters advocated the campaign for social justice. The development of these ideas, however, was not wasted. The national office used many of them as the basis for new programs in the following months.[62]

Evaluations of the conference's success varied. Radicals were comfortable with the open association with the NLF through incidents such as a telegram from Democratic Republic of Vietnam Minister of State Xuan Thuy, a telephone hookup with Madame Nguyen Thi Binh, chief Provisional Revolutionary Government delegate to the Paris peace talks, and the Viet Cong flag at the head of the peace parade. While these ties with America's wartime opponent might attract headlines, moderates criticized them for their potential to alienate CALC's middle-class religious constituency.[63]

Concern about CALC's expansion into other social issues also drew comment. As participant Charles West observed, people attended the conference because of their desire to end the Vietnam War, not by more general concerns for peace or other reforms. He noted that the peace movement's best work had been done in specific, limited areas such as draft counseling and challenging the distorted patriotism that forced men to fight in Vietnam. West criticized the conference for barely addressing its basic purpose of initiating a campaign to penetrate the churches and for failing to analyze what the churches had done. He remarked that only Harvey Cox tried to relate social concerns to Christianity. "Very few people," he concluded, "would have gone away from the conference with a clearer idea of why their faith and churchmanship demanded the kind of action for peace we were talking about. It was not at all clear how God was related to our noble human efforts."[64]

The self-examination of the Ann Arbor conference exposed certain weaknesses in CALC's national structure. CALC was one of the rare peace organizations that maintained a national network of local chapters, but these groups had developed independently and without strong efforts toward integration or centralization. The result was an uneven relationship between New York and the rest of the country. Some locals enjoyed frequent communication, others operated more distantly but in ways that were mutually beneficial. A few worked in relative isolation. By the early 1970s some chapters felt increasingly distant from national decisions or complained that national leaders were out of touch or unaware of how CALC operated at the grassroots level. Although chapters were alienated from the New York office and its decision-making process, support for national initiatives often depended upon local perceptions.[65]

The impact of Ann Arbor on local groups is evident in the Los Angeles chapter's two distinct phases. From late 1967 through 1971, Rev. Harlan Weitzel served as executive director of a group with 300 members and a mailing list of 1,200 that concentrated on individual military and draft counseling and coalition actions. At the time of the Ann Arbor conference when CALC committed itself to long-term organizing, the national office persuaded Weitzel to step aside in favor of someone who could better mobilize the religious community. Most of the existing Los Angeles steering committee members chose to reduce their roles in CALC and a new committee of eighteen, three rabbis and fifteen protestants from six denominations, hired Paul Kittlaus as its staff person of the new Southern California CALC (SC/CALC). The new steering committee was drawn virtually intact from a previously existing organization, the Interreligious Coalition to End the War.[66]

By 1973, SC/CALC served the entire southern California region after the San Diego chapter merged into the Los Angeles group. Its steering committee grew to 65 people and was indicative of the makeup of many local chapters. Over half were lay workers, women made up roughly 25 percent, and liberal Protestants were easily the most heavily represented religious persuasion.[67]

Changes at the regional chapter based in San Francisco further indicated this transition. During the late 1960s, Northern California CALC emphasized educational programs that challenged American cold war ideology and responded to crises such as the Presidio 27 mutiny trials. Philip Farnham, a Presbyterian minister who had worked as the west coast coordinator of Vietnam Summer, served as its director beginning in late 1967. While San Francisco maintained links with the religious community, it operated primarily as a loose ecumenical unit and found it difficult to penetrate local congregations.[68]

By 1970, however, San Francisco's direction had shifted noticeably as it became submerged in the large arena of social justice issues. Farnham's replacement as director, Brian Drolet, was more involved in the leftist politics of the area and focused on workers and others with a more radical orientation at the expense of the religious middle class. Relations between the national office and the northern California staff deteriorated. Drolet complained to Fernandez that his goal of building a new country would not be achieved with "the likes of most of the members of your steering committee." Despite these changes, local CALC retained its links to peace moderates and generally kept its distance from the Mobilization coalitions and Trotskyites.[69]

Caught up in the competition and disputes that frequently characterized the antiwar movement, members of CALC criticized conservative peace organizations as taking a "State Department approved, know everything, do nothing approach," while CALC's critics characterized it as "working for an NLF North Vietnamese victory" and as advocating "the same old Wall Street war monger line."[70] The stridency of antiwar activism in the San Francisco area was matched by the movement's opponents. CALC's office was set on fire twice, had its windows trashed, received bomb threats, and faced increased police surveillance all within the first two months of 1971.[71]

Disturbed at what was happening in the Bay area, CALC's national office finally cut off funding for Drolet's position at the end of the summer in 1971.[72] A new CALC chapter in San Francisco re-emerged near the end of 1971 in the form of the Ecumenical Peace Institute (EPI). The EPI grew out of a meeting between Richard Fernandez and various Bay area religious groups, and was originally the action arm of the San Francisco Conference on Religion and Peace before affiliating with CALC. John Pairman Brown, a 48-year-old former Air Force sergeant with degrees from Dartmouth and Union Theological Seminary, was one of the first staff people hired by EPI, and he remained with the group through the end of the war.[73]

Through early 1974, the EPI worked around a core of about eighty people, a mailing list of up to 2,500, and a staff that grew to seven, including two full-time workers and three part-time people on loan from the AFSC. Once again oriented toward the area religious community, it worked to organize for peace both within congregations and across denominational lines and sought to move religious people into political issues. The EPI functioned basically as a coalition group with representatives from up to thirty religiously based constituencies such as the United Church of Christ Peace Task Force, the Fellowship of Reconciliation, and the Lutheran Peace Fellowship. Only the representative plenary meetings could make major policy decisions, which made for a slower process but kept communications open to a broad range of views within the religious community.[74]

Probably the most important result of the Ann Arbor conference was that it produced a period of intensified, highly coordinated activity within CALC on a national scale. Out of it came the idea of focusing on a national campaign that each chapter would emphasize. Many people on the local level responded enthusiastically, having grown frustrated in carrying out their actions without any sense of national unity.[75]

Kittlaus and Bonthius flew into New York after the Ann Arbor conference and interviewed the national staff to find strengths and weaknesses in CALC. At a subsequent staff retreat in upstate New York, they began developing a more efficient system. A committee headed by Young, Fernandez, Kittlaus, and Bonthius planned two regional conferences for all local and national staff members and representatives from local steering committees. These meetings were held during January 1972 in Denver and Louisville. They developed guidelines to fund local groups, build an integrated church–corporate responsibility program, and establish a more coherent national organization made up of a network of local groups guided by the national steering committee.[76]

Participants at the regional meetings proposed that eight representatives from local groups, one staff person and three steering committee members from both the west and the east, be added as full members to the national steering committee. These eight, plus Young, Fernandez, and one or two other national steering committee members, would form a field development committee (FDC) to implement the items agreed upon at Denver and Louisville and carry out the decisions of the field development program. The national steering committee approved. In February, as a follow-up to the two regional conferences, national and local CALC leaders met in Chicago to more fully develop a coordinated campaign.[77]

In the long run, CALC's program for field development did provide greater national coordination. In the months between Ann Arbor and a conference held the following year in Webster Grove, Missouri, the grassroots organizations came to play a more integral role within CALC. "It was much more functionally related to chapters with a sense of their ownership of what went on in the national office," recalled George Webber.[78] As a result, the local groups gained more influence in CALC's direction.

The greater cooperation between national and local CALC following Ann Arbor did not end the organization's internal tensions. Ideological debates sometimes resulted in acrimonious divisions. Peter Berger left CALC when it began to appear to him a "Maoist chaplaincy to the religious community." He believed that the antiwar movement, including CALC, had become controlled by people less interested in ending the war than in "defeating and humiliating America." Berger's transition substantiates the concern by some that the public would be alienated by controversial tactics. Having opposed the war from a conservative tradition, his sensitivity to such devices was acute. At another meeting of CALC's national committee, he recalled,

> The question was raised by someone whether the unfurling of Vietcong flags at demonstrations might not be counter-productive. . . . In the discussion I suggested that anti-war demonstrations in this country should take place amid oceans of American flags. Most of the individuals there looked at me with blank incomprehension; whatever their tactical notions about the uses of Vietcong flags, it was taken for granted by them that the American flag was the symbol of oppression and inhumanity, and its use in an anti-war demonstration would be morally unthinkable whatever the tactical considerations.[79]

Neuhaus, another prominent figure from a conservative religious background, also found the leftward drift disquieting. His satisfaction with CALC began to wane about 1970 as others advocated a multi-issue approach and the influence of the counterculture became noticeable. In 1971 he left the daily routine behind to spend several months in Africa, and upon his return, found that his philosophical differences with CALC had grown. Influenced perhaps by the cultural changes of those dynamic years, he felt that the organization had become more self-consciously leftist through its occasionally virulent attacks on the United States and its sympathy for America's adversaries. With Vietnamization, Neuhaus felt he no longer had to argue that the war was wrong, only how to get out. His own views, once among the most radical within CALC, lost their strident edge. Believing the cause was less urgent than before, Neuhaus gradually withdrew from a leadership role. His opposition to the radical influence became apparent at a 1974 memorial service for Heschel when Richard Falk delivered what he claimed was "a strident, leftist cliché. It just became appallingly clear to me that in no way did I believe what this organization was about anymore."[80]

For every person who became disillusioned, however, another stepped in, and CALC continued to grow. Kittlaus, for example, joined early in 1971 and described his associates as caring people deeply rooted in the Christian faith who were alarmed at what was happening in American society.[81]

As an active and influential antiwar organization, CALC attracted some extreme views among its newer constituents, but its diversity and strong religious tradition guaranteed that those views would remain in the minority. If some took exception to extremist rhetoric, it never became a real problem for most, who accepted it as part of the national debate over the war. As Minnesota's Joe Selvaggio explained, radicals "weren't really our main people. We tried to stay away from that, the real hard line leftists."[82]

The Ann Arbor conference did more than initiate a stronger voice for local chapters and expose significant ideological differences. CALC's increased visibility at this time kept it under the close scrutiny of various intelligence agencies. The FBI believed the PCPJ was heavily infiltrated by the Communist Party and it particularly feared that Fernandez, a member of the PCPJ steering committee, would make the Bernstein bequest available to that organization. CALC contacts with North Vietnamese officials also disturbed the bureau. Hoover instructed local FBI offices to investigate whether CALC chapters in their areas were infiltrated or controlled by revolutionary subversive, or violence-prone elements. The New York and Washington FBI offices monitored the bank accounts of the NCC, CALC, and the PCPJ to determine if any financial link existed between the latter two.[83]

CALC's relationship with the national coalitions had always been tenuous, as it preferred to work independently and develop its own constituency. Fernandez rebuffed NPAC's effort to attract greater involvement from CALC. Responding to one letter he wrote, "Aside from being [a] Trotskyite front group the National Peace Action Coalition has not over the last six months been deeply involved in organizing the religious community. . . ."[84] To another overture he replied, "I . . . am not particularly interested in 'solidifying our relationships' with NPAC or any other particular coalition at this time. I really believe that our work has to be constituency building first. . . ."[85]

Despite finding no evidence of infiltration by communists, subversive activities, or violation of federal laws, the FBI clearly viewed CALC as an adversary. The Rochester office refused to respond to a letter from the local CALC group regarding an investigation, claiming that to acknowledge the letter "would only give recognition to this group and any reply could be used to further attack the Bureau."[86]

The months after Ann Arbor were among the busiest in CALC's short history. With a variety of methods, CALC tried to reach larger audiences than ever before. One of its major projects focused attention on the war by bringing people into the nation's capital. The

Daily Death Toll joined CALC with the FOR, WILPF, WSP, and WRL in a series of demonstrations at the White House from November 5 through Thanksgiving 1971. Each day a designated city or region sent representatives to Washington to dramatize the 300 Vietnamese who died in the war each day and to encourage public pressure on Nixon to set a date for total withdrawal.[87]

The first day's actions were fairly typical. About 100 Philadelphians arrived at Washington's Lutheran Church of the Reformation at 10:00 A.M. for an orientaton meeting followed by a trip to the Capitol. Roughly half of the protesters met with members of Congress while the others demonstrated on the Capitol steps until shortly after 1:00 P.M., when the growing crowd of about 160 people began a 45-minute walk to the White House. Some dressed in black robes and coolie hats; others carried a large sign reading "three hundred more today killed in Indochina by U.S. bombs." When they arrived at the White House, most lay down on the sidewalk until about 4:00 P.M. to symbolize that day's number of civilian deaths in Indochina. The group remained near the White House until leaving shortly before 6:00, stopping at the home of Senator Hugh Scott (R-Pa.) for a brief demonstration before returning to Philadelphia. No incidents or arrests marred the activities.[88]

Subsequent Daily Death Toll actions followed with a few variations. Most drew smaller crowds than the initial protest but also usually ended with a number of arrests. Police arrested nearly 125 New York protesters for disorderly conduct, for example, when they blocked a White House driveway.[89] The project ended November 25 after eighteen days and 501 arrests. The FBI, having maintained a constant surveillance of the activities, found no evidence of communist infiltration or violence but continued to search for a financial link between CALC and PCPJ.[90]

The escalating air war moved a number of CALC leaders to try to schedule a talk with the cadets at the Air Force Academy on the weekend of November 12–13. Brickner, Harvey Cox, David Hunter, and Sister Mary Luke Tobin wrote to the superintendent of the academy, Lt. General Albert T. Clark, asking to address a mandatory formation of the 4,000 cadets on the topic of "moral aspects of the continuing air war in Indochina." General Clark believed that CALC was interested only in a confrontation and denied the request. He assured the group that the academy's curriculum included discussions of the moral and ethical aspects of warfare. When Clark agreed to meet with a Colorado CALC delegation to discuss the issue and later canceled the meeting, CALC decided to go to the academy anyway.[91]

On Sunday, November 15, about 150 people from the surrounding area entered the Air Force Academy in Colorado Springs to attend the Catholic and Protestant worship services. Military police arrested about 25 of those outside the chapel for distributing an outline of the program they had hoped to present. Another 120 demonstrators stood or kneeled during the services, with one leaving every five minutes to symbolize the civilian death rate in Indochina. The service itself included patriotic martial songs and prayers. Afterward, the group stood on the chapel steps singing hymns and passing out pamphlets. Security forces detained 32 people for refusing to move. This group, which included Fernandez, Cox, Hunter, and Tom Rauch, was photographed, fingerprinted, and held for two hours before being given letters of exclusion prohibiting them from appearing on the grounds without special permission.[92]

A group of thirteen CALC people returned to the Air Force Academy on January 9, 1972 and stood in silent protest throughout the morning worship service. The only incident occurred when military police arrested one of the demonstrators for distributing antiwar literature. Academy authorities then detained and issued letters of exclusion to all thirteen protesters.[93]

Fernandez explained his view of the air war in *Christian Century*. He said that the average tonnage of bombs dropped on Indochina increased from 60,000 tons per month during Lyndon Johnson's term to 95,000 tons per month during the Nixon years. He also quoted a Senate subcommittee *Report on Refugees* that claimed nearly 4,000,000 Indochinese had been killed, injured, or made refugees so far during Nixon's term of office. In criticizing the air war, Fernandez described the erosion of moral restraints upon its combatants. Bomber pilots, isolated by distance from the destruction they created, frequently fell victim to the numbing attitude that their bombs fell only on targets, not on people. These bombings, however, clearly violated the Nuremberg prohibition of "wanton destruction of civilian populations." Drawing a parallel with the highly publicized My Lai massacre, Fernandez argued:

> More and more Americans will no longer put up with the Nixon administration's strange moral calculus, which argues that so long as Americans are not dying, things are getting better and better in Indochina. If it was illegal for Lt. Calley to kill civilians at a distance of 30 feet, it is just as illegal for pilots to kill, injure, and refugee thousands of civilians at 30,000 feet![94]

CALC also maintained a loose relationship with Project Air War, an organization that received its impetus from President Nixon's escalation of the bombing announced on December 26, 1971. Project

Air War was a Washington, D.C. research group sponsored by the American Friends Service Committee and headed by Fred Branfman. It served as an investigative and information group that dealt with the shift in emphasis of the U.S. war effort from the ground to the air. Like CALC, this project kept the antiwar movement aware of the facts of the ongoing American war effort.[95]

Largely through the participation of Fernandez, CALC was involved in the Committee of Liaison, an organization formed to open communication between American prisoners in North Vietnam and their families. On December 21, 1971, Fernandez flew from Paris to New York with nearly 1,000 Christmas letters from over 300 U.S. POWs for distribution through the office of the committee. At a press conference with Cora Weiss of WSP and Dave Dellinger, Fernandez referred to the committee as "the principal vehicle for mail to and from the POWs."[96]

More typical of CALC's tactics from late 1970 to the end of 1972 was a series of long-term national projects that would have been impossible without the income from the Bernstein estate. *American Report* had been the first, and others followed in the succeeding months.

One campaign designed to keep the ongoing air war in front of the public was called Help Unsell the War. In early 1971, CBS broadcast a television special entitled "The Selling of the Pentagon," which exposed the Pentagon's attempts to market its version of the Vietnam War to the public. Amid the controversy that this telecast aroused, Ira Nerken and a group of Yale students and faculty concluded that if the war could be sold, it could also be unsold. In March 1971, this group enlisted the help of David B. McCall, President of McCaffrey-McCall advertising agency in New York, in finding volunteers to work with them. At an April 3 briefing at Yale by Indochina experts, over 300 people from fifty different advertising agencies agreed to donate their time, skills, and facilities to create a series of ad campaigns to end the war. Ultimately they donated over a million dollars worth of talent and materials to this project, what one writer called "the largest contribution ever made to a single peace effort." The project produced a variety of ads for print, posters, television commercials, billboards, and radio spots built around the theme of bringing the troops home by December 31. One ad pleaded: "Let's not just wind it down, for God's sake, let's wind it up."[97]

When Nerken and his group completed the original ads, they sought a national organization with the local strength to increase the visibility of the project around the country. They chose Clergy and Laymen Concerned and in late September began planning for a nationally coordinated campaign. CALC's Carl Rogers headed the Unsell project when Nerken returned to Yale, and the Bernstein money allowed the various advertising materials to be reproduced.

The actual campaign opened with an October 27 news conference. CALC offered samples of magazine and television ads without charge to over 8,500 radio and television stations, magazines, and newspapers. The response was enthusiastic. Eventually 113 television and 450 radio stations ran the Unsell ads as public service announcements[98] and aired them in some of the nation's largest markets, sometimes in choice time slots. CALC even took a cashier's check for $85,000 to ABC TV to buy a minute of Superbowl time, but ABC refused to run the spot.[99] Many newspapers and magazines ran the ads as well. Hugh Hefner donated an entire page of the March issue of *Playboy*, worth $39,000, to an Unsell ad.[100]

The messages effectively conveyed a sense of the war's toll on America. One ad, in a takeoff of the classic military recruiting poster, showed Uncle Sam with his head bandaged, hat under his arm, coat torn, and hand outstretched, with the caption "I want out." Radio commercials featured songs, testimonials from veterans, and Americans at home describing the agony and frustration caused by the war. The Senate appearance of John Kerry, former Navy lieutenant and leader of Vietnam Veterans Against the War, highlighted one television ad. "How do you ask a man to be the last to die in Vietnam?" he queried. "How do you ask a man to be the last to die for a mistake?" Evidence of the quality of the material came with the awarding of a Clio Award, the advertising industry's equivalent to the Oscar, to a television spot entitled "Apple Pie." Uncle Sam serves pie to a group of Americans that includes blacks, hard hats, students, and the elderly. The largest piece goes to a cigar-smoking general who wolfs it down. The announcer is heard over the picture:

> When they divide up the pie in Washington, do you ever wonder who gets the biggest slice? Most of your taxes go to pay for wars past, present, and future.
> What does your money buy? It buys you Viet Nam. And with it, inflation, unemployment, disunity and death.
> It buys you bombs instead of schools, defoliation instead of clean air and water, tanks instead of trains, and destroys homes instead of building them.
> Isn't it time we got out of their country and back into ours?
> Write your Congressman. Tell him you need a bigger piece of the pie—now.

Over 150 stations requested "Apple Pie" to run as a public service announcement.[101]

Unsell ads ran into 1972 when their message became somewhat dated. Their high visibility and additional volunteers from the advertising community convinced CALC to undertake a second series of ads later in the year.

The Bernstein money also allowed CALC to move into radio broadcasting. In the fall of 1971, Fernandez and Robert Lecky met with Robert Maslow and Harold Willens of the Businessmen's Educational Fund to discuss the possibility of CALC taking over sponsorship of the radio program "In the Public Interest." The members of the Businessmen's Educational Fund were liberals opposed to the war; the group had established the radio program in November 1970 to counterbalance the numerous radio broadcasts by the political right. Maslow was the driving force behind the program. He knew that many of the conservatives offered their programs to radio stations without charge as public service features. Liberals could rely on the fairness doctrine of the Federal Communication Commission to require those stations to air without cost their opposing view on the same public questions. Fernandez and Lecky recommended that CALC assume the program's sponsorship by the first of December. The steering committee reviewed the program, approved the recommendation, changed the name to "American Report Radio," and made plans for the following months.[102]

"American Report Radio" was a four-minute news commentary and analysis of public issues that aired six days a week. It was headquartered in Washington, D.C., produced by Maslow, and coordinated by Pat Reis. Commentators included Coffin, John Henry Faulk, John Gardner, Daniel Ellsberg, Edward Kennedy, and Gaylord Nelson. The number of stations carrying the program jumped from 140 before CALC's sponsorship to 460 in mid-1972. In addition, the Mutual Broadcasting Network fed "American Report" to its 555 outlets. Eventually it reached all fifty states and generated over 100 letters per week requesting transcripts and information.[103]

CALC's move into broadcasting was not as successful as it had hoped. While its audience increased quickly, production costs rose from $30,000 to $85,000 per year in less than twelve months. Some within CALC felt the program did not contribute the public relations gains they had envisioned; others felt a need for more advance planning. Financial problems led CALC to include an unsuccessful request for money in the broadcast that coincided with a decrease in program response. The communications committee grew concerned about the lack of control and integration of the program into CALC's overall program. After nearly a year, with its own financial resources limited and the show unable to finance itself, CALC decided to seek additional help for the program.[104]

Maslow and Lecky located an organization, the Fund for Peace, that offered to support half of the program's costs for the next fiscal period. Before an agreement was made, however, the Fund for Peace had second thoughts about cosponsoring the program; so CALC offered to transfer sponsorship of the entire program. The program's name reverted to "In the Public Interest" under funding by Lynn Mattison, and as of November 1, 1972, CALC ties with "American Report Radio" ended.[105]

These projects added a new dimension to CALC's antiwar witness. As impressive as they were in terms of energy and scope, it was left to another project to take best advantage of the stronger network of local chapters that emerged from the Ann Arbor conference. That project was the Honeywell campaign.

6

"AGAINST THEIR MACHINES WE HAVE ONLY . . . A SLENDER PRAYER"

THE CAMPAIGN FOR CORPORATE RESPONSIBILITY

> Ignore us if you dare.
>
> — HONEYWELL AD

On a spring night in 1972 at a Minneapolis church, members of CALC gathered to prepare for their confrontation with representatives of one of the nation's leading manufacturers of weaponry. "We weep for the perversion of conscience that permits good men to act evilly and not feel pain," prayed Rabbi Balfour Brickner. "Against their machines we have only words and hope—a slender prayer."[1] The rabbi's words symbolized one of CALC's most intensive and sustained projects. Choosing corporations that supported the air war and eventually focusing on Honeywell, CALC used moral and economic pressure to try to persuade them to end production of war materials. CALC's use of direct pressure on war-related industries combined with a highly coordinated national effort marked a unique departure from its typical methods of dissent. The campaign for corporate responsibility generated an impressive amount of activity and produced modest achievements on the local level, but it failed to win a conclusive victory.

In July 1970, the steering committee approved a project designed to hasten the end of the war by having religious institutions apply economic pressure to American corporations. CALC leaders reasoned that major religious bodies could use their stock investments for proxy fights to prod war-related corporations into accepting greater social responsibility. CALC would coordinate the entire project and build it around a network that included denominations, seminaries, local churches, and church-related colleges. Although the war remained the central issue, proponents of the multi-issue approach also

131

advocated efforts to influence corporations on overseas investments, racially discriminatory hiring practices, and pollution.[2]

Protests against Dow Chemical Company, which manufactured napalm for the U.S. government, set the precedent for pressuring war-related corporations. Students on numerous college campuses demonstrated against Dow recruiters in 1967, occasionally forming human barricades to prevent interviews from taking place. Protestant bodies such as the Presbyterian and American Baptist Churches divested themselves of thousands of shares of Dow stock.[3] In the fall of 1970, Stephen Rose, a member of CALC's steering committee and associate editor of *Christian Century,* envisioned an expanded role for religious investments. He noted that Protestant denominations had invested over a billion dollars in companies that produced most of the country's armaments. He viewed CALC's corporate campaign as an opening drive to reform the American economic system and counter "U.S. imperialism of the sort that led to our Vietnamese engagement."[4]

By the end of 1970, CALC joined with the Episcopal Peace Fellowship (EPF) to begin planning the campaign for corporate responsibility. The Washington-based Council on Economic Priorities researched and identified corporations with significant military contracts. CALC intended to address the targeted issues primarily through annual stockholder's meetings of these corporations. In November, it began to organize small groups within the various denominations that could represent their churches at the corporate gatherings, and promoted the project during a tour of a dozen cities.[5]

CALC defined its position on corporate responsibility most clearly in a position paper written in conjunction with the Episcopal Peace Fellowship. The paper described corporations as power centers that exerted enormous influence in determining the quality of life for millions of people. It indicated that corporations in general needed to change their priorities toward goods, services, and patterns of production that were more humane and socially useful. Religious institutions could promote those changes by applying pressure through their large investments in corporate securities. To this point, churches had hesitated to initiate significant changes within the corporations primarily because of their dependence on those investments, and the control of religious wealth, estimated at $160 billion, by members of the corporate establishment. CALC quoted from a recent unpublished study on the investments of seventeen national boards and seven Protestant denominations, which found that 123 investment committee members controlled over $3 billion in investments. The most heavily invested companies were IBM ($60,388,713), General

Motors ($18,067,971), Standard Oil of New Jersey ($12,614,445), AT&T ($11,851,492), and General Electric ($11,659,067). Of the 123 investment committee members, 47 percent were businesspeople, 20 percent bankers, 13 percent corporate lawyers, 5 percent business school faculty, and 13 percent church employed. The obvious conclusion was that "most of the management for religious wealth were prominent lay business and professional men holding executive positions and directorships of large business and financial institutions."[6]

CALC believed that religious institutions could make investments based on moral and ethical considerations in spite of their dependence on corporations. The position paper listed a number of strategies for more socially aware investment practices. Individuals or groups could petition corporations to pursue more enlightened social policies. Stock owners could use proxy statements to address shareholder's meetings on the merits of corporate social responsibility or file class-action suits. Church organizations could divest holdings in corporations not meeting their social criteria, or place new investments in companies that did meet those standards. CALC stressed that local organizing was essential regardless of the strategy chosen and that effective use of the media could lead to a duplication of the success against Dow Chemical, which had earlier withdrawn from the production of napalm.[7]

In December 1971, CALC purchased four shares of stock in each of four corporations: ITT, General Electric, Standard Oil of New Jersey, and Honeywell. It selected these businesses because they were involved in the air war, had local outlets, and numbered at least six religious denominations among their stockholders. CALC leaders made plans to attend the 1972 stockholder's meetings and filed three resolutions with each corporation in early June for inclusion on their proxy ballots. These resolutions called on the corporations to cease and desist in manufacturing munitions for the ongoing air war, to appoint an internal committee to study the feasibility of converting from wartime to peacetime development and production, and to disclose all military contracts signed since 1963. General Electric and Standard Oil rejected the resolutions, claiming that they were filed too late, and were upheld by the Securities and Exchange Commission.[8]

In the winter of 1971–72, the campaign's initial attempts to influence national religious agencies to change their investment policies produced encouraging results. Fernandez outlined CALC's future antiwar plans to the General Board of the NCC at its meeting at Charlotte, North Carolina. By late February, two agencies of the United Presbyterian Church voted to support the disclosure of contracts resolution, while the United Church of Christ and American Baptist Convention placed the issue under consideration. National CALC also targeted the U.S. Catholic Bishops' Conference and the General Board of the United Methodist Church, both meeting in Atlanta in mid-April. CALC's Denver chapter prepared for the national conventions of the United Presbyterian and American Baptist Churches planned for that city in the first two weeks of May.[9]

During January 1972, CALC followed up the Ann Arbor convention with two regional conferences in Denver and Louisville. The two groups agreed to focus the campaign for corporate responsibility on the continuing air war. Eight people met in Chicago on February 11–12 to evaluate a proposal from the Louisville conference that would narrow the focus of the corporate campaign by emphasizing one company over the others. The Chicago group adopted the idea and established criteria for selecting the most appropriate corporation. CALC wanted to single out a company involved in ordnance production that could be characterized as "visibly immoral" and that already had several denominations invested in it. To make it more vulnerable to grassroots pressure, it must also manufacture consumer products and take pride in its public image. CALC preferred a corporation that already had organized opposition to it and one that would attract additional allies within the antiwar movement. A CALC victory must have an impact on ending the war, and this campaign must have a legitimate chance of accomplishing its goal.[10]

Of the four corporations, Honeywell best met the criteria. In 1970, 21 percent of its sales went to the military, and as the nation's largest producer of antipersonnel bombs, it was susceptible to charges of participating in immoral actions. The United Church of Christ, United Methodist Church, and United Presbyterian Church all had substantial numbers of shares in Honeywell, which gave CALC a starting point for applying leverage. Honeywell's 1970 annual report stressed its social conscience and concern for oppressed people, and its production of cameras and photographic equipment, thermostats, and computers made it vulnerable to public pressure. Two groups in Minneapolis had already formed to try and stop Honeywell's bomb production. The Honeywell Project was organized in 1968 and centered on the company's blue collar workers, while a spinoff group, the Council for Corporate Review, focused on stockholders. By the time of CALC's involvement, invaluable preliminary research and action had already been done.[11] Stopping Honeywell's production of antipersonnel bombs would be a small but concrete step in ending the war and would warn other electronic warfare suppliers of their vulnerability to public pressure. As the largest of only two producers of complete antipersonnel bombs (outlawed by the Hague Convention), Honeywell was in a morally untenable position, and its status as the second largest company in the computer business made it economically vulnerable beyond its defense contracts.[12]

CALC's selection of the Honeywell campaign came primarily as a method of responding to Nixon's Vietnamization policy. The President's strategy was to gradually remove U.S. troops from Indochina and shift the burden of the fighting to the South Vietnamese. When de-escalation began, it produced a corresponding drop in American casualties, but Nixon compensated for the loss of U.S. soldiers with a drastic increase in bombing and a greater reliance on technology that gave no such relief to the Vietnamese. CALC's challenge was to sustain the interest of an increasingly war-weary public in a conflict that had become less urgent, increasingly automated, and, at least for Americans, waged from the air. It was not an anticorporation campaign for its own sake. The goal was to get Honeywell to announce publicly a decision to stop producing antipersonnel bombs for use in Southeast Asia.[13]

Not everyone embraced the campaign for corporate responsibility. Neuhaus was among the leaders opposed to attacking corporations, believing that it deviated from CALC's central purpose.[14] Many on the field development committee felt overextended with having to do local organizational development and helping to plan the Honeywell program as well. Despite these barriers, CALC went ahead. At its March meeting, the FDC agreed to support the Honeywell campaign as developed in Chicago and also established guidelines for funding local groups. The national staff agreed to send out regular update mailings on the Honeywell campaign and include a detailed organizing manual for integrating the religious community into the project.[15]

The national office worked out a presentation for local groups to build around. CALC relied on a slideshow produced by National Action/Research on the Military-Industrial Complex (NARMIC) entitled "The Automated Battlefield," which depicted the electronic sensors, remote-controlled airplanes, guided bombs, and antipersonnel weapons used in the air war. It also made use of a direct link between Honeywell and many of the nation's churches. "We discovered somewhere around 80 percent of the churches in this country have Honeywell controls on their heating systems," recalled Kittlaus. "You could make a speech and then walk over to the wall in the fellowship hall and there would be a Honeywell thermostat."[16]

CALC spent the early spring of 1972 preparing for the Honeywell stockholder's meeting at the end of April. It publicized the campaign with demonstrations and meetings, literature distributions, ads, and mailings. In late March, 200 Twin City clerics held an antiwar march in St. Paul, site of the Honeywell meeting. Throughout April, CALC representatives visited Honeywell offices in 25 cities. On April 7, Fernandez, Fred Branfman, and Richard Falk, Professor of International Law at Princeton, met with Chairman of the Board James Binger and two Honeywell vice-presidents. They discussed the format of the stockholder's meeting, urged Honeywell to disclose its defense contracts and name a committee for peacetime conversion, and filed three resolutions with the board for inclusion on the proxy statements. Honeywell initially rejected the resolutions but later accepted two of them after a ruling by the Securities and Exchange Commission.[17]

CALC directed some of its efforts toward convincing church bodies to divest their stock in Honeywell. Boston CALC, headed by John Cupples and Mollie Babize, presented resolutions on religious investments at the spring meetings of the statewide organizations of the American Baptists, United Church of Christ, and United Methodists.[18]

On April 25, the night before the Honeywell meeting, Minnesota CALC and the International Affairs Committee cosponsored an ecumenical worship service for the conversion of Honeywell. Several hundred attended the meeting at the Hennepin Avenue Methodist Church in Minneapolis. Robert McAfee Brown led with a sermon based on the fourth chapter of Micah, which read, "they shall beat their swords into plowshares and their spears into pruning hooks." Brown spoke of the need for an outer transformation from war to peace and also an inner transformation, a shift in personal priorities so that people count for more than things. The stockholders of Honeywell, he observed, are "probably, individually, good and decent people. But they have gotten involved in a web of evil of such a sort that individually good and decent people are collectively doing evil and indecent things and that must be stopped when the victims of the collective evil are our fellow human beings."[19]

The next day about twenty people demonstrated outside the Minneapolis Auditorium, site of the shareholder's meeting. Honeywell employees allowed stockholders in two at a time, where their admission cards were checked before private guards led them individually to get admission badges and escorted them to the meeting room. In a prearranged agreement with Honeywell officials, Brickner, Brown, Sister Mary Luke Tobin, and Bishop Walter Schoenerr led a responsive prayer before the meeting's opening asking for corporations to "beat their swords into plowshares." Tobin informed Binger that she had hoped to present him with the "Swords Into Plowshares Award," commending Honeywell for ending production of guava bombs, but the award was not allowed into the room. Binger agreed to accept it after the meeting.[20]

The issues raised by CALC dominated much of the meeting. Its two proposals to the stockholders recommended setting up a committee on economic conversion to peacetime production and forcing disclosure of contracts that supported military actions in Southeast Asia. Over two and a half hours of discussion ensued on Honeywell's production of antipersonnel weapons and its policy of supplying the government with any weapons it requested. CALC made no effort to obstruct the meeting, but with 21 people from twelve chapters in the meeting, it made its presence felt, and several members read speeches condemning the war and Honeywell's contribution to it. The board responded that it also wanted peace but until that time the company would research and develop weapons at government request. Voters defeated both of CALC's proposals.[21]

While CALC's campaign did not produce immediate success, Honeywell received sufficient pressure that it felt compelled to respond publicly. On April 18, it bought local newspaper ads that defended the corporation's position on defense-related activities. CALC responded in July with a pamphlet of its own that rebutted the Honeywell arguments.[22]

Honeywell claimed that decisions regarding America's military requirements rested primarily with the Department of Defense, and it was the duty of corporations to carry out the policy of the nation's elected leaders. Company officials argued that antipersonnel weapons were ethically no worse than more conventional weapons and were more effective militarily because they covered a larger area than standard explosives. Honeywell executives declared that "to the best of our knowledge" their weapons were not used against civilians. They further rejected the idea that producing antipersonnel weapons made their employees war criminals. Honeywell attacked as inaccurate CALC reports listing twelve antipersonnel weapons currently under production. It acknowledged manufacturing only one of those items, the Rockeye II, a small bomb filled with shrapnel, and referred to it as an antitank weapon. The company claimed that it no longer produced any antipersonnel weapons.

CALC emphasized the responsibility of individual citizens to help shape domestic and foreign policy. It was not convinced by Honeywell's "passing the buck" to elected officials on the issue of antipersonnel weapons given the millions of dollars that corporations spent trying to influence government officials regarding their corporate interests. Clergy and Laymen Concerned believed that antipersonnel weapons violated international conventions subscribed to by the United States that prohibited "unnecessary suffering." CALC leaders cited the Senate Subcommittee Report on Refugees of 1970 and 1971 as evidence that the primary victims of the air war were civilians. Honeywell could not deny that its weapons were responsible for much of the death and destruction that continued in Southeast Asia. CALC parried Honeywell's attacks on its facts stating that research for its campaign was carried out by the Corporate Information Center of the NCC and submitted to Honeywell for verification or correction. Honeywell's criticism of CALC's research was based not on the CIC findings but on an article in *American Report* that did not represent the campaign. CALC conceded that the article contained misinformation, but pointed out that its campaign had sought Honeywell's cooperation to avoid any inaccuracies. CALC used company contracts as evidence that Honeywell continued to develop and produce complete or portions of antipersonnel weapons used in Indochina. It referred to the Defense Market Survey as proof that the Rockeye II was also used as an antipersonnel weapon.

CALC attempted to raise the same issues at the annual meetings of the other three corporations it had targeted. Both the national office and Houston CALC planned activities for the General Electric meeting in Houston on April 26. On the night of April 25, they held a panel discussion and teach-in on churches and corporate responsibility that attracted about 100 people. Following the panel, they held a worship service in an excavation site on a university campus to simulate a bomb crater. Several large jets flew overhead during the service, adding to the dramatic impact of the event. On April 26, a number of pickets marched outside the Sheraton-Lincoln Hotel, while seven CALC people participated in the meeting itself. Trudi Young received a nomination for the board of directors but fell short of election. Young and Jhonnye Ste. Angelle of Dallas CALC read three resolutions into the minutes of the meeting and discussed their moral and business implications with Chairman of the Board Fred Borch. David Hunter claimed that General Electric shared responsibility for the war because of its production of equipment used in Indochina. After the meeting, CALC rented a room in the Sheraton Hotel and showed the NARMIC slides to interested stockholders and members of the preess.[23]

Roughly fifty demonstrators picketed the ITT stockholder's gathering on May 10 at the Memphis Sheraton-Peabody Hotel. Dale Oline, a Franciscan priest, represented CALC in the meeting. His two proposals, also imposed by the SEC after ITT's initial rejection, asked for full information on all contracts made with any government and the formation of a committee to study conversion from military to peacetime production. Both were soundly defeated. Unable to exert direct economic pressure on ITT's manufacture of electronic battlefield sensors and targeting devices for F-4 aircraft, CALC added a new tactic. It joined a boycott led by Women Strike for Peace against the Continental Baking Company, an ITT subsidiary that made Wonder Bread, until ITT ceased its manufacture of war-related products.[24]

Fifteen to twenty people participated in a CALC-sponsored demonstration at the May 18 Standard Oil stockholder's meeting in Houston. They gathered at 8:00 A.M. near the Humble Building with signs and a flag-draped coffin before marching to the Houston Music Hall for the 9:30 meeting. Most of the demonstrators attended the meeting, and during a question and answer period several called for Standard Oil to stop furnishing its products to the war effort. Company officials disallowed a proposed resolution to discontinue defense contracts. Following the meeting, CALC held a brief demonstration before dispersing without further incident.[25]

Workers in the Honeywell campaign were temporarily discouraged immediately after the rash of setbacks received at the stockholder's meetings, but gradually local chapters resumed work on the campaign. The national staff took a stronger lead in implementing strategy, while the field development committee sent letters to all CALC chapters reaffirming the Honeywell campaign as the focus of the national program and providing an update on its progress. Building the project at the grassroots, however, proved to be a difficult task. By June, five to eight chapters were heavily involved, eight to twelve others were partially involved, but over half of the 46 local chapters gave it either a low priority or did not work on it at all. CALC attempted to explain the resistance of local chapters to the Honeywell campaign during a retreat for the codirectors and national program staff. They identified two major problems. The first was CALC's lack of a tradition of common, interdependent projects. The national office had done little to coordinate field development in the past and it was unrealistic to expect the more sophisticated strategies of the Honeywell campaign to be learned quickly. The second problem was a grave financial crisis. CALC had to endure drastic budget cuts during both 1972 and 1973, and many on the program staff felt it was inappropriate to demand a more serious effort on the Honeywell project without the national office being able to bear the necessary costs of training. The FDC sent people out in June to visit the twelve areas that had indicated an interest in developing the Honeywell campaign and to better adapt the program at the local level.[26]

Gradually the idea gathered momentum. CALC publicly announced the start of the campaign on April 18, 1972 at sixteen press conferences around the nation, most of which received good coverage by the local media. By that September, half of CALC's fifty chapters were involved to some extent in the campaign, and 80 percent worked actively within religious bodies. By the following May, 27 out of 47 active chapters participated in the project. Activists frequently met with local Honeywell representatives, and convinced a few to advertise CALC showings of the NARMIC slides.[27] The Western Massachusetts CALC chapter sent letters to all Amherst photographic suppliers urging them not to stock Honeywell equipment. Southern California CALC sent small groups to a number of cities in the Los Angeles area, where they held discussions with the management of Honeywell facilities. In Cleveland, thirty people picketed the Honeywell offices, denouncing its production of weapons, while the Kentuckiana chapter picketed once a week for a month at two Louisville stores selling photographic equipment. The Greenville, South Carolina chapter picketed and distributed leaflets at the Greenville Honeywell Electronic Data Processing plant through June 1972 and reemerged in March 1973 for a week-long vigil at a local photo supply store selling Honeywell equipment.[28]

No chapter of Clergy and Laymen Concerned plunged into the Honeywell campaign with greater enthusiasm than Boston. In a region thick with defense industries, CALC carved out its own niche among the ongoing efforts of other social-justice groups advocating corporate responsibility. It opened the campaign in late April 1972, and publicized it with a sixteen-page booklet that combined information on Honeywell's involvement in the war effort and its local locations and activities.[29]

Boston CALC requested meetings with Honeywell's top area managers, but only one joined them for a cordial if uneventful discussion that produced the standard responses heard from other Honeywell officials. CALC found unexpected support among the company's employees, however. About thirty Honeywell workers attended a May 4 program on technological warfare and vented their opposition to Honeywell's production of war materiel. Although sensitive to the issue of corporate responsibility, they recognized the threat to their jobs if they joined, in the company's eyes, a subversive movement. A core of Honeywell employees from that meeting organized an alternative company newspaper, while 35 workers at one of the plants unsuccessfully petitioned the management to show the NARMIC slides at the facility.[30] The Bostonians even polled Honeywell workers at a Waltham plant in August. Of those who returned their secret ballots, 131 said yes to the question "Should Honeywell, Inc. stop research, development, and production of antipersonnel weapons?"; 88 said no.[31] Campaign workers hoped this internal dissent would make Honeywell more vulnerable to its own external pressure.

Most of CALC's Boston contingent viewed the churches as the best place to enlist allies for the Honeywell campaign. CALC stressed moral and economic arguments and used the NARMIC slides in urging the religious community to organize around the issue of corporate responsibility. It spurred the development of congregational peace groups that worked to eliminate church investments in Honeywell or in other war-related manufacturing.[32]

Support within the local congregations aided CALC's effort to have the denominations take a position on corporate responsibility. Denominational committees of social concerns needed the backing of their own churches when their resolutions reached the inevitable debate on the convention floor. During the summer of 1972, state or regional conferences of the American Baptists, United Methodists, and United Church of Christ passed resolutions that called for investigation of their churches' investments. The United Church of Christ state conference also asked Honeywell to stop production of antipersonnel bombs, a move that drew inquiries from the company's management.[33]

Other evidence also suggested Honeywell was beginning to feel the pressure of CALC's campaign. Officials at a Boston plant urged their employees to stay inside for lunch after a nearby Raytheon plant was leafleted one morning, and the main office in Minneapolis defended itself in full-page ads that were reprinted in all the Boston-area plants.[34]

While many of CALC's people pursued negotiation and discussion, others used different tactics. Boston's Daily Death Toll group selected the Lexington Honeywell plant for several days of direct action. During one week from Monday through Thursday, about fifteen people carried posters and passed out leaflets announcing CALC's presence. Each day's leaflets were different and tried to answer the questions raised by employees the day before. After four days, plant workers knew CALC's intentions, and though generally unconverted, were less hostile than at the beginning. On the fifth day CALC members moved into the lobby of the plant's only entrance, staged an hour-long lie-in, forcing employees to step over them, and then left without incident. The next Monday they returned with new leaflets explaining their actions, and two days later served lemonade during the lunch hour and discussed the war and Honeywell's role in it.[35]

During that summer, the Daily Death Toll group made over sixty visits to area plants and sales offices and conducted actions ranging from guerrilla theater to picketing and leafleting without suffering any arrests. CALC personnel differed over the effectiveness of direct action, but continued to support such efforts. Feedback from the plants indicated at least an indirect influence. As one employee remarked, the relative unpopularity of such events made less confrontational efforts seem more legitimate. CALC, however, believed that direct action forced the corporation to think about its participation in the ongoing death and destruction in Indochina.[36]

The most ambitious element of Boston CALC's campaign was its coordination of "Honeywell Day," when it successfully carried out actions at all Honeywell plants and offices in the state of Massachusetts. On Wednesday, October 25, over 300 people converged on 26 sites for demonstrations ranging in size from five to ninety participants. Most activities took place in the morning as employees arrived at work. CALC activists, some dressed in masks and sheets to dramatize the ongoing death toll, distributed thousands of leaflets to Honeywell employees, commuters, and some of the surrounding neighborhoods. Many discussed the production of antipersonnel weapons with Honeywell executives, police, or reporters. CALC members at the Burlington site showed a "60 Minutes" television segment on Honeywell to a small group of employees and police. That afternoon at Tech Square, about 75 people held a service of commemoration, a discussion on war industries, and concluded with an outdoor showing of the "60 Minutes" piece. At one of the Waltham plants, over forty people committed civil disobedience. After a short liturgy at the executive entrance, CALC staged a brief "die-in" beyond the trespass limit and left after pouring blood on the front steps of the plant.[37]

That evening the enthusiastic participants gathered for a potluck supper and to share the day's events. They reported several favorable responses to their efforts and were convinced the simultaneous demonstrations were more effective than a single large protest. Several of the actions attracted attention from local newspapers and radio and television stations; Honeywell photographers also had recorded their activities at each plant.[38]

CALC did remarkably well in carrying out its plans for "Honeywell Day," but there was room for improvement. In rushing to guarantee that the project took place before the presidential election, CALC gave people less than a week's notice about specific times and locations. With more time, CALC leaders felt certain they could have attracted more participation and press coverage. CALC's intelligence on the Honeywell locations was also less than thorough. Five of the locations were unsuitable for demonstrations, one was only an answering service, and another was merely a single room in a larger building. One plant had even been closed! The rally at Tech Square took place in an area that had virtually no employee traffic, and the plant in Wakefield was discovered only by luck. At the last minute a local minister agreed to go there and talk with Honeywell employees.[39]

Not all CALC affiliates were able to tie into Honeywell as effectively as Boston. Some adapted the issue of corporate responsibility to their local situations. Schenectady CALC began its own General Electric project as early as 1971. Seattle CALC made modest efforts in the Honeywell campaign, but dropped out after some initial frustrations. In the fall of 1973, however, it moved to block congressional funding of the Trident submarine that would be built in the Seattle area. When CALC turned its attention to the B-1 bomber, the Seattle chapter participated actively because of its local ties to Boeing. Tempe, Arizona lost the core of its Honeywell task force in 1973 and thereafter focused more on local corporations linked to the war, including Motorola and Marathon Oil. When the lack of local Honeywell plants or offices restricted Dallas' campaign, it expanded the project to include Texas Instrument.[40]

Despite its sometimes sputtering start, the Honeywell project did produce results. Here and there, camera store owners wrote to Honeywell protesting its manufacture of antipersonnel weapons. Several denominational agencies pressured the company to end its production of all such devices, and individual congregations registered their protest as well. Honeywell sales representatives indicated that camera sales had fallen off because of the war's negative impact on the company's image. Even the probing television cameras of "60 Minutes" came to focus on Honeywell.[41]

CALC continued to search for allies in the Honeywell campaign. One opportunity arose in July when Architects Allied for Life, a group of west coast architects, met with Fernandez and Kittlaus in San Francisco about joining the project. Architects could frequently specify whether or not Honeywell equipment should be used in buildings they designed. CALC made this a national project and planned a special mailing to 10,000 architects across the country, but the work was delayed when it could not come up with the $1,500 postal expenses. Some architects, most from California or Massachusetts, wrote directly to Honeywell threatening not to use its equipment because of its involvement in the war, but the company did not respond publicly. The National Student Association adopted a resolution condemning Honeywell's policies, and students targeted Honeywell in actions at a number of colleges across the country.[42]

During September and October, Fernandez became preoccupied with financial and administrative matters, and the Honeywell project slowed down. Attempts to integrate the Honeywell project with American Report Radio and *American Report* proved unsuccessful. However, CALC took its case to two pharmaceutical companies that were considering whether or not to buy Honeywell computers, and local groups continued to hold press conferences. In general, at a time when large-scale protests were not in vogue, the Honeywell campaign served as a concrete program that allowed local chapters to focus on the air war.[43]

In preparation for the upcoming 1973 annual stockholder's meeting, the national office held a series of conference calls with the local chapters most heavily involved in the Honeywell project. These conversations produced a three-pronged strategy to be used before the meeting in Minneapolis. The plan consisted of demonstrating against Honeywell recruiters on college campuses, persuading local congregations to buy a share of stock in order to have a voice in stockholder's meetings, and boycotting local Honeywell camera stores.[44]

On the grassroots level, CALC generated a great deal of activity. Its work within religious institutions produced positive results. Boston CALC influenced the Massachusetts Conference of the United Church of Christ, the Episcopal Diocese Conference Task Force on Honeywell, and Andover-Newton Theological School to pass resolutions condemning Honeywell's involvement in the war. In the Chicago area, fifteen churches passed similar statements. The Detroit chapter persuaded three churches to discontinue their service contracts on Honeywell temperature controls.

The effort to have institutions and individuals purchase shares of stock met with varying success. Eventually hundreds participated, especially in northern California, Boston, Minneapolis, and Washington. Honeywell plants and camera stores across the country received visits, petitions, and pickets, among other actions. Special emphasis on computer, medical, and architectural users of Honeywell products met with only minor success, although limited boycotts did occur in Massachusetts, Indiana, and New York.

The methods and effectiveness of the campaign varied greatly from one area to another. Among its other tactics, the Greenville, South Carolina chapter followed a biblical precedent and tried to knock down the walls of the local Honeywell office by walking around it seven times and blowing trumpets.[45]

In addition to these local actions, CALC sent two resolutions to Honeywell at the end of December for inclusion on the 1973 proxy ballot. CALC leaders were not optimistic about Honeywell's acceptance of the resolutions and anticipated that the Securities and Exchange Commission would have to mediate.[46] Surprisingly, Honeywell did not contest the appearance of CALC's proposal to end manufacture of antipersonnel weapons, and it became the first such proposal to appear on any corporate ballot. CALC argued that production of these weapons could result in a loss of sales because of negative publicity and cited Dow Chemical's production of napalm as an example. Honeywell did object, however, to the resolution that described antipersonnel devices as illegal and implied that the company could be guilty of war crimes.

Diplomatic events around the turn of the year encouraged opponents of the war, but also made a successful conclusion to the Honeywell campaign more difficult to accomplish. In late October 1972, National Security Advisor Henry Kissinger told reporters that "peace is at hand." Despite delays caused by the intransigence of South Vietnamese President Nguyen Van Thieu, the main antagonists finally reached a settlement. On January 27, 1973, the United States, North Vietnam, South Vietnam, and the NLF signed a peace agreement in Paris, achieving what Richard Nixon perversely called "peace with honor." To most of the American public the war was over, and whatever occurred between the rival Vietnamese factions did not greatly concern them. Convincing people in that atmosphere that U.S. corporations were still participating in the destruction of Vietnam would be a monumental feat.

Nevertheless, signs appeared in a number of areas indicating that CALC's year-long effort might be having an impact. At the end of 1972, the peace education division of the American Friends Service Committee decided to adopt the Honeywell campaign, and the Minnesota state legislature introduced a motion to ban the production of all antipersonnel weapons within the state. CALC again contacted the United Methodist Church and United Church of Christ, both of which had supported its resolutioins in 1972, to aid the campaign through the next stockholder's meeting. It also requested the support of the Unitarian Church, which held several thousand shares of stock. All three denominations agreed to support the new resolutions. CALC and the AFSC also pursued other institutions holding stock in Honeywell but with less success.[47]

CALC's Ann Arbor chapter, the Interfaith Council for Peace (ICP), plunged into the Honeywell campaign with a group that, at the time of the Paris accords, numbered over fifty people from about twenty local congregations. The ICP pursued an ambitious plan to have the Ann Arbor city council boycott Honeywell's products and declare its antipersonnel weapons in violation of international law. Members of the ICP contacted dozens of local churches and businesses to build grassroots support for their project. They met with several church boards, presented the NARMIC slideshow, and persuaded four congregations to buy Honeywell stock and protest antipersonnel weapons at the annual shareholder's meeting. At the same time, they talked with local distributors about Honeywell's contracts with the Defense Department and leafleted Honeywell recruiters during a February 1973 visit to the University of Michigan campus.[48]

While these preparations continued, the ICP drafted a resolution charging Honeywell with producing weapons used in violation of international law and called upon the Ann Arbor city council to support CALC's boycott of Honeywell products. At the group's urging, the city council held a public hearing on March 20 regarding Honeywell's weapons production. The council asked CALC to present its allegations and invited Honeywell to defend itself against the charges that its weapons were used illegally. Honeywell declined to send any representatives, responding instead with a letter insisting that it had not produced antipersonnel weapons since January 1972, and equating opposition to the production of antimateriel weapons with unilateral disarmament.[49]

Richard Falk, Professor of International Law at Princeton University, and Erik Prokosch, an AFSC researcher with NARMIC, presented the ICP's case against Honeywell. One of their specific targets was the Rockeye II, designed as an antitank weapon, but Prokosch quoted military officials who admitted to its use against people in Vietnam. Falk testified that the Rockeye II was illegal under international law, which required discrimination between combatants and civilians and prohibited weapons that caused undue suffering. Falk concluded, on the basis of the precedent of certain Nuremberg trial cases after World War II, that Honeywell's knowledge of this illegal use made it criminally liable. The Nuremberg "obligations" required citizens and all levels of government to prevent war crimes from being committed. "The issue of criminal responsibility with respect to war is too important to leave to the government and corporations." The ICP asked the city council to boycott all Honeywell products and urge Ann Arbor residents to boycott consumer products such as cameras, thermostats, and computer equipment.[50]

During a special meeting on March 29 that dragged into the morning hours, Ann Arbor became the first city to boycott Honeywell. Democratic and Human Rights Party council members outvoted Republicans six to four in accepting the Nuremberg obligations. The city council passed the resolution, which claimed that Honeywell produced and developed weapons that were used to "violate international law, treaties and agreements." The resolution prohibited the city from purchasing Honeywell products until the company ended its production of antipersonnel weapons, renounced its position of unquestioned support of Defense Department requests, and agreed to withdraw from production of future products that it believed might be used in violation of international laws of war. The council also urged the citizens and businesses of Ann Arbor to join the Honeywell boycott.[51] Ann Arbor Mayor Robert Harris wrote to James Binger, Honeywell's Chairman of the Board, that "somehow, someone must force American citizens on corporate boards of directors, in city councils, in Congress . . . to question the morality of the daily decisions we make that intimately lead to horrible civilian casualties."[52]

Unfortunately for the ICP, its victory was short-lived. In circumstances indicative of the uphill struggle of the antiwar forces, a newly elected city council with a Republican majority repealed the Honeywell resolution less than two months later.[53]

The Honeywell campaign operated within a larger movement of American business accountability. During the spring of 1973, a number of religious groups submitted resolutions on social issues to major American corporations for inclusion on their proxy statements. Over twenty such statements actually appeared on the ballots. As Edward Fiske of the New York *Times* observed, "The resolutions reflect the growing willingness of religious bodies to use their power as institutions to back up their pronouncements on social issues." These organizations included the United Methodist Church, the Episcopal Church, American Baptist Convention, the United Church of Christ, and the United Presbyterian Church. Several of these bodies appointed staff members or committees to be responsible for following the social implications of their investments. Their primary concerns consisted of investments in South Africa, military production, or environmental policies.[54]

The leaders of the Honeywell campaign established a series of short-term goals for the upcoming stockholder's meeting. CALC would try to have some of its own members appointed to the Honeywell board of directors, find a legal way of getting the antipersonnel issue before the corporation, and reintroduce a new cease-and-desist resolution supported by a confidential Harvard study on corporate recruiting problems.[55]

On her flight from New York to Minneapolis, Trudi Young had a chance meeting with James Binger and gave him a ride to his office.

Binger was surprised that thousands of letters objecting to Honeywell's weapons production were still coming in after the cease-fire agreement. When Young inquired about the campaign's results, he mentioned that Honeywell had been significantly irritated and that the board had discussed the issues raised for the first time. There were no indications, however, that the company intended to alter its policies.[56]

National and regional staff members and representatives from eighteen local CALC groups gathered in Minneapolis during the last week of April for the meeting. On April 24, 1973 the night before the meeting, most of those people supporting the CALC resolutions met at the Hennepin Avenue Methodist Church for a worship and protest service, with Harvey Cox delivering the sermon. The group held a briefing after the service to discuss the strategy for the following day.

Honeywell braced for a confrontation. Security precautions were very tight, as guards searched briefcases and purses and patrolled the hallways. About 150 campaigners from CALC and the AFSC took part in the four-hour meeting, and others came to support their efforts. Some of the participants made extremely harsh statements during the meeting. One motion nominated Honeywell chair Binger "mass murderer of the year" and another suggested he be replaced as chair with South Vietnamese President Thieu. The six Honeywell directors fielded numerous questions about the production of antipersonnel weapons and responded in a generally polite and nonemotional manner.[57]

The real debate came on the proposal that the company withdraw from the design and production of antipersonnel weapons. Shareholders launched a barrage of over seventy statements from the floor as CALC argued that the production of these weapons was immoral and constituted a "violation of international law under the Nuremberg principles." Binger listened courteously as people questioned the moral and ethical criteria of staying in the weapons business. This was, after all, the fourth consecutive year that the issue had been raised at the annual meeting, and 85 percent of the outstanding shares had already been voted in favor of management. The company actually denied having produced antipersonnel weapons since January 1972, but CALC disagreed, citing the Rockeye II.

Binger answered most of the questions by referring to Honeywell's proxy statement on the issue: "the cause of peace in today's world will best be served by a militarily strong United States . . . to that end American industry must participate in supplying needed materiel. . . . Honeywell believes it should continue to support these needs." When the stockholders finally voted, CALC's proposal received less than 1.5 percent of the total. With the proposal defeated, a minister rose to say that CALC was praying for Honeywell and its management "that you may be given the grace of a troubled conscience, and the wisdom to act upon it." When someone called for a moment of silence to honor the Vietnam dead, Binger acquiesced.[58]

After the meeting, over 120 people from CALC, AFSC, the Project on Corporate Responsibility, the Honeywell Project, and the Council for Corporate Review met at the Minnesota Church Center to discuss the shareholder's meeting and evaluate their various campaigns. Phillip Moore of the Project on Corporate Responsibility spoke on the future of corporate activism. He encouraged CALC to continue its Honeywell campaign, but also urged it to address the broader issue of the corporate power structure and its influence on American foreign policy. Moore pointed to a need to go beyond stockholder actions, to get social activists elected to boards of directors and to have corporations provide more information about their work to the public. Corporations, he claimed, were political institutions that must be dealt with through the political process.

The antiwar conference then broke into small groups to discuss the strengths and weaknesses of the various campaigns. The campaign workers seemed most satisfied with the focus on a single company, the camera boycott, the development of a coalition around this issue, and the campaign as an educational experience. On the other hand, some believed that the focus on antipersonnel weapons was too narrow and should be broadened to include the issue of corporate power. Others mentioned the difficulty of influencing Honeywell through a consumer sales boycott and the problems of organizing since the January cease-fire. A few had grown discouraged with their apparent inability to adequately communicate their ideas and assumed a general feeling that "we may be out of touch with the mood of the country." The group set as a future goal a more direct focus on corporate power rather than a view of it as a side effect of the war.[59]

Later, about 35 members of CALC and the AFSC met together for a day and a half to evaluate the campaign and discuss its future directions. Many were concerned that the number of plants, offices, products, and issues were too limited to allow for an effective campaign. They also recognized that reliance on buying single shares of stock made it virtually impossible to vote against management policies.[60] The CALC groups most heavily involved in the Honeywell campaign were: Boston, central Massachusetts, western Massachusetts, Buffalo, Washington, D.C., Greenville, Louisville, Indianapolis, Ann Arbor, Detroit, Chicago, Minnesota, Denver, northern California, and southern California. Out of 40 CALC groups, 25 emphasized the Honeywell program, and they had been joined by the northern and southern California regional offices of the AFSC.[61]

During the Honeywell meetings, members of Denver CALC presented two proposals to the General Electric shareholder's meeting in Denver. The resolutions, calling for the disclosure of military contracts and the conversion to full peacetime production, received less than 1.5 percent of the votes. CALC also succeeded in getting resolutions on manufacturing weapons and conversion to peacetime production on the proxy statement of Exxon.[62]

Following the spring shareholders' meetings, CALC established a Honeywell Campaign Continuation Committee (HCCC), which surveyed local chapters around the country. Out of 24 responses, 16 wanted to continue the Honeywell campaign. Only four groups reported the Honeywell campaign as helpful in local organizing. The HCCC found that 122 local religious congregations had in some way participated in the campaign and that church and synagogue members continued to serve as the major constituencies of local CALC chapters. It also found strong support for a new campaign aimed at preventing the production of the B-1 bomber. In spite of the less-than-enthusiastic response, the program committee proposed that two new national staff people be hired to continue the Honeywell campaign and that the headquarters be moved to Minneapolis. It reasoned that if CALC dropped its support, the national Honeywell project would probably collapse.[63]

By late fall, however, a number of factors combined to end the Honeywell campaign. The 1973 Paris agreement had fundamentally altered the American situation in Vietnam. The removal of U.S. combat troops represented the central goal of most peace activists, and yet the achievement of this victory left them somewhat listless in pursuing their remaining objectives. As the Boston group's project evaluation explained, "The 'post-war' malaise affecting so much of the antiwar movement took its toll on CALC organizers, both nationally and locally." CALC's commitment also suffered because of its ongoing financial problems. Because the pressure on Honeywell had already lasted five years, however, some were reluctant to end it. The Boston chapter assumed the leadership role for those continuing the campaign, but many key contacts around the country had moved on to other issues. Under Boston's direction, the campaign seemed to shift its focus away from antipersonnel weapons toward the larger issue of corporate power, a drift that reflected the growing internal debate over the postwar direction of the organization. With interest waning, national CALC moved to preserve its grassroots network and de-emphasized the Honeywell campaign, cutting off funds for it in June 1974. In its place CALC substituted the goal of preventing the production of the B-1 bomber, which seemed to have greater appeal and hold greater prospects for success.[64]

Occasional protests against corporate involvement in the war continued. Honeywell's 1974 stockholder's meeting in early May attracted 45 demonstrators who rose in unison and briefly recited the Nuremberg principles. Rev. Howard Schomer responded to the board's claim that the government should determine the nation's defense needs by asking Binger why he had entrusted his conscience to Nixon. "Are you not remorseful that you ever relied on such a man for determination of whether such conduct is moral?"[65] At the annual meeting of General Electric, CALC sponsored an amendment to the company's certificate of incorporation stipulating that the company "shall not manufacture and distribute products which are wasteful of the nation's fuel resources or destructive of the human environment." To support this resolution, CALC claimed that the energy crisis underscored that wasteful products should not be made or distributed and that the production of Air Force jet engines "at a time when many basic social needs . . . go unmet, represents a serious distortion of national priorities."[66] General Electric opposed this and three other resolutions, responding that CALC's proposal was part of a campaign to terminate the B-1 bomber program. It also claimed that part of its corporate responsibility was to undertake government contracts which responsible government officials considered important to national security. That direct action against corporations had spread beyond the war was evident in resolutions from agencies of the Episcopal and United Presbyterian churches regarding the numbers of women and minorities in the work force and investments in South Africa.[67]

The Honeywell campaign was significant in the history of CALC for a number of reasons. It was the first successful effort to harness all the organization's resources to work toward a single limited goal. Contributions to a campaign from the local chapters and national coordination reached a new high point. The campaign marked a departure from CALC's usual attempts to convince the general public or the policymakers that the war was wrong and should be stopped. If corporations could be persuaded to limit their support for the war, then perhaps the conflict could be made a little more humane if not altogether ended. The Honeywell campaign established a model later used by CALC and other organizations interested in social change, but it could not be considered an unqualified success. It succeeded in bringing attention to the air war and the frequently inhumane manner in which it was fought, and occasionally convinced individuals of the correctness of CALC's position. However, Honeywell never gave in to CALC's demands, and though it phased out its weapons production, it denied that CALC had any impact on that decision.[68]

While Clergy and Laymen Concerned could claim limited success, the failure to achieve its goal reflected the waning influence of antiwar organizations. For years the antiwar movement had tried to convince the public that the war was either misguided or immoral and advocated an American withdrawal from Vietnam. Most of the nation never accepted this assessment, and the possibility that it was accurate did not increase its appeal. Though people disagreed with the movement's analysis, many could agree that a military exit from Indochina was the best resolution to the country's dilemma. Vietnamization drained away one of the peace forces' major issues. When Nixon declared his intention to de-escalate, passive observers believed that antiwar activists had achieved their goal. A war-weary nation interpreted Vietnamization as the end of the war, ignored the conflict's continuation, and did not understand why dissent persisted. Despite its best efforts, CALC's campaign had less to do with Honeywell's decision than did the war's de-escalation.

7

"A TIME FOR WAR, A TIME FOR PEACE"
(January 1972 to May 1975)

> Where they make a desert, they call it peace.
> — TACITUS

On January 25, 1972, President Nixon announced that, in addition to the formal peace negotiations, Henry Kissinger had been secretly meeting with North Vietnamese representatives in Paris. Though neither set of discussions had yet produced results, the President clearly hoped to impress the public that his administration was sincere in its pursuit of peace. "I think," wrote Richard Fernandez, "Nixon's speech last night again peeled off another layer of the anti-war movement into a state of delusion that the war will somehow end."[1] Fernandez's comment epitomized a growing problem for the peace forces. Antiwar momentum had peaked despite occasional signs of vigor. The policies of the Nixon administration helped to weaken it. Many who opposed the war had witnessed the drastic de-escalation of American ground troops and, feeling that the battle was over, had dropped out of the ranks of activists.

Recognizing that the destruction continued but acknowledging that Vietnamization had undercut the urgency of its message, CALC searched for programs that would generate persistent actions against the war. The Paris accords of 1973 marked the attainment of CALC's primary goal and served as a turning point for the organization. As its antiwar programs ran their course, they were replaced by more peripheral issues and finally by concerns unrelated to Vietnam. Surviving financial crises, a transition of leadership, and a period of decline in motivation and direction, Clergy and Laymen Concerned continued to function as a national organization. As the war drew to a close, however, its existence as strictly an antiwar organization ended.

The religious community produced one of the year's strongest statements on the war when over 600 representatives gathered in Kansas City in early February 1972. This Ecumenical Witness for Peace, coordinated by Robert Bilheimer of the NCC, attracted nearly 350 Protestants, 200 Catholics, 50 Jews, and several Eastern Orthodox. Participants labeled U.S. involvement in the war "unjust and immoral" but also urged China and the Soviet Union to cease military aid so the "Indochinese people can determine their own future." The conferees recommended granting political asylum to Vietnamese refugees after the removal of U.S. troops, the use of civilian clergy rather than military chaplains, and the creation of religious boards to minister to Vietnam veterans. For the war at home they advocated legal recognition for selective conscientious objection, a general amnesty, and abolition of the draft, among other things.[2]

Several denominations addressed these issues at about the same time. The United Presbyterians, United Church of Christ, American Baptists, United Methodists, and Disciples of Christ all established programs to aid returning service personnel in areas like employment, education, drug rehabilitation, and counseling. The United Presbyterian General Assembly criticized American deception regarding the origins of the war, and chastised arguments for staying in Vietnam as immoral. It recommended that Congress limit presidential authority to unilaterally commit U.S. forces and urged church support for peaceful civil disobedience. At their annual convention, the United Methodists called for an immediate bombing halt, release of all POWs, reparations, and the withdrawal of U.S. forces by the end of 1972. They rejected support for draft resistance. American Baptists advocated more government benefits for Vietnam veterans but defeated an anti–Vietnam War resolution.[3]

These actions indicate that mainline churches continued their trend of opposition to American policy in Vietnam but also reflect the difficulty of maintaining a consistent position as convention representatives shifted from year to year. The focus on returning veterans, concern with presidential power, and POWs signified a belief in the imminent conclusion of the war and a desire to address other social issues. The war, however, was not yet finished.

On May 8, 1972, President Nixon intensified American attacks upon North Vietnam through a renewal of massive bombing, a naval blockade, and the mining of Haiphong Harbor, what historian George Herring called "the most drastic escalation of the war since 1968."[4] Writing as editors of *Christianity and Crisis,* John Bennett, Robert McAfee Brown, Harvey Cox, and Michael Novak criticized this move, acknowledging that while the air war required fewer American deaths, more Asians would die as the war continued. The willingness of the administration to resume such a strategy meant that "for an increasing number of Americans the enemies are not overseas. They are now in Washington."[5]

Responding to the President's order, CALC called a May 16 emergency witness demonstration in Washington. More than 500 people turned out to support a congressional effort to cut off funding for the war. Some of the participants lobbied various members of Congress, including a group of twenty that met with Representative Charles Gubser of California. Gubser opposed a number of measures to end the war, and the CALC people hoped to change his vote on these issues. When he asked them to leave, ten people indicated they would remain in his office until he promised to vote for the peace resolutions. Gubser called in the Capitol police, who arrested the ten for unlawful entry.[6] A second group was evicted from the Senate gallery for shouting "end the war" during a Senate session.

The largest demonstration began around 3:00 P.M. when CALC members began a sit-in worship service at the Capitol Rotunda. The singing, speeches, and prayer lasted nearly three hours. Virtually everyone cooperated when Capitol police began making the first of 120 arrests, avoiding any further incidents. Among those arrested was William Sloane Coffin, who not only led the worship service but helped everyone through the arrest process and led the group in hymns all night. That evening the jailers performed their duties with the words of "A Mighty Fortress Is our God" echoing off the walls.[7]

In addition to its one-day emergency demonstration, CALC opened a second phase of the Unsell the War Project. Troop withdrawals under Nixon's Vietnamization program and the passing of the December 31 target date for the total removal of U.S. military forces made the first set of ads appear dated. At the start of 1972, Frank Greer of CALC moved to San Francisco to head phase two, announced to the public on June 13. Roughly 350 people from California ad agencies, film companies, and recording studios volunteered their time and talents to produce eleven television and ten radio spots, eighteen print ads, and four billboard ads. Actors Henry Fonda and James Whitmore were among those contributing to the narration and on-camera work. This second round of ads focused on the continuing air war and pointed toward the upcoming presidential election. This message was typically expressed in a TV ad that followed an ordinary citizen walking his dog along a smalltown street. The voice over explained:

> Charlie Sutton is the foreman of a packing plant in Wilkesville, Ohio, belongs to the All-City Bowling League, and likes to walk his

dog on Sunday morning. He contributes regularly to the United Crusade, the Salvation Army, and the Seventh Street Congregational Church. He also contributes regularly to the new war in Southeast Asia: the air war.

Just last week, Charlie helped pay for the bombing of about seven villages, about 200 farms, about 3,000 men, women, and children.

What can he do about it? Well, this is still a democracy, isn't it?[8]

While it is difficult to measure the impact of a publicity campaign such as this, CALC considered it a success. The project attracted notable public figures to its cause, such as former Attorney General Ramsey Clark, who was the featured guest at a September Unsell fund raiser. Market research indicated that 54 percent of the people tested remembered seeing Unsell ads, which was considered a high percentage. Not everything went smoothly, however. When the National Council of Churches declined to sponsor some of the Unsell ads because of the reluctance of various denominational officials to approve the project, CALC was left to pay for them instead. The Unsell campaign ended in November 1972, and CALC phased out its staff at the end of that month. The program served as a pioneering effort that effectively drew ad executives and personnel into the antiwar movement.[9]

The 1972 presidential election afforded CALC a new opportunity to help influence the war's conclusion. Its enduring faith in the electoral process was one of the things that had set it apart from most radical organizations. By spring, CALC claimed 47 active chapters and a mailing list in excess of 40,000,[10] and many members worked in the campaign with a crusading zeal. Much more than in 1968, the major candidates offered obvious differences on war issues. Nixon's earlier claim of a secret plan to end the war had long since been exposed as a deception, and four additional years of war revealed that he was committed to ending the war only on his own terms. The Nixon administration had stirred up divisions within the nation to the extent that CALC leaders spoke of a potential "demoralization," even a "spiritual crisis" if it remained in power.[11] George McGovern offered the promise of a quick negotiated settlement and a greater possibility of achieving amnesty for draft resisters and resolving other war-related issues along lines desired by CALC.

The clear distinction between the two major candidates attracted allies from unexpected sources. Activists Tom Hayden and Jane Fonda organized the Indochina Peace Campaign in 1972 on the basis of community organizing to pressure Congress to cut off funds for the war. Fonda, Hayden, and others spoke in ninety cities in the two months before the November election urging people to vote against Richard Nixon.[12]

CALC extended its Unsell the War campaign an additional two months through the end of November as an important part of its effort to influence the presidential race. An ad in the New York *Times* quoted one of Nixon's 1968 campaign statements: "Those who have had a chance for four years and could not produce peace, should not be given another chance." It called the war a "nonpartisan issue" and asked the President, "in the name of God, to stop the bombing and end the war now."[13]

Despite the efforts of the peace forces, Nixon won a landslide victory with 60.7 percent of the popular vote. McGovern carried only Massachusetts and Washington, D.C. in the electoral college. This apparent inability to influence national policy discouraged some within CALC and left them with doubts about the feasibility of sustaining the effort against the war. CALC, however, maintained its cohesion. Just after the election the national office hooked up with the local chapters through a pair of conference calls. Young and Coffin spent about an hour each with the groups east and west of the Mississippi River, sharing songs and words of encouragement that helped to alleviate any sense of isolation and hopelessness.[14]

The end of the presidential campaign permitted CALC to address problems that grew out of structural changes within the organization. The money from the Bernstein estate allowed the New York office to expand, but it also imposed a certain rigidity. By 1972, the national staff was composed of over twenty people, including directors, administrative assistants, editors and coordinators of *American Report,* American Report Radio, and the Unsell campaign, and heads of literature services and fund raising. It initiated written bylaws, formal personnel policies, and accounting procedures. Late that same year, George Webber became the first person to be designated chair of the steering committee. CALC's more rigid structure was relative, however, and did not completely replace its flexible tradition. In September, the national office followed the lead of twelve local chapters when it changed its name to Clergy and Laity Concerned, which reflected a greater sensitivity to the growing number of women in the organization.[15]

The increase in both the size and the wealth of the national office sometimes disturbed the more informal chapters, which experienced frequent shortages of funds. Local groups thought the national office made too many decisions without consulting them and that it produced resource material that sometimes alienated the congregations they worked with, if not always in ideas, at least in language and style.[16] Money caused as much friction as programming and decision making. National CALC was a major source of funding for many local chapters, but the uncertainty of the Bernstein estate contributed to a growing credibility problem. The promised financial grants based on income expected from that source were frequently delayed for months, causing budget problems for local groups and producing a lack of confidence in the national office's ability to deliver on its commitments. The funding of two staff persons allowed a Houston chapter to emerge in the summer of 1972, but by the following March both staffers left because of the poor financial situation. Budget restrictions in 1973 forced Nebraskans for Peace to reduce its staff from four to one. By the end of that same year, national CALC fell nearly $4,500 behind in its grants to San Francisco, forcing that chapter to borrow from the AFSC. By 1974, Seattle refused to budget national grant money until it actually arrived.[17] The need for budget cuts after the Berstein money ran out added to the strain between the two sides but helped make the chapters more self-sufficient.

The establishment of the field development committee was designed to lower some of the barriers between local and national CALC. In January 1973 the national leadership absorbed the FDC into the program committee and placed a staff person in each of six regions to oversee the local chapters and act as liaison with the steering committee. In addition to the regional staff, the national office funded staff members for fourteen local CALC chapters. A May 1973 report attested to CALC's organizational strength. Out of 47 existing local groups, 37 were active on a weekly basis and 22 had staff personnel, all but two funded at the national level.[18]

Disputes over bureaucratic proliferation also occurred within the national office. By early 1972, CALC was operating with a system of four codirectors, each with specific duties, and a steering committee that was divided into four or five subcommittees. Fernandez in particular began to feel that the new style handicapped CALC's operation. Because of his long tenure and knowledge of how to get things done, people continued to rely primarily upon him. The subcommittees too often deferred to staff initiatives. Frustrated that CALC was not operating as efficiently as it could, Fernandez recommended that the four-director system be scrapped and he be returned as sole director where he could better use his contacts, organizational skills, and fundraising ability.[19] In November, the steering committee reinstated the executive director position and divided more specific duties among the other three codirectors.

The potential strength of the antiwar movement remained evident following the last escalation of the war. On December 17, American planes began the heaviest bombing of the entire war over North Vietnam's major cities. This so-called Christmas bombing lasted until December 30 and resulted in 1,600 Vietnamese civilian casualties and the loss of fifteen U.S. B-52 bombers. As a response to this and Nixon's reelection, the major antiwar coalitions briefly put aside their differences and cosponsored a demonstration on inauguration day. This last mass rally against the war drew 100,000 people to the nation's capital.[20]

CALC reacted to the bombing by joining with the AFSC and FOR to sponsor a gathering in Washington, the National Religious Convocation and Congressional Visitation for Peace, on January 3–4, 1973. The nearly 3,500 participants attended worship services, lobbied their congressional representatives, and heard speakers such as Philip Berrigan and Ramsey Clark. In the absence of a quick peace agreement, the convocation called on Congress to cut off all war-related funds to Indochina. "Some will argue that such Congressional action will undermine the President's power to negotiate," said William Sloane Coffin. "That is exactly what we have in mind. For if peace was at hand, the President should never have allowed it to slip through our fingers." Nearly 60 percent of those present were over thirty years old, 35 percent were from beyond the east coast, and for 45 percent, it was their first peace action. Clergy, students, educators, and homemakers made up two-thirds of the participants.[21]

On January 27, 1973, the United States and North Vietnam signed the Paris accords that ended America's Indochina War. American troops would withdraw from Vietnam in exchange for the return of U.S. prisoners of war. North Vietnamese forces were permitted to stay in place. Thieu's government in the south remained in power, but the agreement's vague political arrangement virtually guaranteed that the war would resume after the United States left. Although U.S. aid to the south continued, the Paris settlement proved to be the point of no return.

For many antiwar activists, the Paris agreement marked the end of their involvement with Vietnam. The attainment of an American troop withdrawal afforded the opportunity to reflect upon the meaning of the conflict and the opposition that rose against it. Michael Novak felt that the weakness of the nation's political leadership, especially its failure to provide a clear rationale for its decisions, left a gap that the antiwar movement filled. While basically correct in its analysis of the war, the movement became too intertwined with the counterculture, a fact that created within many passive opponents of the war an even stronger objection to war protesters. Novak argued that vague pronouncements about America's duty were insufficient to command public support for any particular policy. Moral reasoning must be a part of explaining why. "Hurrying to ever new frontiers, we have never paused to face our capacity for evil and brutality. The experience of Vietnam is the first time we have been caught."[22]

The Paris peace agreement ended America's combat role in Vietnam, but it produced added benefits at home as well. After conducting internal security and revolutionary activities investigations on CALC since the late 1960s, the FBI ended its spying in April 1973. It based this decision on the assumption that the end of the war and the draft, which ended the same day the accords were signed, took away CALC's issues. The FBI evidently did not consider support for amnesty to be subversive or radical because it was "espoused by many legitimate organizations and individuals." It seems clear that the FBI investigation of CALC was primarily for political rather than security reasons. CALC's constituency and tactics never posed a threat to national security. Even instances of civil disobedience were matters for local authorities. The FBI's own conclusion referred to CALC as primarily a pacifist group that participated in "non-violent anti-war, anti-draft, peace oriented activities." Despite the lack of any serious evidence that CALC threatened domestic safety, the FBI spent years gathering intelligence as part of a coordinated effort to harass and undermine the antiwar movement.[23]

The Central Intelligence Agency maintained surveillance of domestic dissidents through its Operation Chaos, which was encouraged by the White House. The CIA correctly understood the complexity and indigenous nature of the antiwar movement, yet its analysts frequently ignored this diversity and tailored their reports to fit the preconceptions of policymakers. When presented with the facts, government leaders as high as the President deliberately misled the public by portraying antiwar activists as controlled and directed by communists, despite CIA reports to the contrary.[24]

The Paris agreement caused CALC to reflect and reassess, as was expressed in a February position paper entitled "Indochina: The Aftermath." Its sharp rhetoric portrayed the U.S. defeat in Vietnam as a divine judgment on American pride and arrogance and singled out policymakers for their deception exposed in the Pentagon Papers. Warning against renewed U.S. military measures, CALC called on Americans to demand that Saigon release its political prisoners, pressure corporations to stop producing antipersonnel weapons, and influence the U.S. government to end its repression of dissent. Placing Vietnam in a larger context, the paper blamed America's "decline of moral credibility" on its drive for "economic empire" and suggested the nation abandon its anticommunist, counterrevolutionary position in favor of support for stronger multilateral institutions like the United Nations. Surrounded by these criticisms, however, the heart of "Indochina: The Aftermath" called the religious community to a healing mission. It encouraged support for all the war's victims through aid for Indochina's reconstruction and a broad amnesty for war resisters; it urged welcoming Vietnam veterans "with a warmth that has so far been lacking."[25]

In the months that followed the Paris accords, CALC directed an increasing amount of its time and resources toward acquiring amnesty and restoring full legal and political rights to the estimated 100,000 Vietnam-era draft resisters who went into exile or spent time in prison. Amnesty received significant media attention, but opinion polls revealed that a majority of the public opposed a general amnesty. Recognizing the formidable task in overcoming Nixon's opposition and public opinion, CALC prepared for a long struggle. It began an educational program to develop an effective constituency in support of amnesty. The national office built a mailing package around a special supplement of *American Report* and sent it out in May to a list of 56,000 people who had in some way associated themselves with CALC since its inception. CALC made additional plans to place amnesty petitions as ads in ten religious and liberal journals such as *Christian Century* and *New Republic* to attract people not associated with CALC. It also projected a second mailing to reach 225,000 Protestant, Catholic, and Jewish clergy.[26]

Clergy and Laity Concerned sought to increase its chances of building greater popular support for amnesty by aligning itself with similar efforts by other groups. In addition to collaborating with Richard Killmer of the National Council of Churches, CALC joined several other religious peace organizations and denominational groups to form the Inter-Religious Task Force on Amnesty (ITFA). Fernandez and Young served as part of the ITFA leadership. ITFA agreed to develop a core packet of materials on amnesty, organize a series of regional conferences to build grassroots support, and form a coalition for universal and unconditional amnesty with groups outside the religious community.[27]

In May, Trudi Young and William Sloane Coffin participated in a national invitational conference on amnesty held in Washington and sponsored by the NCC and the American Civil Liberties Union. From this conference emerged a new organization, the National Council for Universal and Unconditional Amnesty (NCUUA). CALC joined several antiwar organizations in declaring October 14–22 as National Amnesty Week to acknowledge the men who had served their nation by refusing to fight in the war. NCUUA worked in conjunction with

ITFA during the summer to organize and share resources. Certain that neither Congress nor the President would grant amnesty without sustained public pressure, the coalition, with CALC as a member, prepared for a long campaign and tried to keep the issue in the nation's conscience.[28]

Building around Amnesty Week, southern California CALC targeted regional churches and synagogues and set a goal of preaching 100 amnesty-related sermons on or near the weekend of October 19–21. Like most antiwar activists, southern California CALC supported an unconditional and universal amnesty that would include the largest possible number of war resisters. Its public statement described potential amnesty recipients as one group of the war's victims, along with military casualties, their surviving families, and veterans. In pushing for postwar reconciliation, it discounted claims that amnesty dishonored those who fought while upholding the need to provide educational, economic, medical, and spiritual support for war veterans.[29]

Southern California CALC pursued its goal primarily through mass mailings. Its Amnesty Task Force sent over 500 letters and return cards to selected clergy from the United Church of Christ, United Methodist Church, United Presbyterian Church, Episcopal Church, Disciples of Christ, and Jewish temples urging them to address the question of amnesty. The Social Relations Commission of the Los Angeles Episcopal Diocese supported the amnesty drive and distributed CALC's amnesty letter to over 500 of its clergy. More than 500 churches in the United Methodist Church's regional conference, which covered southern California, Hawaii, and Arizona, received publicity on the amnesty program in their monthly newsletter. Members of southern California CALC complemented these actions with speeches, debates, and panel discussions, and ultimately achieved success; 103 respondents indicated they would address the issue from their pulpits.[30]

In other parts of the country, 22 local churches sent representatives to an October 1973 conference on amnesty sponsored by central Massachusetts CALC, located in Worcester. Detroit CALC visited with draft exiles in Windsor, Canada and encouraged local clergy to preach on amnesty. Greenville, South Carolina CALC provided literature, films, and speakers to interested community groups.[31]

Minnesota CALC pursued the most involved strategy. In June 1973, it began a statewide campaign among religious and political groups to promote unconditional amnesty for Vietnam-era war resisters. Known as Minnesotans for Amnesty (MFA) and coordinated by Carole Nelson, the campaign favored a national amnesty for a wide variety of war resisters but focused on the impact amnesty would have in its own state. According to its own estimates, nearly 12,000 Minnesotans would be candidates for an unconditional amnesty. Most were veterans who received less than honorable discharges during the war, but the number included 673 war resisters, 280 civilian war protesters who had been arrested, 602 deserters, and 1,880 who failed to register for the draft.[32]

Minnesotans for Amnesty divided into committees, each responsible for a particular aspect of the campaign. The religious committee supplied liturgies, bulletin inserts, slide shows, and speakers for churches, seminaries, and other religious groups. At the same time it prodded state church bodies to pass resolutions in favor of unconditional amnesty, gaining the support of the annual conference of the United Methodist Church, and the Committee on International Relations of the Minnesota Council of Churches, among others.[33]

Initial plans to have the state legislature recommend that Congress support amnesty were changed when the legislative committee ascertained from sympathetic lawmakers that such a resolution would not pass. Instead it concentrated on building grassroots support within state party caucuses and from Minnesota congressional representatives. Campaign workers spent most of late 1973 and early 1974 trying to elect proamnesty delegates to the February 1974 political caucuses of both the Republican and Democratic Farmer Labor parties.[34]

The campaign contacted Minnesota war resisters through the "task force resister liaison committee." It was the least publicized aspect of the campaign because of fears of government surveillance. Task force members made regular contacts with imprisoned or underground Minnesota resisters and communicated with exiles in Canada through the Winnipeg Committee to Assist War Resisters.[35]

The media committee prepared radio ads, films, a slide presentation, educational packets, buttons, and bumper stickers for circulation around the state. It identified proamnesty newspapers, television, and radio stations through a survey of 600 editors and managers and channeled publicity through those sources. In early 1974 for example, 12 percent of the state's radio stations were running six four-minute amnesty commentaries produced by "In the Public Interest."[36]

Minnesotans for Amnesty formed a speakers' bureau of about twenty people trained and experienced in the issues, questions, and strategies of amnesty. Representatives of the campaign, including both war resisters and Vietnam veterans, addressed well over 100 groups in the following months.[37]

This statewide project was one of CALC's most successful efforts at mobilizing public opinion around an issue. After a year of activity the campaign had grown to 1,700 people, two-thirds of whom were not members of CALC. Amnesty workers formed local groups in numerous outstate communities as well as the Twin Cities area. Campaign speakers addressed church, school, and political groups in 160 cities and towns across the state. A typical contact in the outstate area occurred at Owatonna. One woman there ran proamnesty ads in the local newspaper until a team of Carole Nelson, Louise Ransom, director of Americans for Amnesty, and Michele Morley, wife of a Vietnam MIA, visited the town for a speaking engagement. After their departure, a group of fifteen remained to work in the amnesty program.[38]

Minnesotans for Amnesty burrowed into the political system at the grassroots level. In addition to its other actions, it hoped to create additional leverage by having the state convention of the Democratic Farmer Labor Party (DFL) pass an amnesty resolution in 1974. Workers made initial contacts with the chairs of the state's eight congressional districts and received invitations to speak at two district meetings. All county chairs received a November mailing explaining the campaign. MFA representatives spoke and presented amnesty resolutions to twenty precaucus meetings in Minneapolis and nearly 20 percent of outstate meetings. Both CALC and MFA encouraged their members to attend the February precinct caucuses, which resulted in the passage of roughly 100 unconditional amnesty resolutions at that level. MFA publicized the precinct results among delegates to district and county conventions, and participants at that stage produced about forty similar resolutions.[39]

Before the state convention, the state DFL platform committee accepted MFA's universal and unconditional amnesty plank as part of the party platform for presentation on the convention floor. Two weeks before the convention, the campaign reminded about 130 targeted delegates to back the resolution, and a week later sponsored amnesty forums around the state to generate more support and publicity. MFA members lobbied delegates at the convention, urging them especially to oppose any amendments that would have made amnesty conditional, and pushed for a floor vote rather than have the issue deferred to the central committee. Although confident the central committee would pass the resolution, MFA wanted a more accurate gauge of the delegates' convictions. From September 1973 to June 1974, Minnesotans for Amnesty worked through the party apparatus for a clear statement in favor of universal and unconditional amnesty. On June 16, the resolution passed without amendments with 70 percent of the votes.[40]

CALC, however, found amnesty a difficult issue to champion. Public opinion polls consistently revealed that large majorities of Americans opposed amnesty for draft resisters and deserters, and the religious community expressed similar thoughts. Although some denominations had officially supported amnesty as early as 1969, they did not necessarily reflect the attitudes of their constituents. At their convention in late 1973, the lay representatives in the Episcopal House of Deputies rejected a general amnesty resolution. Congregations of the Pennsylvania Southeast Conference of the United Church of Christ voted roughly two to one against endorsing amnesty in the spring of 1974.[41]

Another issue further reflected the difficulty of stirring support for war-related activities by 1973. CALC's Religious Convocation and Congressional Visitation for Peace on January 3–4 attempted to raise money for medical aid to the Vietnamese. The coordinators intended to divide the proceeds among the Medical Aid to Indochina Committee, which bought medical equipment and supplies for North Vietnam, the AFSC's Quang Ngai Hospital, and the School of Youth for Social Services, but the sponsors raised less than $5,000.[42] Local efforts were occasionally more successful. Western Massachusetts CALC, centered in Amherst, was one of the most financially stable of all CALC chapters and worked closely with the AFSC in that area. The two organizations attracted significant community support in a 1973 campaign for medical aid to the war's victims. They raised more than $20,000, including over $5,000 in donated hospital equipment.[43] Even under the best of circumstances CALC could not have expected much better. Few Americans shared the ideal of international unity to the degree of providing aid to America's current enemies, even to save lives.

Individual chapters continued to devise creative programs but with limited success. In 1973, San Francisco CALC (Ecumenical Peace Institute, or EPI), focused on eliminating Junior ROTC programs from area high schools. As a realistic goal, EPI hoped to reduce the number of high school ROTC programs in northern California, an area where they proliferated. As the military prepared for the end of the draft, it tried to compensate for the significant decreases in college ROTC enrollments by increasing its number of recruiters and Junior ROTC units. EPI tried to organize communities against the high school programs by exposing the local costs of supporting ROTC programs, questioning their educational value, suggesting alternate employment for ROTC instructors and alternate courses for ROTC, and sending mailings to high school seniors to counter military recruiting.[44]

EPI's efforts to reduce the number of high school ROTC programs made little headway, and attempts to have public schools post alternatives to military service failed completely. CALC contacted 100 social studies departments and not one was willing to participate in a counterrecruitment program. Similar results came when they tried to introduce peace studies into the educational curriculum.[45]

As interest in the war declined, CALC's situation became increasingly difficult. When funds began to dry up, its financial picture deteriorated even further. The accumulation of a $200,000 deficit in 1972 curtailed its ability to meet programming obligations such as its medical aid project and support for American deserters in Sweden. CALC tried to fill the gap by urging denominational bodies to increase their financial support of war-related projects.[46] The 1972 Christmas bombing caught the religious antiwar movement with its political resources nearly exhausted. In January 1973, Harvey Cox, Robert McAfee Brown, and Sister Mary Luke Tobin accompanied a small group of U.S. religious leaders to enlist the help of the European religious community. They were well received by key leaders in England, Belgium, West Germany, and the Netherlands, but despite careful planning were denied an audience with Pope Paul VI. Unknown to the Americans, the U.S. State Department had secretly intervened with the Vatican to prevent the meeting.[47]

Working to overcome dwindling resources, the antiwar movement continued to plan and act. Two hundred fifteen people from fifteen organizations, including CALC, convened in Germantown, Ohio on October 26–28, 1973 and agreed to lobby Congress to cut off further aid to the Thieu government.[48] Later that same year CALC briefly considered a merger with SANE, but after preliminary discussions the organizations decided to limit their association to occasional joint planning and programming.[49]

Compounding the problems caused by growing apathy and financial troubles, CALC suffered the loss of some of its key personnel. Three years after surviving a heart attack, Abraham Heschel died of a second attack at age 65 just before Christmas 1972. An essential part of CALC since its inception, Heschel had been instrumental in rallying and maintaining Jewish support for the organization.[50] Another loss to CALC during this time came from people such as Neuhaus, Novak, and Berger who had come out of conservative traditions to oppose the war. As the war drew to an end and CALC drifted more to the political left, conservatives became less comfortable and withdrew.

As important as these losses were, none had as great an impact as when Richard Fernandez shocked CALC by resigning his position as executive director in June 1973. He cited a loss of challenge and interest in the job as his reason for leaving, though in retrospect he admitted that the organization's financial problems were also an important factor.[51] CALC leaders cited the keen organizational skills, boundless energy, and inspirational vision of Fernandez as the key to the growth and success of Clergy and Laity Concerned. He was never one to back away from a challenge, but at the same time, his peers respected his willingness to abide by the group consensus. As Brown recounted, "He never tried to push any of us beyond where we could in conscience at the moment be."[52]

The decision by Fernandez to step down marked a major transition for CALC. In the ensuing months and for various reasons, a number of CALC's leaders moved on. Denver codirectors Duane Gall and Tom Rauch, burned out from years of activism and weary of financial problems, resigned at the end of 1973. John Cupples of Boston left in mid-1974, victimized by bureaucratic routine and the post–Ann Arbor organizational battles.[53] Its activity limited by America's extrication from Vietnam and a lack of money, the organization struggled to remain in existence. Local groups faced uncertainty as they sought new direction or questioned their continuation. With the movement's apparent victory came difficulty in maintaining constituents and raising money. Chapters reduced or eliminated their paid staff members as human and financial resources drained away, and several dissolved entirely.[54] Following Richard Van Voorhis' interim leadership, Don Luce served as executive director from mid-1974 to 1976. Luce was shocked to find CALC in excess of a quarter of a million dollars in debt. When the money from the Bernstein estate finally ran out, CALC's national office was forced to reduce the size of the staff and its salaries and make drastic operating cuts. *American Report,* which had earlier been changed from a weekly to a biweekly paper, was discontinued altogether in 1974. By raising funds through loans from its board members, church grants, and direct appeals, CALC eventually managed to pay off its debts. Its survival was nothing short of miraculous, George Webber recalled.[55]

During 1974, CALC sponsored two trips to Vietnam. In January, George Webber led about half a dozen people on a two-week tour to investigate the high rate of casualties under the Paris accords. Luce led another small group to North Vietnam for twelve days in December. While observing the damage and shortages caused by the war, Luce and his party were impressed by the relative freedom and efficiency. They were aware, however, that North Vietnam still intended to unify the nation.[56]

Fearful that the United States government might consider increasing its support for the Thieu regime, CALC joined the AFSC in Washington to hold an Assembly to Save the Peace Agreement, January 25–27, 1975. When a North Vietnamese offensive in the spring threatened to overrun the south, President Gerald Ford indeed requested additional aid to both Vietnam and Cambodia. CALC opposed the increase as an immoral intrusion into Vietnamese affairs.[57]

When Saigon fell to North Vietnamese forces on May 1, 1975, the Vietnam War ended and the cutting of U.S. ties to that country was complete. Until that time, CALC's attention had remained focused almost solely on the war, but the end of the war marked something of a turning point. Since the Ann Arbor conference, tensions within the organization had grown. Perhaps the major irritant was the debate over whether to focus strictly on ending the war or to become a multi-issue organization. The attraction to CALC of newer and frequently younger members in the 1970s brought an infusion of thought tinged with the ideas of the counterculture and the New Left. Some of these supported the National Liberation Front and the North Vietnamese without qualification. This constituency generally viewed the war as merely one symptom of a fundamentally flawed system and wanted CALC to address a broader critique of American society. The decision to launch a campaign against the production of the B-1 bomber in late 1973 reflected a small step in that direction.[58]

Antiwar veterans in CALC maintained the organization's theological perspective and commitment to end the war despite a tendency among some of its younger members to give up, drop out, or become more radical. Throughout the Vietnam period CALC's orientation remained predominantly white, middle class, and religiously motivated, a constituency that generally criticized the radical interpretation as inaccurate. As the war drew to a close, however, some viewed their work as complete and left to pursue other interests. The influence of the multi-issue element grew after Fernandez resigned and increased further in the more than two years between the Paris agreement and the fall of Saigon as staunch moderates turned their attentions elsewhere.[59]

After 1975, CALC's focus on Indochina disappeared, but a progressive organization concerned with issues of peace and justice remained. The years immediately after the Vietnam War were difficult ones for Clergy and Laity Concerned. At one point, the entire national office went on unemployment insurance when money for salaries ran out. The number of local chapters dropped to 25. By the late 1970s, however, continued organizing efforts began to turn its fortunes around. It supported economic sanctions against South Africa, was one of the organizational leaders of the nuclear freeze campaign, and was a founder of the Witness for Peace program in Nicaragua that opposed U.S. involvement in Central America. Locally, CALC won a legal precedent in Chicago's federal district court regarding the practice of public schools' bringing in military recruiters. The court ruled that counselors on the draft and the military, who had previously been systematically denied entrance, be given equal access. Clergy and Laity Concerned also spearheaded the drafting and passage of a Chicago ordinance banning the design, production, or storage of nuclear weapons within city limits. In recent years it has become increasingly concerned with economic issues and the fight against racism. In the summer of 1985, CALC counted 54 local chapters in 28 states and claimed 35,000 members and supporters.[60]

The transformation of CALC from a single-issue antiwar group to a multi-issue social-justice organization was complete by 1975. Having persevered during the trying years of the war's de-escalation, many veterans left to pursue new challenges. Others remained, hoping to direct the existing network into new directions. CALC survived and moved into the future, but its crusade against the Vietnam War was part of the past.

8

"TOGETHER IN A WORTHWHILE STRUGGLE"

> To sin by silence when they should protest
> makes cowards of men.
>
> — ABRAHAM LINCOLN

In January 1975, Richard Neuhaus and Peter Berger drafted the Hartford Statement signed by 18 prominent church leaders including William Sloane Coffin. This document deplored the recent secular influences upon liberal religious bodies and stressed the reality of the supernatural. Referring to the NCC and liberal Protestantism as the captive of the "white, middle-class cultural elite," Neuhaus accused the antiwar leadership of occasionally ignoring the majority and alienating many parishioners. He did not call for a retreat from social action, only for its grounding in a deeper spiritual conviction. "Bill Coffin and I are not repudiating our activism of the 60s," Neuhaus stated. "There are historical times when evil is so clearly defined that all Christians are called to come to witness. The 60s was one of those times. But we are concerned with reexamining some of the excesses and mistakes of the movement."[1]

A year later, 21 members of the Boston religious community, including Harvey Cox, issued a response known as the Boston Affirmations. This group detected a strong backlash in the churches against social involvement and pleaded for increased social militancy, suggesting that God's work is most forcefully achieved in struggles for the poor and oppressed.[2]

These statements by themselves did not erect theological barriers between former allies, but they do indicate something that happened to CALC and much of American society as Vietnam receded from the nation's immediate attention. Millions of people from diverse backgrounds had banded together to concentrate their social activism into an intense opposition to the Vietnam War. When that common link disappeared, an avalanche of deferred concerns tested those ties.

170

As the antiwar movement passed from the scene, what was left behind.

Perhaps CALC's most impressive achievement during the war years was its construction of an ecumenical organization against American policy in Vietnam. The common struggle in support of civil rights reinforced by the recent ecumenical advances had established a strong precedent of interfaith social activism. CALC built upon that momentum, and the presence of Martin Luther King, Jr. gave it the most visible symbol linking the civil rights and antiwar movements. Churches with a history of social activism often addressed the war in Indochina, but many others feared this controversial issue and left their constituents with no outlet for their antiwar sentiment.

CALC appealed primarily to theological and social liberals from America's mainstream religious groups, but attracted conservatives and radicals as well. If Protestant denominations provided the majority of its members, it also served as one of the first important channels for Jewish and Catholic peace activism. Jews initially formed a disproportionate percentage of CALC's leadership, not unusual for a reform movement, while Catholics were temporarily underrepresented. Time brought some notable changes. A significant number of Jews dropped out of the movement when Christians failed to give strong support to Israel during the 1967 middle east war and because of Nixon's veiled threat to tie U.S. support for Israel to Jewish silence on Vietnam. Catholic bishops, increasingly convinced that Vietnam failed to meet the standards of a just war, joined the growing ranks of priests and laity that were already active.

American ecumenism benefited from CALC's role in the antiwar movement. The war sometimes threatened formal ecumenical ventures as fragile interfaith groups sometimes feared the divisive potential of a new controversy so soon after civil rights. Frustrated by the hesitancy of local councils of churches, socially concerned clergy and laity often turned to informal single-issue coalitions. CALC's antiwar focus provided an urgent moral cause that solidified the ecumenical cooperation nurtured by the civil rights movement. Clergy and Laity Concerned found it easier to unite individuals than institutions; yet its close relationship with the NCC gave it legitimacy within religious circles.[3]

Mobilizing antiwar sentiment within the major churches was among CALC's most important and difficult challenges. The task of ending the Vietnam conflict invigorated some elements and infuriated others, as debates at denominational conventions clearly indicate. More than any other organization, however, CALC linked the diverse religious community together and permitted it to speak out on the war with a united voice. This ability derived partly from its prominent membership, people who served in leadership positions of many of the largest and most influential denominations, ecumenical bodies, religious publications, and peace organizations in American religion. By external pressure and from within national church boards and agencies, Clergy and Laity Concerned pushed various denominations to debate and formulate positions that advocated a quicker end to the war or a more humanitarian solution to the problems that it left behind. It reinforced the idea that clerics could appropriately address social action as part of their ministry, and for Christians and Jews who felt isolated within their own churches and synagogues, it provided a supportive outlet for their antiwar views and a platform from which to influence their local communities.

Clergy and Laity Concerned mobilized thousands of people, spent millions of dollars, and worked for ten years to end the war in Vietnam. By the mid-1970s, the American phase of the Indochina War was over. All the combatants, including the National Liberation Front, had reached a negotiated arrangement. American troops had been withdrawn. The Vietnamese revolution, begun during World War II, had finally succeeded. The impact of the estimated four million Americans who publicly demonstrated against the war has been assessed in different ways. Some critics and supporters of the movement have stated that this massive show of concern finally convinced the public and the government to abandon its mistaken and immoral policy in Indochina. Yet a number of studies conclude that the antiwar demonstrations had no significant impact on the presidential handling of the war, Senate votes, or public opinion. Some even suggest that the movement was counterproductive.[4]

Peace activists achieved only limited success in reversing the course of the war. In the end, the conflict they worked so hard to stop dragged on for several years. Much of the reason lies in the antiwar movement's limited base. Public opinion analysts have identified a number of groups that were inclined to oppose the war: women, blacks, Jews, graduate students, students attending the nation's leading universities, and the lower socioeconomic classes.[5] Opposition to the war, however, did not necessarily imply participation in the antiwar movement. Blacks and working-class people did not provide large numbers to the movement. Activists were generally upper-middle-class college students and professionals.[6] As a rule, the people who marched in demonstrations and actively opposed the war in their communities argued from a moral perspective that the United States had no right to intervene in Vietnamese affairs, use excessive force, or prop up a corrupt government against the will of the people. Passive antiwar sentiment reflected in the public opinion polls was largely pragmatic and influenced by specific events. These people objected to the war because they were not sure why it was being fought, because it dragged on too long and cost too many American lives, and because it seemed unable to produce victory. Where activists saw the misguided application of cold war policies, the general antiwar public saw only an isolated mistake.[7]

The passive antiwar public frequently disapproved of the movement's tactics and was offended by its moral analysis, its attacks on conformist patriotism, and its ties with the counterculture. It also shared much of the general public's aversion to the antiwar movement.[8] "Nobody in America," declared Balfour Brickner, "was prepared to learn or to hear that their president lied to them or that the authorities of their government were dissemblers, deceivers, masters of the coverup, and liars."[9] The fact that this was sometimes part of the movement's message brought it the enmity that often goes to the messenger who carries bad news. These ideological differences sometimes divided families;[10] in other instances they divided communities. Leslie Withers, a CALC worker in Greenville, South Carolina in the early 1970s recalled, "Active hostility was therefore something that I had to count on. We used to encounter hatred on a personal level when we demonstrated, leafletted, or conducted programs in churches."[11] This hostility was exploited by national figures who took the opposite view. "At best, dissenters in America are thought to be eccentrics," comments Leslie Gelb. "At worst, they are equated with the devil. The New American Puritans . . . had little difficulty convincing most Americans that those who opposed Vietnam policy were the enemy."[12]

Historians Charles DeBenedetti and Charles Chatfield cite additional problems. For the war's duration, the antiwar movement remained disorganized and divided. This amorphous quality subjected it to abuse by prorevolutionary elements and radicals who used the movement for their own purposes. In addition, antiwar groups relied too heavily on mass demonstrations rather than on long-term political organizing. They also proved susceptible to the American government's efforts to subvert their activities.[13]

Clergy and Laity Concerned managed to avoid some of the pitfalls of the larger antiwar movement, but it encountered strong opposition despite its religious base and moderate approach. The public's habit of ignoring the differences between various antiwar groups diluted

CALC's message. Government and media presented a misleading picture of the movement by focusing on the radical groups and violent actions, and CALC suffered in the process.

CALC may also be faulted for committing some tactical errors. The violence committed by their nation and the silence emanating from their churches offended the faith of many religious Americans. These occurrences eroded trust in the government for some and left others estranged from organized religion. CALC served as a comfortable haven for some of these. When lobbying, petitions, and articles failed to prevent the war's expansion and government deception, activists responded with progressively stronger measures. This tactical and rhetorical escalation, however, did not always produce the desired results. Just as the institutional church's reluctance to challenge the war alienated dissidents, the actions of CALC sometimes antagonized the very people it tried to reach. Its message did acquire a degree of critical rhetoric and radical thought as the war progressed, as some of its own members observed. Perhaps the organization would have been more effective by placing greater emphasis on reaching the apathetic majority within its constituency. In the end CALC was preaching primarily to the converted. Its abrasiveness with the government and the military, the attacks on corporate irresponsibility, and the championing of unpopular causes may or may not have been morally sound, but they were not designed to capture the approval of a public less willing than they to leave the myths of American altruism and invincibility behind.

The hostility sometimes directed toward the U.S. government raised concerns about the antiwar movement's allegiance, but attempts to portray CALC as disloyal are unsubstantiated. While the goals of independence and self-determination certainly attracted sympathy for the Vietnamese revolution, few held illusions about the beneficence of a communist regime. There are instances where CALC's membership was guilty of ill-advised or excessive remarks, and these comments damaged their influence within the churches and synagogues, but they do not translate into sympathy for communist goals. CALC leaders, whatever their political views, were frequently subjected to overt hostility from the far left and sought to maintain their distance. CALC remained neutral regarding the outcome of the Vietnam War, believing the Vietnamese should be the ones to determine their nation's fate. As George Webber remarked in 1974, "We do not support Thieu and we do not support Hanoi; as citizens our primary task is to address the evil wrought by our own government." [14]

Among the claims made by the war's supporters is that the public protests actually prolonged the war by preventing a tougher military policy and encouraging Hanoi to hold out for reunification. Historian Melvin Small refutes this argument,[15] but the original assertion ignores the commitment of North Vietnam and the NLF. William Sloane Coffin recalled listening to the North Vietnamese liaison to France in the mid–1960s. "We have no illusions, Reverend. This question will be settled on the battlefield." When Coffin asked how many years that would take, he replied, "About ten."[16]

Despite its limitations, the antiwar movement achieved certain successes. While Presidents Johnson and Nixon publicly disavowed being influenced by protests against the war, both were concerned enough about the potential impact of dissent that they went to great lengths to undermine the credibility of the antiwar movement. These efforts contributed to both men's fall from power. It is probable that the protests limited military options for prosecuting the war and restrained further escalations.[17]

Dissent against the war combined with the civil rights struggle and the counterculture of the 1960s and early 1970s to create a period of domestic turbulence unparalleled in recent American history. The constant tensions of social disruption threatened to split American society and contributed to a national weariness that eventually made it impossible for the government to continue the conflict in Vietnam.[18]

Scholars further subscribe to the movement's effectiveness. Melvin Small credits it with restraining military escalation and imposing Vietnamization upon Nixon as the only strategy acceptable to the nation. Arguments made by the antiwar movement had general public acceptance by the mid–1970s, reflected in opinion polls that showed that a majority agreed that the war had been a mistake, perhaps even immoral. This strong backing permitted Congress to refuse a renewed combat role for U.S. troops as the Vietnam War moved to a conclusion.[19] Charles DeBenedetti and Charles Chatfield insist that through a flow of accurate information that contradicted the administration's position, activists established public skepticism, legitimized dissent, undermined the government's credibility, and created political action within the legislative and executive branches.[20]

If none of these claims were directly responsible for ending the conflict, they all certainly contributed to that decision. "The dissidents did not stop the war," observed DeBenedetti, "But they made it stoppable."[21]

CALC played a significant role in the effectiveness of the larger movement. Its religious, ecumenical, and nonpacifist nature made it more resistant than most antiwar groups to the public's negative attitudes and allowed it to communicate with a moderate, middle-class constituency that would not begin to listen to the radical left. Clergy and Laity Concerned cultivated the American mainstream. It allied itself with traditional religiously oriented peace organizations and avoided close ties with the left. Many of its members made it a point to wear coats and ties during public demonstrations and rallies. This helped to legitimize concerns about the war among the general public. The government could not ignore CALC's influence with this constituency as it could most student and radical groups.[22] This legitimacy brought CALC access to government officials usually denied to most other antiwar organizations. Congressional doves supported CALC's efforts, and in return, it provided a visible constituency for antiwar legislators to draw upon when confronting the prowar forces in government. The personal effort and financial resources provided by antiwar activists helped elect a number of doves to national office who played an essential role in changing U.S. policy in Indochina.

At the same time CALC bridged the gap between activists and passive observers, it linked the extremes within the movement. Between exclusionary conservatives and radical ideologists, CALC served as a moderating force and tried to avoid the hardening of lines between Americans. Its willingness to help fund coalition actions was a great benefit to organizations that typically existed on minimal financial support.

The members of CALC did not discriminate in their ministerial responsibilities of comforting the victims of the war. They visited imprisoned American war resisters, provided for the physical needs of deserters and draft resisters, established links between American prisoners of war and their families, and intervened to curb the harshness of the military judicial system. CALC continually urged the U.S. government to provide for the safety of those Vietnamese who had backed the southern regime, and it raised funds for the purchase of medical supplies destined for both North and South Vietnam.

Clergy and Laity Concerned affected the larger society around it, but many people found it to be a very personal experience as well. CALC offered a new perspective for those discontented with organized religion. Richard Fernandez was one who found new possibilities and gained a greater appreciation for the institutional church.[23] Others found their work against the war to be at the heart of their religious commitment. "Its very hard to convey . . . the fantastic feeling of fellowship and camaraderie and being together in a worthwhile struggle that had real spiritual dimensions to it," explained Harvey Cox. "It was a profoundly important religious experience for many people. It was not a peripheral experience. It was a way of really serving God, of expressing faith, of really feeling the presence of God."[24] Uncertain of what their impact might be, thousands of Americans felt compelled to act on their beliefs. "We've simply got to say something," remarked Barbara Fuller, "because of who we are and because of our faith."[25]

The ability to influence American foreign policy is elusive for people without direct access to the levers of power. Even in a democratic system, sometimes all that can be done is to express concern and hope to be heard. In a time of national crisis, when silence would have been a betrayal of their religious faith, the people of CALC spoke up.

CHRONOLOGY

1945

Sept. 2 Ho Chi Minh declares independence of Vietnam.

1946

Nov. 23 French war against Vietminh begins.

1950

July 26 United States begins sending military aid for the French war effort in Indochina.

1954

May 7 French defeated at Dienbienphu.
July Geneva Accords call for an end to hostilities in Indochina and national elections in Vietnam.

1955

Jan. United States begins sending aid directly to the South Vietnamese government.

1957

Oct. Communist insurgency begins in South Vietnam.

1963

Nov. 1 South Vietnamese President Diem overthrown in coup.

1964

Aug. 2 Tonkin Gulf incident between North Vietnamese boats and American ship *Maddox*.
Aug. 7 Congress passes Gulf of Tonkin resolution giving President Johnson greater power to act in Vietnam.

1965

Feb. 24 Operation Rolling Thunder begins, sustained bombing of North Vietnam.
Mar. 8 Marines land in South Vietnam.
Mar. 24 Teach-ins begin at the University of Michigan.
Apr. 17 SDS antiwar march, Washington, D.C.
Oct. 25 Ad hoc Clergy Concerned About Vietnam holds New York news conference to support dissent.
Dec. 24 President Johnson initiates bombing pause.
Dec. Clergy Concerned About Vietnam contacts people across the nation to support bombing pause.

1966

Jan. 11 Meeting in John Bennett's apartment produces National Emergency Committee of Clergy Concerned About Vietnam.
Apr. 1 National Emergency Committee decides to remain in existence for the duration of the war.
May Name changed to Clergy and Laymen Concerned About Vietnam.
May Richard Fernandez hired as CALCAV's executive director.
Summer CALCAV begins to establish local chapter network.
Nov. Publication of *Washington and Vietnam*.

1967

Jan. 31–Feb. 1 CALCAV's first national mobilization, Washington, D.C.
Feb. 8–10 Fast for the Rebirth of Compassion.
Apr. 4 Riverside Church speeches by Martin Luther King, Jr., John Bennett, Abraham Heschel, and Henry Steele Commager.
Apr. 15 Spring Mobilization Committee demonstrations, New York and San Francisco.
May Publication of *Vietnam: Crisis of Conscience*.
May Vietnam Summer begins.
Oct. 21–22 March on the Pentagon.
Oct. 25 Statement on Conscience and Conscription released.

1968

Jan. Booklet developed, *Who's Right, Who's Wrong on Vietnam*.
Jan. 31 Tet offensive begins.
Feb. 5 Release of *In the Name of America*.

Feb. 5–6 CALCAV's second national mobilization, Washington, D.C.
Apr. 8–12 CALCAV Holy Week Fast.
May CALCAV attends Dow Chemical stockholders meeting.
Summer National office of CALCAV organizes paid field staff workers.
Autumn CALCAV campaign for postwar amnesty.
Nov. 3 Observance of Vietnam Sunday.
Dec. 21 Celebration of Conscience service, Allenwood Federal Prison.

1969

Jan. 27 San Francisco CALCAV releases statement on the Presidio Mutiny Trials.
Feb. 3–5 CALCAV's third national mobilization, Washington, D.C.
Mar. 20 Thomas Hayes begins ministry to U.S. deserters in Sweden.
May 7 CALCAV attends Dow Chemical stockholders meeting.
May 23 CALCAV cosponsors over thirty press conferences to focus on the political/religious repression of the Saigon government.
May 30 Memorial Day actions for repeal of the draft.
June 17–18 CALCAV cosponsors demonstration for the rights of U.S. soldiers, Washington, D.C.
August 27–28 CALCAV national committee holds Cambridge conference.
Oct. 15 Nationwide Moratorium.
Nov. 14 CALCAV sponsors worship service at Washington National Cathedral as part of National Mobilization.
Nov. 15 Washington, D.C. Mobilization.
Dec. Financial grants presented by CALCAV to Canadian antidraft centers.

1970

Feb. 11–Apr. 28 CALCAV cosponsors 75-day Lenten-Passover Fast Action Project.
Mar. 13–15 CALCAV field staff conference, Clinton, Michigan.
Apr. 30 Cambodian invasion.
May 4 Kent State killings.
May 26–27 CALCAV cosponsors mobilization in Washington, D.C. in response to Cambodia and Kent State.
Oct. 2 First issue of *American Report* newspaper.

1971

Feb. 8 Invasion of Laos.
Mar. Set the Date campaign begins.
Apr. 24 Coalition demonstration, Washington, D.C.
May CALCAV conference on war crimes, New York City.
Summer Name change to Clergy and Laymen Concerned becomes generally accepted.
Aug. 17–22 Ann Arbor conference.
Oct. 27 Phase one of Unsell the War campaign begins.

Nov. 5 Daily Death Toll action begins.
Nov. 15 First CALC demonstration at Air Force Academy.
Dec. American Report Radio begins under CALC direction.

1972

Jan. 9 Second CALC demonstration at Air Force Academy.
Feb. Ecumenical Witness for Peace, Kansas City.
Apr. 18 Beginning of CALC's Honeywell campaign.
Apr. 26 CALC attends Honeywell stockholders meeting.
May 16 Emergency Witness demonstration, Washington, D.C.
June 13 Phase two of Unsell the War campaign begins.
Sept. Name changed to Clergy and Laity Concerned.

1973

Jan. 3–4 CALC cosponsors Religious Convocation and Congressional Visitations for Peace.
Jan. CALC establishes regional field staff.
Jan. 27 Signing of Paris Agreement.
Apr. 25 CALC attends Honeywell stockholders meeting.
May CALC initiates amnesty program.
June Richard Van Voorhis named CALC's interim executive director.
Oct. 26–28 Germantown, Ohio conference.

1974

Jan. George Webber leads group to Vietnam.
May CALC attends Honeywell stockholders meeting.
June Don Luce named CALC's executive director.
Dec. Don Luce leads group to Vietnam.

1975

Jan. 25–27 CALC cosponsors Assembly to Save the Peace Agreement.
May 1 Saigon captured by North Vietnamese.

NOTES

PREFACE

1. Michael Kilian, "Fun with Tom and Jane: Building an Anti-War Monument," Lexington *Herald-Leader,* April 30, 1985.
2. Skolnick, *The Politics of Protest,* pp. xx, 59, 61; Long, "Communication and Social Change," p. 47.

1. A NATIONAL EMERGENCY COMMITTEE

1. "Clergy Concerned About Vietnam," p. 99.
2. Two excellent books dealing with American involvement in Vietnam are Herring, *America's Longest War,* and Karnow, *Vietnam.*
3. DeBenedetti, "On the Significance of Citizen Peace Activism," p. 12.
4. Halstead, *Out Now!* pp. 19–22; Zaroulis and Sullivan, *Who Spoke Up?* pp. 12–15.
5. Powers, *The War at Home,* pp. 61–66; Halstead, *Out Now!* pp. 51–54.
6. Powers, *The War at Home,* pp. 69–70.
7. DeBenedetti, *Peace Reform,* p. 171.
8. *Ibid.,* pp. 138–64.
9. Jacquet, *Yearbook of American Churches.*
10. Marty, *Pilgrims,* esp. pp. 403–26; Marty, *Public Church,* pp. 70–93.
11. Webber, "CALC: The Anti-War Years"; Hadden, *Gathering Storm,* pp. 123–36; Gallup, *The Gallup Poll,* 3:1933, 3:2120; Hero, *American Religious Groups,* esp. pp. 165–208.
12. See, for example, Reinitz, *Irony and Consciousness,* pp. 115–16.
13. Cox, "The 'New Breed' "; Webber, "CALC: The Anti-War Years"; Hero, *American Religious Groups,* pp. 151–57, 207–8.
14. Marty, et al., *The Religious Press in America.*
15. New York *Times,* September 15, 1963, p. E5.
16. Bennett, "Questions About Vietnam."
17. Bennett, "Where Are We Headed in Vietnam?"

18. Lachman, "Barry Goldwater and the 1964 Religious Issue."

19. New York *Times,* December 15, 1964, p. 9.

20. New York *Times,* April 4, 1965, p. 3, E5.

21. "Protest Trends in Foreign Policy."

22. "Call to Vigil on Vietnam."

23. "U.S. Policy in Vietnam."

24. "Fifth General Synod Sets Forward Course"; "CCSA Takes Stand on Vietnam"; Slemp, "San Francisco, 1965"; "Council Scores Draft Evasion."

25. "Weighty Unanimity."

26. "Battle of Conscience."

27. Powers, *The War at Home,* pp. 38–53.

28. New York *Times,* July 3, 1965, p. 6; August 13, 1965, p. 1.

29. Oates, *Let the Trumpet Sound,* pp. 375–76.

30. A. J. Muste to John C. Bennett, October 15, 1965, Muste Papers, box 52.

31. Halstead, *Out Now!* pp. 131–35.

32. Zaroulis and Sullivan, *Who Spoke Up?* pp. 76–86.

33. Two important books dealing with these and other peace organizations in the twentieth century are Chatfield, *For Peace and Justice,* and Wittner, *Rebels Against War.*

34. Coffin, *Once to Every Man,* pp. 211–12.

35. New York *Times,* October 17, 1965, p. 9.

36. New York *Times,* November 2, 1965, p. 9.

37. New York *Times,* October 26, 1965, p. 4.

38. *Ibid.*

39. John C. Bennett to Robert Bilheimer, June 18, 1966, CALC Records, ser. 2, box 1.

40. Neuhaus interview.

41. "Battle of Conscience."

42. Gray, "Profiles," pp. 94–98.

43. " 'Peace' Priest Muzzled."

44. *Ibid.*

45. Gray, "Profiles," pp. 98–100.

46. Coffin, *Once to Every Man,* pp. 216–17; William Sloane Coffin to Fellow Clergy, January 24, 1966, CALC Records, ser. 2, box 1.

47. Coffin, *Once to Every Man,* p. 219; Edward G. Murray to John C. Bennett, January 14, 1966, CALC Records, ser. 2, box 1.

48. Balswick, "Theology and Political Attitudes"; Baer and Mosele, "Political and Religious Beliefs of Catholics"; Lewis, "A Contemporary Religious Enigma."

49. Carroll, Johnson, and Marty, *Religion in America,* esp. pp. 11–16, 28–34.

50. *Ibid.*

51. Quinley, "The Protestant Clergy and the War in Vietnam." In another study, Ellis E. Long found that among Protestants, the Episcopal, Methodist, and United Church of Christ denominations were most heavily represented in antiwar activity. Long, "Communication and Social Change."

52. Granberg, "Jewish-Nonjewish Differences on the Vietnam War"; Starr, "Religious Preference, Religiosity, and Opposition to War"; Erskine, "The Polls: Is War a Mistake?"

53. Gallup International, Inc., *Gallup Opinion Index: Political, Social, and Economic Trends,* report 26, August 1967, p. 6; report 29, November 1967, p. 11; report 33, March 1968, p. 8; Report 35, May 1968, p. 20.

54. *Ibid.,* report 35, May 1968, p. 20.

55. See Coffin, *Once to Every Man.*

56. Brown, "Benisons on Bennett"; Moritz, *Current Biography*, pp. 40–42; Fernandez interview.

57. *Who's Who in Religion*, 3d ed. (Chicago: Marquis Who's Who, 1985), p. 272.

58. Long, "Communication and Social Change," p. 94.

59. Brickner interview.

60. Brown, *Religion and Violence*, pp. xii–xv; Brown, "Benisons on Bennett," pp. 663–64; *Who's Who in Religion*, p. 42.

61. Richard R. Fernandez, "Proposal. Clergy and Laymen Concerned About Vietnam—A National Emergency Committee—Its History and Future," September 21, 1966, CALC Records, ser. 2, box 2.

62. "Telegram to President Johnson," January 11, 1966, CALC Records, ser. 2, box 2; William Sloane Coffin to Fellow Clergy, January 24, 1966, CALC Records, ser. 2, box 1.

63. "Telegram to President Johnson," January 13, 1966, CALC Records, ser. 2, box 2.

64. "National Emergency Committee of Clergy Concerned About Vietnam," January 18, 1966, CALC Records, ser. 2, box 2.

65. Clarence E. Tygart found a very strong correlation among Protestants between civil rights activism and antiwar activism. Tygart, "Social Movement Participation."

66. William Sloane Coffin to Fellow Clergy, January 24, 1966, CALC Records, ser. 2, box 1; "Clergy Concerned About Vietnam," p. 99; Coffin, *Once to Every Man*, pp. 217–18.

67. "Press Release from National Emergency Committee of Clergy Concerned About Vietnam," January 18, 1966, CALC Records, ser. 2, box 2; "What We Have Done," n.d., CALC Records, ser. 2, box 2.

68. Brown interview.

69. William Sloane Coffin to Fellow Clergy, January 24, 1966, CALC Records, ser. 2, box 1; Coffin, *Once to Every Man*, pp. 220–21.

70. New York *Times*, February 15, 1966, p. 2.

71. "Statement from the Steering Committee of the National Emergency Committee of Clergy Concerned About Vietnam," February 1, 1966, CALC Records, ser. 2, box 2.

72. Bennett, "From Supporter of War."

73. "We Protest the National Policy."

74. Bennett, "From Supporter of War"; "We Protest the National Policy"; Bennett, "Christian Realism"; "A Statement Developed by the Steering Committee," March 15, 1966, CALC Records, ser. 2, box 2.

75. "A Statement Developed by the Steering Committee," March 15, 1966, CALC Records, ser. 2, box 2.

76. Bennett, "Christian Realism"; "A Statement Developed by the Steering Committee," March 15, 1966, CALC Records, ser. 2, box 2.

77. Bennett, "Christian Realism"; "We Protest the National Policy"; Bennett, "From Supporter of War."

78. Bennett, "Christian Realism."

79. William S. Coffin, Jr. to Fellow Clergy, February 2, 1966, CALC Records, ser. 2, box 2.

80. Brown, "Treating Dissent Seriously."

81. John C. Bennett to A. J. Muste, February 22, 1966, Muste Papers, box 42.

82. New York *Times*, March 30, 1966, p. 13.

83. Tim Light to Bill [Coffin], March 21, 1966; Timothy Light to Association d'Amitie Franco-Vietnamienne, March 31, 1966, CALC Records, ser. 2, box 1.

2. TAKING THE MIDDLE GROUND: MARCH 1966 TO SEPTEMBER 1967

1. Brown, Heschel, and Novak, *Vietnam*, p. 8.
2. New York *Times*, February 15, 1966, p. 2; Steering Committee to Fathers and Brothers, April 7, 1966, CALC Records, ser. 2, box 2; Timothy Light to William C. King, April 7, 1966, CALC Records, ser. 2, box 1.
3. Steering Committee to Fathers and Brothers, April 7, 1966, CALC Records, ser. 2, box 2.
4. Richard J. Neuhaus to Chief Area Contact Men, February 14, 1966, CALC Records, ser. 2, box 2.
5. Fernandez interview.
6. Coffin, *Once to Every Man*, pp. 216–17, 223.
7. "Fernandez, Dick. Biographical sketch," 1971, CALC Records, ser. 3, box 4; Richard Fernandez to Al Hassler, May 17, 1966, CALC Records, ser. 2, box 1.
8. John C. Bennett to Robert Bilheimer, June 18, 1966; Bennett to George Sommaripa, July 3, 1967; Bennett to John Leo, May 5, 1966; Fernandez to Howard Schomer, May 16, 1966, CALC Records, ser. 2, box 1.
9. "Political and Economic History of Clergy and Laymen Concerned," 1972, p. 1; "A History of Clergy and Laymen Concerned About Vietnam," August 22, 1969, p. 2, CALC Records, ser. 1, box 1; and Fernandez interview.
10. "Boston Area Clergy and Laity Concerned: History of CALC," November 30, 1972, CALC records, ser. 5, box 5.
11. Fernandez interview.
12. "Political and Economic History of Clergy and Laymen Concerned," 1972, p. 1; and "A History of Clergy and Laymen Concerned About Vietnam," August 22, 1969, p. 2, CALC Records, ser. 1, box 1; Richard R. Fernandez, "Proposal: Clergy and Laymen Concerned About Viet Nam—A National Emergency Committee—Its History and Future," September 21, 1966, CALC Records, ser. 2, box 2.
13. Fernandez interview.
14. DeBenedetti and Chatfield find this same conversion-like experience in their book, *An American Ordeal*, p. 74.
15. Fuller interview.
16. William E. Hershey to Fernandez, February 21, 1967; Geoffrey Butcher to Fernandez, March 22, 1967, CALC Records, ser. 2, box 3.
17. Fernandez interview.
18. New York *Times*, July 4, 1966, p. 2.
19. Bennett, "It Is Difficult to Be an American," p. 165.
20. Fox, *Reinhold Niebuhr*, p. 285.
21. Fernandez, "Proposal," September 21, 1966, CALC Records, ser. 2, box 2.
22. "Lutheran World Relief to Aid Refugees in South Vietnam"; "Churchmen View Escalation in Vietnam"; "Uphold Right to Protest"; "The Dallas Assembly"; "CCSA Protests Bombing, Urges Negotiation."
23. Slemp, "Be Disciples . . . Make Disciples"; "LCA 3rd Biennial Convention"; "Catholic Bishops Speak Out on Vietnam, Birth Control"; McCorkle, "Pain and Promise."
24. Halstead, *Out Now!* pp. 189–98.
25. Halstead, *Out Now!* pp. 208–15, 226–35; Zaroulis and Sullivan, *Who Spoke Up?* pp. 96–98.
26. Fernandez to A. J. Muste, September 26, 1966, CALC Records, ser. 2, box 1.

27. Fernandez to Sidney Peck, September 15, 1966, CALC Records, ser. 2, box 1.

28. "Executive Committee of CALCAV to Contact People," February 24, 1967, CALC Records, ser. 3, box 8.

29. Fernandez to Rev. D. Eugene Lichty, April 27, 1967; Dick [Fernandez] to Tom Nichols, March 21, 1967, CALC Records, ser. 2, box 3.

30. Fernandez to William A. Slater, May 3, 1966; Timothy Light to Philip Scharper, April 6, 1966, CALC Records, ser. 2, box 1.

31. Fernandez to Bill Whit, November 21, 1966, CALC Records, ser. 2, box 1.

32. Powers, *The War at Home,* pp. 121–34.

33. *Ibid.,* p. 167.

34. "Clergy Mobilize for Peace"; "Minutes of Executive Committee of CALCAV," September 27, 1966, CALC Records, ser. 1, box 1.

35. Fernandez to Clergy Concerned Executive Committee, et al., December 21, 1966, CALC Records, ser. 2, box 2.

36. Brown, "An Open Letter to the U.S. Bishops," p. 548; Fernandez to A. V. Krebs, Jr., March 21, 1967; Fernandez to Rev. Glenn H. Turner, March 14, 1967; Fernandez to Rev. Paul Archambault, April 21, 1967, CALC Records, ser. 2, box 3.

37. Elston interview.

38. "The Religious Community and the War in Vietnam," February 1967, CALC Records, ser. 4, box 1.

39. *Ibid.*

40. Coffin, *Once to Every Man,* p. 224.

41. Haselden, "Concerned and Committed."

42. *Ibid.;* "Instructions for Vigil and Walk to Capitol," 1967, Muste Papers, box 42.

43. Haselden, "Concerned and Committed," p. 197.

44. *Ibid.,* pp. 197–98.

45. Coffin, *Once to Every Man,* pp. 224–26.

46. Haselden, "Concerned and Committed", p. 198.

47. *Ibid.*

48. LN to Walt Rostow, February 1, 1967, Executive ND 19/CO312, White House Central Files—Subject File.

49. William J. Jorden to Walt Rostow, January 30, 1967, Executive ND 19/CO312, White House Central Files—Subject File.

50. Coffin, *Once to Every Man,* pp. 226–29.

51. Small, *Johnson, Nixon, and the Doves,* pp. 41–49, 71, 84. Small elaborates on these points throughout chapters 2 and 3.

52. "Political and Economic History of Clergy and Laymen Concerned," 1972, p. 1, CALC Records, ser. 1, box 1; Haselden, "Concerned and Committed," p. 197.

53. Charlton and Moncrieff, *Many Reasons Why,* pp. 164–65.

54. Fernandez to Clergy and Laymen Concerned About Vietnam, March 10, 1967, Records of the Episcopal Peace Fellowship, box 11; Richard Killmer, "A Report of the Activities of Minnesota Clergy and Laymen Concerned About Vietnam, June, 1969 Through March, 1969," n.d.; "Buffalo Field Report," n.d., CALC Records, ser. 4, box 1.

55. New York *Times,* February 9, 1967, p. 2, and February 12, 1967, p. 9; "Minutes of the Executive Committee of CALCAV," February 16, 1967, CALC Records, ser. 1, box 1.

56. "A Second Selma."

57. New York *Times,* March 19, 1967, p. 3. For a more extensive treatment of this transition, see Au, *The Cross, the Flag, and the Bomb.*

58. Sheerin, "Bishop Shannon, Exile?"; "A Sense of Freedom, Joy, and Rightness."

59. Sheerin, "The Morality of the Vietnam War," p. 330.

60. *Ibid.*, pp. 326–30.

61. Sheerin, "The Vietcong as Negotiators?"

62. Sheerin, "Is Peace Coming Tomorrow?"

63. Fernandez to Jim Estes, April 18, 1967, CALC Records, ser. 2, box 3.

64. Fernandez to Jeanne Ballantine, April 12, 1967, CALC Records, ser. 2, box 3.

65. Fernandez to Timothy Light, June 19, 1967, CALC Records, ser. 2, box 3.

66. Oates, *Let the Trumpet Sound*, p. 395.

67. "Dr. Martin Luther King, Jr., Dr. John C. Bennett, Dr. Henry Steele Commager, Rabbi Abraham Heschel Speak on the War in Vietnam," April 1967, pp. 5–9, Peace Movement Collection.

68. Garrow, *Bearing the Cross*, p. 550; Fernandez interview.

69. Fernandez interview.

70. "King, Bennett, Commager, Heschel Speak on the War," April 1967, pp. 10–17, Peace Movement Collection.

71. *Ibid.*

72. *Ibid.*

73. *Ibid.*

74. Powers, *The War at Home*, p. 161.

75. Fernandez interview.

76. Fernandez to Constituency, May 1967, Muste Papers, box 42; Garrow, *Bearing the Cross,* p. 555; "Operating Costs of CALCAV National Office," October 1, 1967, CALC Records, ser. 1, box 1.

77. See, for example, "No Nobel for This Logic," Atlanta *Constitution,* April 6, 1967, p. 4; "Inflammatory Talk," Chicago *Tribune,* April 6, 1967, p. 20; "Dr. King's Boycott," *Christian Science Monitor,* April 7, 1967, p. 20; "Dr. King's Error," New York *Times,* April 7, 1967, p. 36; "A Tragedy," Washington *Post,* April 6, 1967, p. A20.

78. Oates, *Let the Trumpet Sound,* pp. 437–39. For more information on government attempts to undermine King's credibility, see Garrow, *The FBI and Martin Luther King, Jr.*

79. Halstead, *Out Now!* p. 278.

80. Oates, *Let the Trumpet Sound,* p. 440.

81. Halstead, *Out Now!* pp. 278–80.

82. Halstead, *Out Now!* p. 291; Zaroulis and Sullivan, *Who Spoke Up?* pp. 117–18; Katz, *Ban the Bomb,* pp. 105–6.

83. Fernandez to Constituency, May 1967, Muste Papers, box 42; and Halstead, *Out Now!* pp. 291–93.

84. "History of Clergy and Laymen Concerned About Vietnam," August 22, 1969, p. 3, and "Political and Economic History of Clergy and Laymen Concerned," 1972, p. 1, CALC Records, ser. 1, box 1; Nelson, "Vietnam Summer"; "Progress Report on Vietnam Summer," July 31, 1967, CALC Records, ser. 2, box 3.

85. Fernandez to Marcus Raskin, August 9, 1967, CALC Records, ser. 2, box 3.

86. Elston interview.

87. "A Plea for Openness and Flexibility."

88. "Mission Board Urges Candor on Viet Nam"; Marshall, "We Have Opened Another Door"; "Excerpts From the Resolutions at Pittsburgh"; "A Declaration of Conscience"; "We Resolve"; "What Did We Actually Do?"

89. Furlow, "General Assembly Highlights"; "Churches Continue to Call for Vietnam Peace"; "When Compromise Is Progress."

90. "Getting Close to Home"; "The Assembly Views War, Peace, Justice at Home and Abroad"; "Herbster Explains Synod Actions on War Service"; "Houston Church Threatens to Withdraw from Denomination."

91. Fernandez to Constituency, May 1967, Muste Papers, box 42; Fernandez to CALCAV Constituency, October 22, 1967, CALC Records; and Fernandez to Constituency, May 1967, Muste Papers, box 42.

92. "Operating Costs of CALCAV National Office," July 1967, CALC Records, ser. 1, box 1; Bennett to Robert Bilheimer, June 18, 1966, CALC Records, ser. 2, box 1.

93. Brown, Heschel, and Novak, *Vietnam*, p. 8; Fernandez to Mark F. Cassel, August 22, 1968, CALC Records, ser. 2, box 5.

94. Fernandez to Timothy Light, June 19, 1967, CALC Records, ser. 2, box 3.

95. Brown, Heschel, and Novak, *Vietnam*, pp. 61, 53.

96. *Ibid.*, pp. 90–93; Elston, "Vietnam."

97. Brown, Heschel, and Novak, *Vietnam*, pp. 45, 90–93.

98. *Ibid.*, p. 87.

99. Brown, "The Church and Vietnam."

100. Brown, "Vietnam," p. 5.

101. Powers, *The War at Home*, p. 185.

102. Brown, "Vietnam," pp. 6–7.

103. Neuhaus, "American Religion and the War."

104. Brown, Heschel, and Novak, *Vietnam*, p. 84.

105. *Ibid.*, p. 88.

106. Brown, "Vietnam," pp. 7–10.

107. *Ibid.*, pp. 9–10.

108. Brown, Heschel, and Novak, *Vietnam*, pp. 58–59.

109. Elston, "Vietnam," pp. 78–82.

110. Brown, Heschel, and Novak, *Vietnam*, pp. 84–85.

111. Elston, "Vietnam," pp. 78–82.

112. Brown, Heschel, and Novak, *Vietnam*, pp. 52, 54.

113. Brown, "Vietnam," pp. 7–10.

114. Brown, Heschel, and Novak, *Vietnam*, p. 15.

115. *Ibid.*, p. 46.

3. "IN CONSCIENCE I MUST BREAK THE LAW": SEPTEMBER 1967 TO DECEMBER 1968

1. New York *Times*, July 3, 1968, p. 37; Barry Johnson, "Seminarian in 'The Resistance.' "

2. Powers, *The War at Home*, pp. 134–35.

3. Zaroulis and Sullivan, *Who Spoke Up?* p. 115.

4. "Clergy and Laymen Concerned About Vietnam," report from Norfolk, Virginia, FBI office, February 5, 1968, FBI Files.

5. Powers, *The War at Home*, pp. 85–87. For background on the draft resistance movement, see Ferber and Lynd, *The Resistance*.

6. Halstead, *Out Now!* pp. 321–25.

7. DeBenedetti, *Peace Reform*, p. 180.

8. Zaroulis and Sullivan, *Who Spoke Up?* p. 142.

9. "A Call to Resist Illegitimate Authority," *New Republic* (October 7, 1967), 157:34–35.

10. Brown, "In Conscience, I Must Break the Law," p. 50.

11. "Minutes of Executive Committee of CALCAV," September 6, 1967, CALC Records, ser. 1, box 1.

12. Richard R. Fernandez memorandum, October 22, 1967, CALC Records, ser. 4, box 2.

13. New York *Times,* October 26, 1967, p. 10.

14. "Conscience and Conscription," n.d., CALC Records, ser. 4, box 1.

15. William H. Maness to Fernandez, November 15, 1967, CALC Records, ser. 2, box 4.

16. New York *Times,* February 11, 1968, p. E11.

17. Brown interview.

18. Brown, "In Conscience," p. 52.

19. Bennett, "The Place of Civil Disobedience."

20. Sheerin, "The Limits of Civil Disobedience." On May 17, 1968, nine people, including Daniel and Philip Berrigan, seized hundreds of classification files from a Catonsville, Maryland draft board and burned them with homemade napalm.

21. Coffin, "Civil Disobedience, the Draft, and the War."

22. Coffin, *Once to Every Man,* p. 234.

23. *Ibid.,* p. 244.

24. Coffin, *Once to Every Man,* pp. 243–44; Powers, *The War at Home,* pp. 192–94; Zaroulis and Sullivan, *Who Spoke Up?* pp. 133–35.

25. Zaroulis and Sullivan, *Who Spoke Up?* p. 149; Halstead, *Out Now!* pp. 377–78.

26. Shapiro, "God and That Man at Yale," p. 74.

27. Neuhaus, "Super-General Hershey."

28. Sheerin, "From Vietnam to Isolation?"; Sheerin, "Must Conscientious Objectors Be Pacifists?"; Sheerin, "Silent Church and the Endless War."

29. Dellinger, *More Power Than We Know,* p. 116.

30. "CALCAV's Contributions to the Anti-War Efforts," *CALC Report* (August–October 1985), 11:9–11; Bennett interview.

31. Delwin Brown to Fernandez, May 25, 1967, CALC Records, ser. 2, box 3; Fernandez to Clergy and Laymen Concerned About Viet Nam Constituency, October 22, 1967, CALC Records, ser. 4, box 2.

32. Barbara Fuller, "Regional Field Staff Program, Evaluation of Central Region," 1973, CALC Records, ser. 3, box 19.

33. Press release, January 18, 1966, CALC Records, ser. 2, box 2; Fernandez to Clergy and Laymen Concerned About Vietnam, March 10, 1967, Records of the Episcopal Peace Fellowship, box 11; Jack von Mettenheim to Fernandez, May 9, 1967, CALC Records, ser. 2, box 3; Betsy Gwynn to Fernandez, December 13, 1967, CALC Records, ser. 2, box 4.

34. "Minutes of Executive Committee of CALCAV," November 21, 1967, CALC Records, ser. 1, box 1.

35. New York *Times,* January 13, 1968, p. 4.

36. *Ibid.*

37. Clergy and Laymen Concerned About Vietnam, *In the Name of America,* pp. 1–11.

38. Fernandez to Irving J. Fain, November 28, 1967, CALC Records, ser. 2, box 1.

39. New York *Times,* February 4, 1968, p. 1; February 11, 1968, p. E11.

40. "Protest Activity by Clergy and Laymen Concerned About Vietnam, Washington, D.C., February 5 and 6, 1968," February 5, 1968, FBI Files.

41. *Ibid.,* February 6, 1968.

42. *Ibid.*

43. Powers, *The War at Home,* p. 178.

44. MacKaye, "Clergy in the Capitol."
45. "Protest Activity . . . February 5 and 6, 1968," February 5, 1968, FBI Files; Washington *Post*, February 6, 1968, p. B1.
46. New York *Times*, February 6, 1968, p. 15.
47. "Silent March."
48. Washington *Post*, February 10, 1968, p. D9; "Protest Activity . . . February 5 and 6, 1968," February 6, 1968, FBI Files.
49. John R. McDonough and Hugh Durham to the Attorney General, February 28, 1968, FBI Files.
50. Director, FBI to SACs [Special Agents in Charge], Atlanta, New York, WFO [Washington Field Office], January 17, 1968; SAC, New York to Director, FBI, January 19, 1968; C. D. Brennan to W. C. Sullivan, February 1, 1968; SAC, WFO to Director, FBI, February 5, 1968; February 6, 1968, FBI Files.
51. J. Edgar Hoover to Mr. Crowley, May 7, 1968; Cleveland to Director, July 1, 1968; "Protest Activity . . . February 5 and 6, 1968," February 6, 1968; J. Edgar Hoover to [censored], December 2, 1968, FBI Files.
52. Small, *Johnson, Nixon, and the Doves*, pp. 104–6. Small concludes that the use of intelligence agencies was partially motivated by the desire to undermine political opposition.
53. Bennett to Herman Will, Jr., March 18, 1968, CALC Records, ser. 2, box 4.
54. John C. Platt to Fernandez, October 29, 1968, CALC Records, ser. 2, box 6.
55. Washington *Post*, February 10, 1968, p. D9; Mackaye, "Clergy in the Capitol," p. 36.
56. "Churchmen Welcome Pope Paul's New Year's Plea for Peace"; "Action at Atlanta"; "Business—'Internal' and 'External' "; "Excerpts from the Resolutions at Boston"; "A Union . . . and Much More"; "Vietnam Report: Looking Toward the Future"; "Church and Society."
57. "The Opinion Poll on Vietnam"; Stauderman, "Editor's Opinion"; "Hawks in the Pews." The denominations represented were the United Church of Christ, United Church of Canada, Presbyterian Church of the United States, Methodist Church, United Presbyterian Church, Episcopal Church, Lutheran Church in America, Christian Churches (Disciples of Christ), and Evangelical United Brethren.
58. Quinley, "The Protestant Clergy"; Tygart, "Social Movement Participation." Tygart's study of Protestant pastors indicated that they were twice as likely to be participants in the antiwar movement than the general public.
59. Hall, "A Time for War"; Blevens, "Southern Baptist Attitudes Toward the Vietnam War."
60. Quinley, "The Protestant Clergy."
61. Neuhaus, "The War, the Churches, and Civil Religion."
62. Quoted in Zaroulis and Sullivan, *Who Spoke Up?* p. 147.
63. New York *Times*, April 10, 1968, p. 36.
64. Halstead, *Out Now!* pp. 386–90.
65. *Wall Street Journal*, May 9, 1968, p. 4; "Dow (May 1968)," CALC Records, ser. 3, box 22.
66. Fernandez to Clergy and Laymen Concerned About Vietnam Constituency, October 22, 1967, CALC Records, ser. 4, box 2.
67. Duane Gall and Tom Rauch, "Evaluation of RFS [Regional Field Staff] Program," December 19, 1973, CALC Records, ser. 3, box 19; Duane Gall, "September–October Report, Denver CALCAV," 1969; Duane Gall, "September Report, Denver CALCAV," n.d., CALC Records, ser. 5, box 3.
68. "A Proposal for a Campaign to End the Draft," May 1968, CALC Records, ser. 5, box 2; Northern California Clergy and Laymen Concerned About Vietnam,

"Debate on the Draft in America: Is Conscription Necessary for or Destructive of a Free Society?" n.d., CALC Records, ser. 5, box 2.

69. "Special Report on the Work of the Northern California Clergy and Laymen Concerned About Vietnam," March 21, 1969, CALC Records, ser. 4, box 1.

70. Homer A. Jack to Fernandez, April 24, 1967; Fernandez to Homer Jack, April 28, 1967, CALC Records, ser. 2, box 3.

71. Fernandez to Rosemary Stahlka, July 9, 1971, CALC Records, ser. 2, box 9.

72. Elston interview.

73. Bennett to Herman Will, Jr., March 18, 1968, CALC Records, ser. 2, box 4; Fernandez to John F. Taplin, June 26, 1968, CALC Records, ser. 2, box 5; form letter from Fernandez, November 1968, FBI Files; *Issues and Actions,* October 18, 1968, p. 3, Periodicals Collection.

74. Fernandez to K. Sherwood McKee, May 16, 1966, CALC Records, ser. 2, box 1; Richard L. Deats, "Clergy and Laymen Concerned About Vietnam Dallas Area Report," August 1968–March 1969, CALC Records, ser. 4, box 1; Duane Gall and Tom Rauch, "Regional Field Staff Report," December 19, 1973, CALC Records, ser. 3, box 19.

75. Fernandez to Clergy and Laymen Concerned About Vietnam Constituency, October 22, 1967, CALC Records, ser. 4, box 2; Paul Kittlaus, "Regional Field Staff Reflections 1973," CALC Records, ser. 3, box 19.

76. Harold R. Fray, Jr. to Dear Friends, June 14, 1968; "Local Clergy Call for Churches and Synagogues to Consider Sanctuary," June 18, 1968, CALC Records, ser. 5, box 5.

77. New York *Times,* December 1, 1967, p. 1.

78. Zaroulis and Sullivan, *Who Spoke Up?* pp. 157–58.

79. "Who's Right? Who's Wrong? on Vietnam," n.d., Records of Friends Committee on National Legislation, box 12.

80. John B. Paine, Jr. to Fernandez, March 6, 1968, CALC Records, ser. 2, box 4; Fernandez to John F. Taplin, June 26, 1968, CALC Records, ser. 2, box 5; John W. Sonnenday to Fernandez, August 21, 1968, CALC Records, ser. 3, box 3; Fernandez to Robert K. Dubroff, August 13, 1970, CALC Records, ser. 2, box 7.

81. Zaroulis and Sullivan, *Who Spoke Up?* pp. 159–60.

82. *Ibid.,* pp. 162–63.

83. *Issues and Actions,* December 1968, p. 1, Periodicals Collection; Fernandez to Gretchen Hahn, August 16, 1968, CALC Records, ser. 2, box 5.

84. Walker, et al., *Rights in Conflict,* pp. 5, 343–44, 351–58.

85. Page and Brody, "Policy Voting and the Electoral Process."

86. Fernandez to Abbey Rockefeller, September 23, 1968, CALC Records, ser. 2, box 6.

87. Fernandez to Mrs. Gardner Cox, September 24, 1968, CALC Records, ser. 2, box 6.

88. "Vietnam Sunday—A Call for Reflection—and Action!" November 3, 1968, Records of Friends Committee on National Legislation, box 12; *Issues and Actions,* December 1968, p. 2, Periodicals Collection.

89. Theodore W. Johnson to Richard Earl Lanning, November 5, 1968, CALC Records, ser. 2, box 6; "Proposal for Amnesty Campaign August 25, 1968–January 1, 1969," n.d., CALC Records, ser. 3, box 25; Director, FBI to Legat, London, October 25, 1968; SAC, New York to Director, FBI, December 27, 1968; Director, FBI to SAC, New York, November 19, 1968, FBI Files.

90. Los Angeles *Times,* August 16, 1968, p. 3.

91. Fernandez to Vera Rubin, September 23, 1968, CALC Records, ser. 2, box 6.

92. Fernandez to President Johnson, December 18, 1968, White House Central Files—Subject File, General ND 9-4-1.

93. Minutes of Steering Committee," September 30, 1968, CALC Records, ser. 1, box 1.

94. Fernandez to Coretta Scott King, December 4, 1968, CALC Records, ser. 2, box 6; New York *Times,* December 22, 1968, p. 5; Washington *Post,* December 28, 1968, p. E7.

95. Small, *Johnson, Nixon, and the Doves,* pp. 96, 157.

4. "HOW PATIENT MUST WE BE, MR. NIXON?": JANUARY 1969 TO MAY 1970

1. Berger and Neuhaus, *Movement and Revolution,* p. 8.

2. Halstead, *Out Now!* pp. 441–44; Zaroulis and Sullivan, *Who Spoke Up?* pp. 209–10.

3. *Issues and Actions,* January 13, 1969, p. 1, Periodicals Collection.

4. New York *Times,* February 4, 1969, p. 24; "Mobilizing for Peace."

5. Rose, "From Viet Nam to Empire"; Washington *Post,* February 4, 1969, p. A11; New York *Times,* February 4, 1969, p. 24; Washington *Post,* February 5, 1969, p. A20.

6. Kuttner, "Recharging the Peace Movement," p. 669; SAC, WFO [Special Agent in Charge, Washington Field Office] to Director, FBI and SACs, San Francisco and New York, February 3, 1969, FBI Files.

7. "The Reconciliation We Seek," 1969, CALC Records, ser. 4, box 1; Washington *Post,* February 5, 1969, p. A20.

8. New York *Times,* February 5, 1969, p. 8.

9. Kuttner, "Recharging the Peace Movement," p. 670.

10. SAC, WFO to Director, FBI and SACs, New York and San Francisco, February 4, 1969; SAC, WFO to Director, FBI, February 11, 1969, FBI Files.

11. Washington *Post,* February 6, 1969, p. A14.

12. Kuttner, "Recharging the Peace Movement."

13. SAC, WFO to Director, FBI, February 11, 1968, FBI Files.

14. Hayes, *American Deserters,* p. 37; Washington *Post,* February 6, 1969, p. A14.

15. Hayes, *American Deserters,* pp. 26–27.

16. Novak, "Alive and Well in Paris," p. 278.

17. *Christian Science Monitor,* November 8, 1968, p. 20.

18. *Lutheran Forum,* December 1968, p. 7.

19. *Issues and Actions,* December 1968, p. 2, Periodicals Collection.

20. "Tom Hayes Biographical Sketch," n.d., CALC Records, ser. 3, box 6.

21. New York *Times,* March 19, 1969, p. 2.

22. Hayes, *American Deserters,* pp. 40–42.

23. "Report to CALCAV from T. L. Hayes and the Sweden Project," June 6, 1969, CALC Records, ser. 3, box 3; Hayes, *American Deserters,* p. 79.

24. "Report to CALCAV from T. L. Hayes and the Sweden Project," June 6, 1969, CALC Records, ser. 3, box 3.

25. *Ibid.*

26. *Ibid.;* Fernandez interview.

27. "Speech by Mrs. Bea Seitzman," August 27–28, 1969, CALC Records, ser. 3, box 2.

28. Richard Fernandez to Staff and Contact People," December 17, 1969, CALC Records, ser. 3, box 6; Hayes, *American Deserters,* p. 185.

29. "Minutes of Steering Committee," January 13, 1970, CALC Records, ser. 1, box 1.

30. Fernandez to Gerald M. Condon, April 27, 1971, CALC Records, ser. 2, box 8.

31. "Minutes of Steering Committee," January 13, 1970, CALC Records, ser. 1, box 1.

32. "Americans in Exile in Canada," May 9, 1969, CALC Records, ser. 3, box 3.

33. "Americans in Exile in Canada," May 9, 1969, CALC Records, ser. 3, box 3; Fernandez to Dear Friend, May 14, 1969, CALC Records, ser. 3, box 2; Killmer, Lecky, and Wiley, *They Can't Go Home Again*, p. 20–24.

34. *Issues and Actions*, December 4, 1969, pp. 1, 6, Periodicals Collection.

35. News Release, "Over $5,000 Raised for Deserters in Canada," December 15, 1969, CALC Records, ser. 3, box 3; *Issues and Actions*, December 4, 1969, pp. 1, 6, Periodicals Collections.

36. *Issues and Actions*, December 4, 1969, p. 1, 6, Periodicals Collection; Killmer, Lecky, and Wiley, *They Can't Go Home Again*, pp. 35–37; "Political and Economic History of Clergy and Laymen Concerned," 1972, CALC Records, ser. 1, box 1; "Minutes of Steering Committee," November 10, 1970, CALC Records, ser. 1, box 1.

37. "Fact Sheet in the Killing of Richard Bunch and Mutiny Charges Against 27 Soldiers Who Protested His Death," n.d., FBI Files.

38. New York *Times,* January 28, 1969, p. 23; "CALCAV News Release—Religious Leaders Demand Mutiny Trial Stop," January 27, 1969, FBI Files; "Clergy and Laymen Concerned About Vietnam" pamphlet, 1969, CALC Records, ser. 1, box 1.

39. Kuttner, "Recharging the Peace Movement," p. 670.

40. "Special Report on the Work of the Northern California Clergy and Laymen Concerned About Vietnam," March 21, 1969, CALC Records, ser. 4, box 1; "Fact Sheet Concerning Presidio Stockade," n.d.; "Why Be Concerned," n.d., FBI Files.

41. New York *Times,* February 22, 1969, p. 4.

42. New York *Times,* March 30, 1969, p. E7.

43. Halstead, *Out Now!* pp. 451–52.

44. New York *Times,* May 8, 1969, p. 12.

45. *Ibid.*

46. Fernandez interview.

47. Fernandez to Herbert Doan, December 11, 1969, CALC Records, ser. 3, box 22.

48. *Issues and Actions,* June 5, 1969, CALC Records, ser. 4, box 1.

49. *Ibid.*

50. *Issues and Actions,* May 1, 1969, FBI Files.

51. "History of Clergy and Laymen Concerned About Vietnam," August 22, 1969, CALC Records, ser. 1, box 1.

52. "Clergy and Laymen Concerned About Vietnam," pamphlet, 1969, CALC Records, ser. 1, box 1.

53. Fernandez interview.

54. "Clergy and Laymen Concerned About Vietnam," pamphlet, 1969, CALC Records, ser. 1, box 1.

55. Fernandez interview.

56. Carson, *In Struggle,* p. 294–95.

57. "Churches Asked to Provide Draft Counseling"; "Church and Society Papers"; "Issues at General Synod"; "American Baptists at Seattle"; "The Business of the Christian Church."

58. "Notes on Planning Meeting for Boston Conference," July 25, 1969, CALC Records, ser. 3, box 2.

59. "The Future of Clergy and Laymen Concerned, Some Proposals," August 20, 1969, CALC Records, ser. 3, box 1; "Specific Programmatic Items," August 22, 1969, CALC Records, ser. 3, box 2.

60. *Issues and Actions*, September 26, 1969, p. 3, Periodicals Collection.

61. "Report on Clergy and Laymen Concerned Regional Conferences," n.d., CALC Records, ser. 3, box 11; "Specific Programmatic Items," August 22, 1969, CALC Records, ser. 3, box 2.

62. *Issues and Actions*, May 1, 1969, FBI Files.

63. Director, FBI to SAC, New York, May 20, 1969; Colonel John W. Downie and Merrill T. Kelly to Director, FBI, June 23, 1969; SAC, New York to Director, FBI, July 31, 1969; SAC, New York to Director, FBI, September 29, 1969; SAC, WFO to Director, FBI, October 6, 1969; SAC, WFO to Director, FBI, November 24, 1969; J. Edgar Hoover to [censored], October 22, 1969, FBI Files.

64. Interviews with Brown, Fernandez, and Elston.

65. Halstead, *Out Now!* pp. 467–73.

66. Halstead, *Out Now!* pp. 473–74; Zaroulis and Sullivan, *Who Spoke Up?* pp. 257–58.

67. Halstead, *Out Now!* pp. 488–90.

68. *Ibid.*, pp. 494–95, 511.

69. Fuller interview.

70. Zaroulis and Sullivan, *Who Spoke Up?* p. 288–89.

71. Elston interview.

72. Brown interview.

73. Elston interview.

74. Coffin, *Once to Every Man*, p. 297; Hoffman, *Moratorium*, pp. 170–71.

75. Coffin, *Once to Every Man*, p. 298.

76. DeBenedetti, *Peace Reform*, p. 185.

77. Halstead, *Out Now!* pp. 522–23; Dellinger, *More Power Than We Know*, p. 17.

78. Halstead, *Out Now!* pp. 525–27; Zaroulis and Sullivan, *Who Spoke Up?* pp. 297–98.

79. Brickner, "Vietnam and the Jewish Community," pp. 531–34.

80. Bennett, "End the War Now!" pp. 261–63. His views were unchanged six months later. See Bennett, "The President's Folly."

81. Novak, "Vietnam's Tomorrow."

82. Bennett, "End the War Now!"; Novak, "Vietnam's Tomorrow"; Sheerin, "A Cease-Fire Now in Vietnam."

83. Neuhaus, "The Good Sense of Amnesty."

84. "Clergy and Laymen Concerned About Vietnam, Fellowship of Reconciliation" report from Washington, D.C., February 10, 1970, FBI Files; New York *Times*, February 12, 1970, p. 5.

85. "Clergy and Laymen Concerned About Vietnam, Fellowship of Reconciliation" report from Washington, D.C., February 10, 1970, FBI Files; *Issues and Actions*, March 11, 1970, Periodicals Collection.

86. "Lenten-Passover Fast Action," n.d., FBI Files; New York *Times*, February 12, 1970, p. 5; Washington *Post*, February 12, 1970, p. A3.

87. SAC, WFO to Director, and SAC, New York, February 11, 1970, FBI Files; "The Washington Fast"; New York *Times*, February 12, 1970, p. 5; Washington *Post*, February 12, 1970, p. A3; SAC, WFO to Director, FBI and SAC, New York, March 27, 1970, FBI Files.

88. *Issues and Actions,* January 26, 1970, Periodicals Collection.

89. "Minutes of Steering Committee," February 16, 1970, CALC Records, ser. 1, box 1; *Issues and Actions,* March 11, 1970, Periodicals Collection.

90. Falk, "The Circle of Responsibility."

91. Director, FBI to SAC, New York, May 22, 1970, FBI Files.

92. Berger, "Indochina and the American Conscience."

93. SAC, WFO to Director, FBI, May 28, 1970, FBI Files.

94. DeBenedetti, *Peace Reform,* p. 186; Halstead, *Out Now!* pp. 538–40.

95. Wittner, *Rebels Against War,* p. 290.

96. Zaroulis and Sullivan, *Who Spoke Up?* p. 328.

97. *Issues and Actions,* June–July 1970, Periodicals Collection; Washington *Post,* May 27, 1970, p. A15.

98. Bryan, *Friendly Fire,* pp. 166–81.

99. *Ibid.*

100. Elizabeth Stowe, "Eight Descriptive Studies: How Churches and Synagogues Act on the Issue of Peace," August 17, 1971, CALC Records, ser. 4, box 1.

101. "On War, Peace, and Dissent"; "Too Much, Too Little"; Willis, "A Summary of General Convention Actions."

102. "Listening to Some New Voices"; "Assembly Speaks on Indochina, Proxies; 'Receives' Balance of Church and Society Report."

103. Zaroulis and Sullivan, *Who Spoke Up?* pp. 335–36.

5. FROM MOVEMENT TO ORGANIZATION: JUNE 1970 TO DECEMBER 1971

1. Coffin, *Once to Every Man,* p. 223.

2. Fernandez to Coffin, October 27, 1966, CALC Records, ser. 3, box 1.

3. Elston interview.

4. Fernandez to Balfour Brickner, September 20, 1967, CALC Records, ser. 2, box 3; Fernandez to Rev. John Giannini, March 22, 1968, CALC Records, ser. 2, box 4; "Minutes of Executive Committee," September 6, 1967, November 2, 1967, November 21, 1967, CALC Records, ser. 1, box 1.

5. Fernandez interview.

6. "Staff Meeting, Clinton, Michigan, March 13–15, 1970 and Steering Committee, New York City, March 30, 1970," CALC Records, ser. 3, box 2.

7. Fernandez interview; Webber interview.

8. "Minutes of Steering Committee," November 10, 1970; March 15, 1971; "Minutes of Meeting Between Seminarians, Theologians, and CALC National Staff," December 9, 1971, CALC Records, ser. 1, box 1..

9. "Minutes of Steering Committee," September 11, 1972; November 14, 1972, CALC Records, ser. 1, box 1; "Minutes of Steering Committee," January 9, 1973, CALC Records, ser. 1, box 2.

10. National Steering Committee to Regional Field Staff, February 19, 1973; "Minutes of Steering Committee," July 26, 1973, CALC Records, ser. 1, box 2.

11. Fernandez interview.

12. *Ibid.*

13. "Staff Meeting, Clinton, Michigan, March 13–15, 1970 and Steering Committee, New York City, March 30, 1970," CALC Records, ser. 3, box 2; "Agenda of Steering Committee," May 19, 1970, CALC Records, ser. 1, box 1.

14. "Clergy and Laymen Concerned About Vietnam," June 19, 1970, CALC

Records, ser. 1, box 1; *American Report,* October 2, 1970, October 9, 1970, October 16, 1970; "Newspaper Committee to Members of the Steering Committee, July 15, 1970, CALC Records, ser. 1, box 1.

15. "Minutes of Steering Committee," November 10, 1970, CALC Records, ser. 1, box 1. Some readers felt the same way. See *American Report,* October 23, 1970.

16. "American Report Newspaper," n.d., CALC Records, ser. 1, box 1.

17. "Minutes of Steering Committee," September 11, 1972, CALC Records, ser. 1, box 1; *American Report,* October 9, 1972; "Minutes of Finance Committee," October 18, 1972, CALC Records, ser. 1, box 2; "Minutes of Steering Committee," June 13, 1973, June 25, 1973, CALC Records, ser. 1, box 2.

18. "Minutes of Communications Committee," November 3, 1972, CALC Records, ser. 1, box 1.

19. Lecky, "Requiem of an Editor."

20. "Minutes of Steering Committee," January 9, 1973, July 26, 1973, November 7, 1973, CALC Records, ser. 1, box 2. See file folder "Subscriptions, samples of 'cancel my subscription' letters 1972," CALC Records, ser. 4, box 13.

21. Elston interview.

22. "American Report Readership Survey," November 1973, CALC Records, ser. 4, box 18.

23. Fernandez to Jane Fonda, August 12, 1970, CALC Records, ser. 2, box 7.

24. Fernandez interview.

25. Brown, "An Open Letter to Spiro T. Agnew."

26. DeBenedetti, *Peace Reform,* pp. 187–88; Halstead, *Out Now!* pp. 563–70; Zaroulis and Sullivan, *Who Spoke Up?* pp. 336–37.

27. SAC [Special Agent in Charge], Philadelphia to Director, FBI, March 23, 1971, FBI Files.

28. "Minutes of Steering Committee," January 12, 1971; March 15, 1971, CALC Records, ser. 1, box 1.

29. Zaroulis and Sullivan, *Who Spoke Up?* pp. 346–47.

30. Robert McAfee Brown, et al. to Steering Committee, National Committee, Contact People, February 10, 1971, CALC Records, ser. 3, box 3.

31. "Minutes of Steering Committee," April 20, 1971; "Minutes of Program Committee," March 2, 1971, CALC Records, ser. 1, box 1.

32. Halstead, *Out Now!* pp. 587–614; Zaroulis and Sullivan, *Who Spoke Up?* pp. 343–60.

33. Halstead, *Out Now!,* pp. 617–23; Zaroulis and Sullivan, *Who Spoke Up?* pp. 360–65; DeBenedetti, *Peace Reform,* pp. 189–90.

34. Zaroulis and Sullivan, *Who Spoke Up?* pp. 351–52.

35. DeBenedetti, *Peace Reform,* p. 188.

36. "Minutes of Meeting," May 21–22, 1971; "Minutes of Steering Committee," April 20, 1971; May 25, 1971, CALC Records, ser. 1, box 1.

37. Sheerin, "War Crimes in High Places."

38. "Vietnam and America: From Bondage to Liberation: A Call to a National Organizing Conference," June 1971, CALC Records, ser. 1, box 1.

39. "Religious Groups Call for Withdrawal."

40. "Vietnam Statement Causes Anguish"; "Convention Roundup"; *United Church Herald* (August 1971), 14:3, 30.

41. "Minnesota Campaign to Set the Date for Total Withdrawal from All of S.E. Asia," n.d.; "Special Report" from Minnesota Clergy and Laymen Concerned, n.d., CALC Records, ser. 5, box 8.

42. *Ibid.*

43. *Ibid.*

44. *Ibid.*

45. "Staff Meeting, Clinton, Michigan, March 13–15, 1970 and Steering Meeting, New York City, March 30, 1970," CALC Records, ser. 3, box 2.

46. "Givens, 1971—Pre Ann Arbor," n.d., CALC Records, ser. 1, box 1; "Minutes of Steering Committee," April 20, 1971, May 25, 1971, CALC Records, ser. 1, box 1; Webber, "CALC: The Anti-War Years."

47. Brickner, "On Calley . . . and Silence."

48. "Givens, 1971—Pre Ann Arbor," n.d.; "Report on Field Development and Honeywell Campaign Development Since Ann Arbor Conference and Planning, 1971–September, 1972," July 14, 1972, CALC Records, ser. 1, box 1; Webber, "CALC: The Anti-War Years"; "CALCAV's Contributions to the Anti-War Efforts," *CALC Report* (August–October 1985), 11:9–11; Webber and Kittlaus interviews.

49. "Givens, 1971—Pre Ann Arbor," n.d., CALC Records, ser. 1, box 1; Carl, "Old Testament Prophecy and the Question of Prophetic Preaching," p. 193.

50. "Some Background Information on the Conference," n.d., CALC Records, ser. 5, box 4.

51. Fernandez to prospective contacts, May 14, 1971, CALC Records, ser. 1, box 1.

52. "Minutes of Steering Committee," April 20, 1971 and May 25, 1971, CALC Records, ser. 1, box 1; "Givens, 1971—Pre Ann Arbor," n.d., CALC Records, ser. 1, box 1.

53. "Minutes of Steering Committee," June 15, 1971, CALC Records, ser. 1, box 1; "Steps in Field and Honeywell Campaign Development Since Ann Arbor Planning, 1971," n.d., CALC Records, ser. 1, box 1.

54. "Overview of National Organizing Project," May 25, 1971, CALC Records, ser. 1, box 1; "Vietnam and America: From Bondage to Liberation: A Call to a National Organizing Conference," June 1971, CALC Records, ser. 1, box 1.

55. Kittlaus interview; Los Angeles *Times,* January 13, 1974, p. VII-6.

56. "Vietnam and America: From Bondage to Liberation: A National Organizing Conference Update," n.d., FBI Files; "Steps in Field and Honeywell Campaign Development Since Ann Arbor Planning, 1971," n.d., CALC Records, ser. 1, box 1.

57. Lecky, "From Emergency Committee to Protracted Struggle"; "Some Background Information on the Conference," n.d., CALC Records, ser. 5, box 4.

58. Lecky, "From Emergency Committee to Protracted Struggle"; "Some Background Information on the Conference," n.d., CALC Records, ser. 5, box 4; "Who was at Ann Arbor," n.d., CALC Records, ser. 1, box 1.

59. "Vietnam and America," n.d., FBI Files; "Some Background Information on the Conference," n.d., CALC Records, ser. 5, box 4; "CALC Renews Antiwar Push."

60. "Ann Arbor Conference Sets Agenda for Future," *American Report,* September 3, 1971, p. 7; "Clergy and Laymen Concerned Campaign for Social Justice," n.d., FBI Files.

61. "Ann Arbor Conference Sets Agenda for Future"; Fernandez and Young, "CALC After Ann Arbor"; "Priority Setting Agenda Sheet, Ann Arbor," n.d., CALC Records, ser. 5, box 4.

62. "Preparing for Protracted Struggle"; Fernandez interview.

63. "Robert A. Cleland to Trudi Young and Dick Fernandez," August 24, 1971, CALC Records, ser. 5, box 4.

64. Charles C. West, "Report to the Steering Committee of Clergy and Laymen Concerned About the Ann Arbor Conference," n.d., CALC Records, ser. 1, box 1.

65. John Cupples, "Report of the Regional Field Staff," December 12, 1973; Michael Riesch, "Regional Field Staff Report," 1973; Ron Freund, "Midwest Regional

Report," December 28, 1973; Barbara Fuller, "Regional Field Staff Program," 1973; Duane Gall and Tom Rauch, "Evaluation of the RFS Program," December 19, 1973; Paul Kittlaus, "Regional Field Staff Reflections," 1973, CALC Records, ser. 3, box 19; John Pairman Brown to George W. Webber, July 10, 1973, CALC Records, ser. 5, box 2.

66. "Directory of Peace Organizations, Los Angeles Area," July 23, 1971. CALC Records, ser. 5, box 1; Fernandez to Harlan Weitzel, September 15, 1971; Fernandez to Paul Kittlaus, October 15, 1971; Proposal to National Clergy and Laymen Concerned from Southern California Clergy and Laymen Concerned, February 9, 1972, CALC Records, ser. 5, box 1.

67. "SC/CALC Steering Committee," September 24, 1972, CALC Records, ser. 5, box 1; Paul Kittlaus, "Regional Field Staff Report," 1973, CALC Records, ser. 3, box 19; "Southern California Clergy and Laity Concerned Program and Structure Plan," March 12, 1973, CALC Records, ser. 5, box 1.

68. Fernandez to Clergy and Laymen Concerned About Viet Nam Constituency," October 22, 1967, CALC Records, ser. 4, box 2; "To Clergy and Laymen and other people," May 2, 1969, CALC Records, ser. 5, box 2.

69. Fernandez to D. Clifford Crummey, n.d. CALC Records, ser. 2, box 8; Brian [Drolet] to Dick [Fernandez], February 17, 1971, CALC Records, ser. 5, box 2.

70. Lyle W. Grosjean to Fernandez, July 20, 1971, CALC Records, ser. 5, box 2.

71. Brian [Drolet] to Dick [Fernandez], February 17, 1971, CALC Records, ser. 5, box 2.

72. Fernandez to Brian Drolet, July 6, 1971, CALC Records, ser. 5, box 2.

73. John Pairman Brown to Trudi Young, October 5, 1971; "Ecumenical Peace Institute New Funding Proposal: May 1972"; "Résumé, John Pairman Brown," n.d., CALC Records, ser. 5, box 2.

74. "The Ecumenical Peace Institute: Prospectus 1973," n.d.; Steve Hart, "Proposal for Linkage Funding for 1974," October 28, 1973; "Minutes of Pacific Region CALC Conference," March 29–31, 1974; "Ecumenical Peace Institute New Funding Proposal: May 1972," CALC Records, ser. 5, box 2.

75. Kittlaus interview.

76. Ibid.; "Steps in Field and Honeywell Campaign Development Since Ann Arbor Planning, 1971," n.d., CALC Records, ser. 1, box 1.

77. "Steps in Field and Honeywell Campaign Development Since Ann Arbor Planning, 1971," n.d., CALC Records, ser. 1, box 1.

78. Webber interview.

79. Berger, "Indochina and the American Conscience."

80. Neuhaus interview.

81. Kittlaus interview.

82. Fuller interview; Selvaggio interview.

83. R. L. Shackelford to C. D. Brennan, August 31, 1971; Director, FBI to SAC, Albany, September 2, 1971, FBI Files.

84. Fernandez to Alan Geyer, July 9, 1971, CALC Records, ser. 2, box 9.

85. Fernandez to Jerry Gordon, July 22, 1971, CALC Records, ser. 2, box 9.

86. J. B. Engelstad to Mr. Cleveland, January 26, 1972, FBI Files.

87. Fernandez, "The Air War," p. 1404; Richard Fernandez and Trudi Young to Clergy and Laymen Concerned, November 1, 1971, CALC Records, ser. 3, box 15; "The Dying Continues."

88. Washington Field to Director, Philadelphia, November 11, 1971, FBI Files.

89. Washington Field to Director, New York, November 9, 1971, FBI Files.

90. SAC, WFO [Special Agent in Charge, Washington Field Office] to Director, FBI, December 28, 1971, FBI Files.

91. Fernandez, "The Air War"; Religious News Service press release, "Anti-War, Academy Officials Set Talks: Air Force Rejected 'Mandatory Formation,' " November 5, 1971, CALC Records, ser. 3, box 1; Denver to Director, November 15, 1971, FBI Files.

92. Fernandez, "The Air War"; Religious News Service press release, "Anti-War, Academy Officials Set Talks: Air Force Rejected 'Mandatory Formation' " November 5, 1971, CALC Records, ser. 3, box 1; Denver to Director, November 15, 1971, FBI Files.

93. "Clergy and Laymen Concerned," January 12, 1972, FBI Files.

94. Fernandez, "The Air War."

95. DeBenedetti, *Peace Reform*, p. 192; Halstead, *Out Now!* p. 655.

96. "Committee of Liaison with Families of Servicemen Detained in North Vietnam," January 20, 1972, FBI Files; "UCC Minister Brings Letters from American POWs."

97. "Help Unsell the War," n.d., CALC Records, ser. 3, box 15.

98. " 'Unsell the War' Ads Are Unveiled"; "End the War Ads Available for Use on Local Stations"; "New Ads Offer Alternatives to 'Selling of the Pentagon' "; "CALC Takes Lead in Unsell Campaign."

99. Fernandez interview.

100. *An Occasional Memo,* March 20, 1972, CALC Records, ser. 4, box 1.

101. Radio Commercials to Unsell the War," n.d., Records of Friends Committee on National Legislation, box 17; *American Report,* November 5, 1981, p. 8-S; "Unsell TV Spot Wins Add Award."

102. "Trying to Level Scales"; Washington *Post,* November 10, 1970, p. A19; "Minutes of Program Committee," October 14, 1971, CALC Records, ser. 1, box 1.

103. "American Report Radio," n.d., CALC Records, ser. 1, box 1; "Trying to Level Scales."

104. "American Report Radio," n.d.; "Minutes of Steering Committee," September 11, 1972; "Minutes of Communications Committee," November 3, 1972, CALC Records, ser. 1, box 1.

105. "Minutes of Finance Committee," October 18, 1972, CALC Records, ser. 1, box 2; "Minutes of Steering Committee," November 14, 1972, CALC Records, ser. 1, box 1.

6. "AGAINST THEIR MACHINES WE HAVE ONLY . . . A SLENDER PRAYER": THE CAMPAIGN FOR CORPORATE RESPONSIBILITY

1. *An Occasional Memo,* May 10, 1972, CALC Records, ser. 4, box 1; "Minneapolis, Minnesota 'Clergy and Laymen Concerned,' " June 29, 1972, FBI Files.

2. "Clergy and Laymen Concerned About Vietnam," June 19, 1970, CALC Records, ser. 3, box 3; Fernandez to David Hunter, August 14, 1970, CALC Records, ser. 3, box 22; Fernandez to Program Committee Members, September 17, 1970, CALC Records, ser. 1, box 1.

3. Fernandez to Muriel C. Hyman, May 16, 1968, CALC Records, ser. 2, box 5.

4. Rose, "The Coming Confrontation on the Church's War Investments."

5. "Religious Institutions and Corporate Responsibility," n.d., CALC Records, ser. 4, box 1; *An Occasional Memo,* May 10, 1972, CALC Records, ser. 4, box 1; "Minneapolis, Minnesota 'Clergy and Laymen Concerned,' " June 29, 1972, FBI Files.

6. "Religious Institutions and Corporate Responsibility," n.d., CALC Records, ser. 4, box 1.

7. *Ibid.*

8. "CALC vs. Honeywell"; "Update on Church and Corporate Responsibility"; "Program and the Question of Integration—Dick Fernandez and Barbara Armentrout," October 16, 1972, CALC Records, ser. 1, box 2; "Report of (censored), New York, New York, 'Clergy and Laymen Concerned,' " April 27, 1972, FBI Files.

9. SAC [Special Agent in Charge], Charlotte [N.C.] to Director, FBI, February 16, 1972, FBI Files; Barbara Armentrout, Dick Fernandez, Trudi Young to CALC Field Staff and Local Groups, February 23, 1971, CALC Records, ser. 3, box 16; "The Air War and Church Investments," *An Occasional Memo,* March 20, 1972, CALC Records, ser. 4, box 1.

10. Armentrout, Fernandez, Young to CALC Field Staff and Local Groups, February 23, 1971, CALC Records, ser. 3, box 16.

11. "Continuing the Honeywell Campaign," November 6, 1973, CALC Records, ser. 1, box 2.

12. Armentrout, Fernandez, Young to CALC Field Staff and Local Groups, February 23, 1971, CALC Records, ser. 3, box 16.

13. "Continuing the Honeywell Campaign," November 6, 1973; "Notes from the Ad Hoc AFSC-CALC Conference #2 in Minneapolis, April 26–27, 1973, CALC Records, ser. 1, box 2; "The Air War and Church Investments," *An Occasional Memo,* March 20, 1972, CALC Records, ser. 4, box 1.

14. Fernandez interview.

15. "Steps in Field and Honeywell Campaign Development Since Ann Arbor Planning, 1971," n.d., CALC Records, ser. 1, box 1.

16. "CALC Circulating NARMIC Slide Show"; Kittlaus interview.

17. "Honeywell Responds"; "Honeywell Campaign: An Update"; "Minneapolis, Minnesota 'Clergy and Laymen Concerned,' " June 29, 1972, FBI Files; "CALC vs. Honeywell."

18. Kittlaus interview; "The Air War and Church Investments," *An Occasional Memo,* March 20, 1972, CALC Records, ser. 4, box 1.

19. *An Occasional Memo,* May 10, 1972, CALC Records, ser. 4, box 1; "Minneapolis, Minnesota 'Clergy and Laymen Concerned,' " June 29, 1972, FBI Files.

20. *An Occasional Memo,* May 10, 1972, CALC Records, ser. 4, box 1; "Minneapolis, Minnesota 'Clergy and Laymen Concerned,' " June 29, 1972, FBI Files. Honeywell stopped making guava bombs because the Air Force stopped buying them, as they were testing even more destructive bombs. *Business Week,* April 15, 1972, pp. 42–43.

21. *An Occasional Memo,* May 10, 1972, CALC Records, ser. 4, box 1.

22. "Honeywell Responds," *American Report,* May 5, 1972, p. 9; "Should Honeywell Stop Making Munitions? A Response from Clergy and Laymen Concerned to Honeywell," July 1972, CALC Records, ser. 3, box 23.

23. *An Occasional Memo,* May 10, 1972, CALC Records, ser. 4, box 1.

24. "CALC Corporate Campaign Aimed at Major Military Contractors"; SAC, Memphis to Acting Director, FBI, May 23, 1972, FBI Files; "Don't Buy Bombs When You Buy Bread," n.d., Peace Movement Collection.

25. Houston to Acting Director, May 18, 1972, FBI Files.

26. "Steps in Field and Honeywell Campaign Development Since Ann Arbor Planning, 1971," n.d., CALC Records, ser. 1, box 1.

27. "Local Groups Press Honeywell to 'Cease and Desist' "; "Minutes of Steering Committee," September 11, 1972, CALC Records, ser. 1, box 1; "Minutes of Program Committee," May 3, 1973, CALC Records, ser. 1, box 2; *An Occasional Memo,* n.d., CALC Records, ser. 4, box 1.

28. See file folder "Honeywell Campaign, CALC Reports (1972–1973)," CALC

Records, ser. 3, box 23; Los Angeles to Director, April 18, 1972, FBI Files; Cleveland to Director, April 26, 1972, FBI Files; "Louisville, Kentucky 'Clergy and Laymen Concerned of Kentuckiana (CLCK) Internal Security—Revolutionary Activities.' " October 6, 1972, FBI Files; "Columbia, South Carolina 'Clergy and Laymen Concerned, South Carolina Chapter, Greenville, South Carolina,' " March 9, 1973, FBI Files.

29. Mollie Babize, "The Honeywell Campaign: A Case Study of Boston Area Clergy and Laity Concerned," June 28, 1972, CALC Records, ser. 5, box 6.

30. Kernodle, "Update on Honeywell."

31. Babize, "The Honeywell Campaign," June 28, 1972, CALC Records, ser. 5, box 6.

32. *Ibid.*

33. *Ibid.*

34. *Ibid.*

35. *Ibid.*

36. *Ibid.;* "Boston Area Clergy and Laity Concerned: Program Outline: Honeywell Campaign," November 30, 1972, CALC Records, ser. 5, box 5.

37. "Reports on October 25th: Honeywell, Nixon, and the War," October 27, 1972, CALC Records, ser. 5, box 5.

38. *Ibid.*

39. *Ibid.*

40. John Cupples, "Regional Field Staff Report," December 27, 1973; Paul Kittlaus, "Regional Field Staff Reflections: 1973"; Duane Gall and Tom Rauch, "Evaluation of RFS Program," December 19, 1973, CALC Records, ser. 3, box 19.

41. "Local Groups Press Honeywell to 'Cease and Desist' "; Trudi [Young] to Barbara [Armentrout] and Dick [Fernandez], July 10, 1972, CALC Records, ser. 5, box 7; Joseph Miko to Honeywell, Inc., December 20, 1972, CALC Records, ser. 5, box 1; "Honeywell: New Pressure," *American Report,* January 1–15, 1973, p. 21.

42. "Program and the Question of Integration—Dick Fernandez & Barbara Armentrout," October 16, 1972, CALC Records, ser. 1, box 2; John Pairman Brown, "Presentation to Northern California Ecumenical Council," October 26, 1972, CALC Records, ser. 5, box 2; "Honeywell Campaign: An Update"; Kernodle, "Update on Honeywell."

43. "Program and the Question of Integration—Dick Fernandez & Barbara Armentrout," October 16, 1972, CALC Records, ser. 1, box 2.

44. "Notes for the Program and Steering Committees," January 9, 1973, CALC Records, ser. 1, box 2; "Honeywell: New Pressure," *American Report,* January 1–15, 1973, p. 21; Kernodle, "Update on Honeywell."

45. "Inventory of Honeywell Campaign Activities," n.d., CALC Records, ser. 1, box 2.

46. "Notes for the Program and Steering Committees," January 9, 1973, CALC Records, ser. 1, box 2.

47. "Notes for the Program and Steering Committees," January 9, 1973, CALC Records, ser. 1, box 2; "Report on General Program from Trudi Young and Barbara Armentrout," February 18, 1973, CALC Records, ser. 1, box 2.

48. "Interfaith Council for Peace," n.d.; "Report of the Interfaith Council for Peace Meeting," January 11, 1973; Form letter from Barbara Fuller and David Houseman, March 23, 1973, CALC Records, ser. 5, box 7.

49. "Ann Arbor: Boycott Honeywell?"

50. Interfaith Council for Peace press release, March 26, 1973; Glen Harris, "City

Boycott of Firm Urged," Ann Arbor *News,* March 21, 1973, CALC Records, ser. 5, box 7.

51. "Ann Arbor Boycotts Honeywell"; "Ann Arbor Accepts Nuremberg Obligations," Ann Arbor *News,* April 9, 1973, CALC Records, ser. 5, box 7; Barbara Fuller to Richard Falk and Eric Prokosch, March 30, 1973, CALC Records, ser. 5, box 7.

52. Interfaith Council for Peace press release, April 23, 1973. CALC Records, ser. 5, box 7.

53. Barbara Fuller to James Binger, May 18, 1973, CALC Records, ser. 5, box 7.

54. New York *Times,* March 11, 1973, p. 25.

55. "Minutes of Steering Committee," November 14, 1972, CALC Records, ser. 1, box 1.

56. Rieke, "Honeywell's Annual Meeting."

57. Minneapolis *Tribune,* April 26, 1973, p. 12A; *An Occasional Memo,* May 30, 1973, CALC Records, ser. 4, box 1; Rieke, "Honeywell's Annual Meeting," pp. 7, 15; Claire Gorfinkel, "Report on Honeywell Shareholders' Meeting, Minneapolis, Minnesota, April 25, '73 and CALC-AFSC evaluation meetings," May 15, 1973, CALC Records, ser. 5, box 2.

58. Minneapolis *Tribune,* April 26, 1973, p. 12A; *An Occasional Memo,* May 30, 1973, CALC Records, ser. 4, box 1; Rieke, "Honeywell's Annual Meeting," pp. 7, 15; Gorfinkel, "Report on Honeywell Stockholders' Meeting," May 15, 1973, CALC Records, ser. 5, box 2.

59. "Conference #1—Wednesday, April 25," April 25, 1973, CALC Records, ser. 1, box 2; Rieke, "Honeywell's Annual Meeting," pp. 7, 15; Gorfinkel, "Report on Honeywell Shareholders' Meeting," May 15, 1973, CALC Records, ser. 5, box 2.

60. Gorfinkel, "Report on Honeywell Shareholders' Meeting," May 15, 1973, CALC Records, ser. 5, box 2.

61. "Conference #1—Wednesday, April 25, 1973; "Notes from the Ad Hoc AFSC-CALC Conference #2 in Minneapolis, April 26–27, 1973," CALC Records, ser. 1, box 2.

62. *An Occasional Memo,* May 30, 1973, CALC Records, ser. 4, box 1; Minneapolis *Tribune,* April 26, 1973, p. 12A.

63. "Minutes of Program Committee," June 13, 1973, CALC Records, ser. 1, box 2.

64. "Continuing the Honeywell Campaign," November 6, 1973, CALC Records, ser. 1, box 2; Farren, "The Honeywell Corporation Learns About Nuremburg"; "AFSC, CALC Launch 'Peace Conversion' Drive Against B-1 Bomber."

65. Farren, "The Honeywell Corporation Learns About Nuremberg," pp. 13, 15.

66. New York *Times,* March 15, 1974, p. 45.

67. *Ibid.*

68. Kittlaus interview.

7. "A TIME FOR WAR, A TIME FOR PEACE": JANUARY 1972 TO MAY 1975

1. Fernandez to Robert Cleland, January 31, 1972, CALC Records, ser. 2, box 10.

2. "Ecumenical Meeting of Churchmen Urges End to Vietnam War."

3. "Emergency Ministry Initiated for Services to Veterans"; "Presbyterian Group to Help Returning Vietnam Servicemen"; "Face-Saving or Life-Saving"; Ranck, "The Atlanta Pinata"; "A Message to United Presbyterians"; Sharp, "Denver Wrap-Up."

4. Herring, *America's Longest War,* p. 248.

5. "The Bombing of America."

6. Washington *Post,* May 17, 1972, pp. B1, B7.

7. New York *Times,* May 17, 1972, p. 20; Kittlaus interview.

8. McGraw, "Unselling of the Pentagon"; Branfman, "Unselling the Air War"; " 'Unsell the War' Ads"; *An Occasional Memo,* March 20, 1972, CALC Records, ser. 4, box 1.

9. "Minutes of Steering Committee," September 11, 1972; "Minutes of Communications Committee," November 3, 1972, CALC Records, ser. 1, box 1.

10. "Charlotte, North Carolina 'Clergy and Laymen Concerned,' " February 16, 1972, FBI Files; Report from New York, N.Y. "Clergy and Laymen Concerned," April 27, 1972, FBI Files.

11. "Steering Committee Retreat," July 20–22, 1972, CALC Records, ser. 1, box 1.

12. Zaroulis and Sullivan, *Who Spoke Up?* pp. 393–94.

13. New York *Times,* September 17, 1972, p. 12E.

14. Kittlaus interview.

15. "Minutes of Steering Committee," September 9, 1972, CALC Records, ser. 1, box 1.

16. Luce, "How CALC Humanized the War"; "CALC Chapters and the National Office: Conflict or Symbiosis?"; "Steering Committee Retreat," July 20–22, 1972, CALC Records, ser. 1, box 1.

17. Ron Freund, "Midwest Regional Report," December 27, 1973, CALC Records, ser. 3, box 19; Paul Kittlaus, "Regional Field Staff Reflections," 1973; Duane Gall and Tom Rauch, "Evaluation of RFS Program," December 19, 1973, CALC Records, ser. 3, box 19; "EPI/CALC Minutes of Board Meeting," October 18, 1973, CALC Records, ser. 5, box 2.

18. "Notes for the Program and Steering Committees," January 9, 1973; "Minutes of Program Committee," May 3, 1973, CALC Records, ser. 1, box 2.

19. Fernandez to Steering Committee, n.d.; "Program and the Question of Integration—Dick Fernandez & Barbara Armentrout," October 16, 1972, CALC Records, ser. 1, box 2.

20. Halstead, *Out Now!* pp. 694–700; Herring, *America's Longest War,* p. 254.

21. "Religious Leaders Assail Escalation of Vietnam War," December 22, 1972, Records of SANE, Box PB 1; Maurer, "Religious Convocation for Peace." See file folder "Washington D.C. Convocation (January 3–4, 1973)," CALC Records, ser. 3, box 19.

22. Novak, "Rights and Wrongs."

23. "New York Office 'Clergy and Laity Concerned' Internal Security-Activities," April 9, 1973, FBI Files.

24. DeBenedetti, "A CIA Analysis of the Anti–Vietnam War Movement."

25. "Indochina: The Aftermath," February 1973, CALC Records, ser. 5, box 7.

26. "Amnesty Proposal Clergy and Laity Concerned, May 1, 1973–December 31, 1973," n.d., CALC Records, ser. 3, box 25; "National Program Report to the Steering Committee," May 3, 1973, CALC Records, ser. 1, box 2.

27. "Minutes of Program Committee," January 9, 1973, CALC Records, ser. 1, box 2; "Minutes of Interreligious Task Force on Amnesty," March 20, 1973, CALC Records, ser. 3, box 25; "National Program Report to the Steering Committee," May 3, 1973, CALC Records, ser. 1, box 2; "Amnesty Proposal Clergy and Laity Concerned, May 1, 1973–December 31, 1973," n.d., CALC Records, ser. 3, box 25.

28. "National Program Report to the Steering Committee," May 3, 1973, CALC Records, ser. 1, box 2; "Amnesty Week Organizing Packet," n.d., CALC Records,

ser. 3, box 25. See file folder "Walk of Concern, Press Conference (September 1974), CALC Records, ser. 3, box 35.

29. "Regional Field Staff Report," 1973; "SC/CALC Newsletter," October 1973, CALC Records, ser. 5, box 1.

30. "SC/CALC Newsletter," October 1973, CALC Records, ser. 5, box 1; "Regional Field Staff Report," 1973, CALC Records, ser. 5, box 1.

31. John Cupples, "Regional Field Staff Report," December 17, 1973; Barbara Fuller, "Regional Field Staff Program," 1973; Michael Riesch, "Regional Field Staff Report," 1973, CALC Records, ser. 3, box 19.

32. *Minnesota Report,* September 1973, CALC Records, ser. 5, box 8; Pat Camp, "Year-old Amnesty Group Reports Membership Gain," *Minneapolis Tribune,* June 30, 1974, copy in CALC Records, ser. 5, box 8; "Minnesota Clergy & Laymen Concerned Amnesty Campaign, Statement of Philosophy," n.d.; "Minnesotans Who Need Amnesty," February 25, 1974; unidentified newspaper article, copy in CALC Records, ser. 5, box 8.

33. *Minnesota Report,* September 1973, CALC Records, ser. 5, box 8.

34. *Ibid.*

35. *Ibid.*

36. *Minnesota Report,* September 1973; "Amnesty Campaign: Minnesota Clergy and Laity Concerned," May 1974, CALC Records, ser. 5, box 8.

37. *Minnesota Report,* September 1973; "What Have We Done So Far?" n.d., CALC Records, ser. 5, box 8.

38. Camp, "Year-old Amnesty Group," June 30, 1974, copy in CALC Records, ser. 5, box 8.

39. "Amnesty Action Idea: Organizing Within Electoral Politics," n.d., CALC Records, ser. 5, box 8.

40. *Ibid.*

41. "The Amnesty Issue"; Richard Fernandez to All Churches in the Pennsylvania Southeast Conference of the United Church of Christ, April 3, 1974, CALC Records, ser. 3, box 26.

42. "Program and the Question of Integration—Dick Fernandez and Barbara Armentrout," October 16, 1972; "Minutes of Program Committee," January 9, 1973; "Notes for the Program and Steering Committees," January 9, 1973, CALC Records, ser. 1, box 2.

43. John Cupples, "Regional Field Staff Report," December 17, 1973, CALC Records, ser. 3, box 19.

44. Steve Hart, "Proposal for Linkage Funding for 1974," October 28, 1973; Dennis Allen and Sandra Farley, "EPI Project Proposal: U.S. Military Manpower Task Force," n.d.; Dennis Allen, "Ecumenical Peace Institute Communicator," vol. 1, no. 4, n.d., CALC Records, ser. 5, box 2.

45. "Minutes of EPI Military Manpower Taskforce," August 9, 1973, CALC Records, ser. 5, box 2.

46. Richard R. Fernandez to American Deserters Committee, January 25, 1973, CALC Records, ser. 2, box 11; "Minutes of Program Committee," May 3, 1973, CALC Records, ser. 1, box 2.

47. "Notes for the Program and Steering Committees," January 9, 1973, CALC Records, ser. 1, box 2; Cox interview.

48. "Indochina Conference Report," October 26–28, 1973, Records of Friends Committee on National Legislation, Box 17.

49. Richard Van Voorhis to National Board, Staff of SANE, March 13, 1974; "CALC-SANE Basic Data," December 1973, Records of SANE, Box PB 1.

50. Woodward, "A Foretaste of Eternity."

51. "Minutes of Steering Committee," June 25, 1973, CALC Records, ser. 1, box 2; Fernandez interview.

52. Brown interview.

53. Tom Rauch to Rick [Boardman], July 17, 1974, CALC Records, ser. 5, box 3; John Cupples to All Persons Concerned in CALC Network, March 20, 1974, CALC Records, ser. 5, box 6.

54. John Cupples, "Report of the Regional Field Staff," December 12, 1973; Michael Riesch, "Regional Field Staff Report," 1973; Barbara Fuller, "Regional Field Staff Program," 1973; Paul Kittlaus, "Regional Field Staff Reflections," 1973, CALC Records, ser. 3, box 19.

55. "Luce Named CALC Director"; Webber, "CALC: The Anti-War Years"; Luce, "How CALC Humanized the War."

56. Webber interview; "Press release," January 9, 1975, CALC Records, ser. 3, box 35; transcript of the Reasoner Report, January 11, 1975, CALC Records, ser. 1, box 2.

57. See file folder "The Convocation (January 6–7, 1975)"; Press release, March 12, 1975, CALC Records, ser. 3, box 35.

58. Luce, "How CALC Humanized the War."

59. Interviews with Kittlaus, Bennett, Brickner, Neuhaus, and Webber.

60. Collins, "CALC Transformed"; Blast, "Conscience Comes to the Classroom"; Brockopp and Freund, "No Nukes in the Windy City"; *CALC Report* (August–October 1985), 11:32.

8. "TOGETHER IN A WORTHWHILE STRUGGLE"

1. Gray, "To March or Not to March."

2. *Ibid.*

3. These sentiments are reflected in interviews with Fernandez, Cox, Fuller, and Coffin.

4. Mandelbaum, "Vietnam: The Television War"; Schreiber, "Anti-War Demonstrations"; Burstein, "Senate Voting on the Vietnam War"; Berkowitz, "The Impact of Anti-Vietnam Demonstrations."

5. Lunch and Sperlich, "American Public Opinion and the War in Vietnam"; Converse and Schuman, " 'Silent Majorities' and the Vietnam War"; Hahn, "Correlates of Public Sentiment About War"; Verba, et al., "Public Opinion and the War in Vietnam."

6. O'Brien, "The Anti-War Movement and the War"; Walzer, "Peace Movement"; Katz, "Peace Liberals."

7. Schuman, "Two Sources of Antiwar Sentiment"; Converse and Schuman, " 'Silent Majorities' "; Mandelbaum, "Vietnam: The Television War"; Katz, "Peace Liberals."

8. Converse and Schuman, " 'Silent Majorities' "; Walzer, "Peace Movement"; Schreiber, "Anti-War Demonstrations and American Public Opinion"; Erskine, "The Polls: Freedom of Speech"; Robinson, "Public Reaction to Political Protest"; Schuman, "Two Sources of Antiwar Sentiment," pp. 516–17.

9. Brickner interview.

10. Kittlaus interview.

11. "CALC Chapters and the National Office: Conflict or Symbiosis?"

12. Gelb, "Dissenting on Consensus."

13. Charles DeBenedetti and Charles Chatfield, *An American Ordeal,* pp. 355–56.

14. "Webber to Martin: Our Country Fuels This Evil War," *American Report*, April 15, 1974, p. 10.

15. Small, *Johnson, Nixon, and the Doves*, pp. 230–31.

16. Coffin interview.

17. Gitlin, "Seizing History"; Small, "The Impact of the Antiwar Movement on Lyndon Johnson"; Nixon, *RN*, esp. pp. 434–41, 493–97, 616.

18. Levering, *The Public and American Foreign Policy*, pp. 130–36; Mandelbaum, "Vietnam: The Television War"; O'Brien, "The Anti-War Movement."

19. Small, *Johnson, Nixon, and the Doves*, pp. 224–28.

20. DeBenedetti and Chatfield, *An American Ordeal*, p. 356.

21. Charles DeBenedetti, "On the Significance of Citizen Peace Activism," p. 14.

22. Brown interview; Brickner interview.

23. Fernandez to Harry Applewhite, April 2, 1971, CALC Records, ser. 2, box 8.

24. Cox interview.

25. Fuller interview.

BIBLIOGRAPHY

MANUSCRIPT COLLECTIONS

Business Executives Move for Vietnam Peace. Swarthmore College Peace Collection, Swarthmore, Pennsylvania.

Clergy and Laity Concerned. (CALC Records.) Swarthmore College Peace Collection, Swarthmore, Pennsylvania.

Episcopal Peace Fellowship. Swarthmore College Peace Collection, Swarthmore, Pennsylvania.

Federal Bureau of Investigation Files on Clergy and Laity Concerned. (FBI Files.) University of Kentucky Library Special Collections, Lexington, Kentucky.

Friends Committee on National Legislation. Swarthmore College Peace Collection, Swarthmore, Pennsylvania.

A. J. Muste Papers. Swarthmore College Peace Collection, Swarthmore, Pennsylvania.

Peace Movement Collection. Gettysburg College Library, Gettysburg, Pennsylvania.

Periodicals Collection. Swarthmore College Peace Collection, Swarthmore, Pennsylvania.

A Quaker Action Group. Swarthmore College Peace Collection, Swarthmore, Pennsylvania.

SANE, A Citizens' Organization for a Sane World. Swarthmore College Peace Collection, Swarthmore, Pennsylvania.

Hugh Scott Papers. University of Virginia Library, Charlottesville, Virginia.

Vietnam Summer. Swarthmore College Peace Collection, Swarthmore, Pennsylvania.

White House Central Files—Name File. The Lyndon Baines Johnson Library, Austin, Texas.

White House Central Files—Subject File. The Lyndon Baines Johnson Library, Austin, Texas.

PERSONAL COMMUNICATIONS

Bennett, John C. Telephone interview, May 21, 1985.

Brickner, Balfour. Telephone interview, August 21, 1985; August 22, 1985.

Brown, Robert McAfee. Telephone interview, August 12, 1985.
Coffin, William Sloane. Telephone interview, September 16, 1988.
Cox, Harvey. Telephone interview, September 22, 1988.
Cupples, John. Telephone interview, August 16, 1988.
Elston, Gerhard. Personal interview, Philadelphia, Pennsylvania, May 10, 1985.
Fernandez, Richard. Personal interview, Philadelphia, Pennsylvania, May 10, 1985.
   Telephone interview, September 10, 1988.
Fuller, Barbara. Telephone interview, September 13, 1988.
Kittlaus, Paul. Telephone interview, May 23, 1985.
Neuhaus, Richard John. Telephone interview, August 15, 1985.
Rauch, Thomas. Telephone interview, September 7, 1988.
Selvaggio, Joseph. Telephone interview, August 15, 1988.
Tobin, Mary Luke. Telephone interview, May 24, 1985.
Webber, George W. Telephone interview, May 30, 1985.

BOOKS

Andrews, Bruce. *Public Constraint and American Policy in Vietnam.* Beverly Hills, Calif.:
   Sage, 1976.
Arlen, Michael. *The Living Room War.* New York: Viking, 1969.
Au, William A. *The Cross, the Flag, and the Bomb: American Catholics Debate War and
   Peace, 1960–1983.* Westport, Conn.: Greenwood Press, 1985.
Baritz, Loren, *Backfire.* New York: Ballantine, 1985.
Baskir, Lawrence M., and William A. Strauss. *Chance and Circumstance: The Draft, the
   War, and the Vietnam Generation.* New York: Vintage Books, 1978.
Bennett, John C. *The Radical Imperative: From Theology to Social Ethics.* Philadelphia:
   Westminster Press, 1975.
Berger, Peter L., and Richard John Neuhaus. *Movement and Revolution.* Garden City,
   N.Y.: Doubleday, 1970.
Berrigan, Daniel. *To Dwell in Peace.* San Francisco: Harper and Row, 1987.
Braestrup, Peter. *Big Story: How the American Press and Television Reported and Interpreted
   the Crisis of Tet 1968 in Vietnam and Washington.* Rev. ed. New Haven: Yale
   University Press, 1983.
Brown, Robert McAfee. *Creative Dislocation—The Movement of Grace.* Nashville:
   Abingdon, 1980.
—— *Frontiers for the Church Today.* New York: Oxford University Press, 1973.
—— *Religion and Violence: A Primer for White Americans.* Philadelphia: Westminster
   Press, 1973.
Brown, Robert McAfee, Abraham J. Heschel, and Michael Novak. *Vietnam: Crisis of
   Conscience.* New York: Association Press, Behrman House, and Herder and Herder,
   1967.
Bryan, C.D.B. *Friendly Fire.* New York: Bantam, 1976.
Burns, Richard Dean, and Milton Leitenberg. *The Wars in Vietnam, Cambodia, and
   Laos, 1945–1982: A Bibliographic Guide.* Santa Barbara, Calif.: ABC-Clio, 1983.
Carroll, Jackson W., Douglas W. Johnson, and Martin E. Marty. *Religion in America:
   1950 to the Present.* San Francisco: Harper and Row, 1979.
Carson, Clayborne. *In Struggle: SNCC and the Black Awakening of the 1960s.* Cam-
   bridge: Harvard University Press, 1981.
Charlton, Michael, and Anthony Moncrieff. *Many Reasons Why: The American Involve-
   ment in Vietnam.* New York: Hill and Wang, 1978.

Chatfield, Charles. *For Peace and Justice: Pacifism in America, 1914–1941.* Knoxville: University of Tennessee Press, 1971.

Clergy and Laymen Concerned About Vietnam. *In the Name of America.* Annandale, VA.: Turnpike Press, 1968.

Coffin, William Sloane, Jr. *Once to Every Man: A Memoir.* New York: Atheneum, 1977.

Coffin, William Sloane, Jr., and Morris I. Liebman. *Civil Disobedience: Aid or Hindrance to Justice?* Washington: American Enterprise Institute for Public Policy Research, 1972.

Cohen, Mitchell, and Dennis Hale. *The New Student Left.* Boston: Beacon Press, 1966.

Cox, Harvey Gallagher. *Just As I Am.* Nashville: Abingdon, 1983.

——, ed. *Military Chaplains: From a Religious Military to a Military Religion.* New York: American Report Press, 1972.

DeBenedetti, Charles. *An American Ordeal: The Antiwar Movement of the Vietnam Era.* Charles Chatfield, assisting author. Syracuse, N.Y.: Syracuse University Press, 1990.

—— *The Peace Reform in American History.* Bloomington: Indiana University Press, 1980.

Dellinger, Dave. *More Power Than We Know: The People's Movement Toward Democracy.* Garden City, N.Y.: Anchor Press/Doubleday, 1975.

Emerson, Gloria. *Winners and Losers.* New York: Random House, 1976.

Ferber, Michael, and Staughton Lynd. *The Resistance.* Boston: Beacon Press, 1971.

Finn, James. *Protest: Pacifism and Politics.* New York: Random House, 1967.

——, ed. *A Conflict of Loyalties: The Case for Selective Conscientious Objection.* New York: Pegasus, 1968.

—— *Conscience and Command: Justice and Discipline in the Military.* New York: Random House, 1971.

Fisher, Randall M. *Rhetoric and American Democracy: Black Protest Through Vietnam Dissent.* Lanham, Md.: University Press of America, 1985.

Fox, Richard Wightman. *Reinhold Niebuhr: A Biography.* New York: Pantheon, 1985.

Fray, Harold R., Jr. *Conflict and Change in the Church.* Philadelphia: Pilgrim Press, 1969.

—— *The Pain and Joy of Ministry.* Philadelphia: Pilgrim Press, 1972.

Gallup, George. *The Gallup Poll: Public Opinion, 1935–1971.* New York: Random House, 1972.

Garrow, David J. *Bearing the Cross: Martin Luther King, Jr., and the Southern Christian Leadership Conference.* New York: William Morrow, 1986.

—— *The FBI and Martin Luther King, Jr..* New York: Penguin, 1981.

Gitlin, Todd. *The Sixties: Years of Hope, Days of Rage.* Toronto: Bantam, 1987.

Hadden, Jeffrey K. *The Gathering Storm in the Churches.* Garden City, N.Y.: Doubleday, 1969.

Halstead, Fred, *Out Now! A Participant's Account of the American Movement Against the Vietnam War.* New York: Monad Press, 1978.

Hayes, Thomas Lee. *American Deserters in Sweden.* New York: Association Press, 1971.

Heath, G. Louis, ed. *Mutiny Does Not Happen Lightly: The Literature of the American Resistance to the Vietnam War.* Metuchen, N.J.: Scarecrow Press, 1976.

Hero, Alfred O., Jr. *American Religious Groups View Foreign Policy: Trends in Rank-and-File Opinion, 1937–1969.* Durham, N.C.: Duke University Press, 1973.

Herring, George C. *America's Longest War: The United States and Vietnam, 1950–1975.* Rev. ed. New York: Knopf, 1986.

Hoffman, Paul. *Moratorium: An American Protest.* New York: Tower, 1970.

Horowitz, Irving Louis. *The Struggle Is the Message: The Organization and Ideology of the Anti-War Movement*. Berkeley: Glendessary Press, 1970.

Jacquet, Constant H., Jr., ed. *Yearbook of American Churches*. New York: Council Press, 1970.

Karnow, Stanley. *Vietnam: A History*. New York: Viking Press, 1983.

Katz, Milton S. *Ban the Bomb: A History of SANE, the Committee for a Sane Nuclear Policy, 1957–1985*. Westport, Conn.: Greenwood Press, 1986.

Keniston, Kenneth. *Young Radicals: Notes on Committed Youth*. New York: Harcourt, Brace, and World, 1968.

Killmer, Richard L., Robert S. Lecky, and Debrah S. Wiley. *They Can't Go Home Again*. Philadelphia: Pilgrim Press, 1971.

Kohn, Stephen M. *Jailed for Peace: The History of American Draft Law Violators, 1658–1985*. Westport, Conn.: Greenwood Press, 1986.

Lake, Anthony, ed. *The Vietnam Legacy*. New York: New York University Press, 1976.

Lewy, Guenter. *Peace and Revolution: The Moral Crisis of American Pacifism*. Grand Rapids, Mich.: William B. Eerdmans, 1988.

MacPherson, Myra. *Long Time Passing: Vietnam and the Haunted Generation*. Garden City, N.Y.: Doubleday, 1984.

Marty, Martin E. *By Way of Response*. Nashville: Abingdon, 1981.

—— *Pilgrims in Their Own Land*. Boston: Little, Brown, 1984.

—— *The Public Church*. New York: Crossroad, 1981.

Marty, Martin E., John G. Deedy, Jr., David Wolf Silverman, and Robert Lekachman. *The Religious Press in America*. Westport, Conn.: Greenwood Press, 1963.

Menashe, Louis, and Ronald Radosh, eds. *Teach-Ins: U.S.A.* New York: Praeger, 1967.

Moritz, Charles, ed. *Current Biography*. New York: H. H. Wilson, 1961.

Mueller, John E. *War, Presidents, and Public Opinion*. New York: Wiley, 1973.

Neuhaus, Richard John. *In Defense of People: Ecology and the Seduction of Radicalism*. New York: Macmillan, 1971.

—— *The Naked Public Square: Religion and Democracy in America*. Grand Rapids, Mich.: William B. Eerdmans, 1984.

Nixon, Richard. *RN: The Memoirs of Richard Nixon*. New York: Warner Books, 1978.

Oates, Stephen B. *Let the Trumpet Sound: The Life of Martin Luther King, Jr*. New York: Harper and Row, 1982.

Podhoretz, Norman. *Why We Were in Vietnam*. New York: Simon and Schuster, 1982.

Powers, Thomas. *The War at Home: Vietnam and the American People, 1964–1968*. New York: Grossman, 1973.

Quigley, Thomas E., ed. *American Catholics and Vietnam*. Grand Rapids, Mich.: William B. Eerdmans, 1968.

Reinitz, Richard. *Irony and Consciousness*. Cranbury, N.J.: Associated University Presses, 1980.

Robinson, Jo Ann Ooiman. *Abraham Went Out: A Biography of A. J. Muste*. Philadelphia: Temple University Press, 1981.

Sheehan, Neil, et al. *The Pentagon Papers as Published by the New York Times*. New York: Bantam, 1971.

Skolnick, Jerome H. *The Politics of Protest*. New York: Ballantine, 1969.

Small, Melvin. *Johnson, Nixon, and the Doves*. New Brunswick, N.J.: Rutgers University Press, 1988.

Stone, I. F. *In a Time of Torment*. New York: Random House, 1967.

Strout, Cushing. *The New Heavens and New Earth: Political Religion in America.* New York: Harper and Row, 1974.

Tobin, Mary Luke. *Hope is an Open Door.* Nashville: Abingdon, 1981.

Walker, Daniel, et al. *Rights in Conflict.* New York: Bantam, 1968.

Wittner, Lawrence S. *Rebels Against War: The American Peace Movement, 1933–1983.* Philadelphia: Temple University Press, 1984.

Zaroulis, Nancy and Gerald Sullivan. *Who Spoke Up? American Protest Against the War in Vietnam, 1963–1975.* Garden City, N.Y.: Doubleday, 1984.

ARTICLES AND ESSAYS

"Action at Atlanta." *Lutheran* (July 17, 1968), 6:5–8, 26–29.

"AFSC, CALC Launch 'Peace Conversion' Drive Against B-1 Bomber." *American Report,* January 21, 1974. p. 9.

"American Baptists at Seattle." *Crusader* (June 1969), 24:7.

"Amnesty As Reconciliation." *Christian Century* (November 24, 1977), 88:1371.

"The Amnesty Issue." *Episcopalian* (November 1973), 138:10.

"Ann Arbor: Boycott Honeywell?" *American Report,* March 26, 1973, pp. 16, 22.

"Ann Arbor Boycotts Honeywell." *American Report,* April 10, 1973, p. 20.

"Ann Arbor Conference Sets Agenda for Future." *American Report,* September 3, 1971, p. 7.

"Assembly Speaks on Indochina, Proxies; 'Receives' Balance of Church and Society Report." *Presbyterian Life* (June 15, 1970), 23:28–29.

"The Assembly Views War, Peace, Justice at Home and Abroad." *Presbyterian Life* (June 15, 1967), 20:25–27, 42.

Baer, Daniel J., and Victor F. Mosele. "Political and Religious Beliefs of Catholics and Attitudes Toward Involvement in the Vietnam War." *Journal of Psychology* (July 1971), 78:161–64.

Bailey, George. "Television War: Trends in Network Coverage of Vietnam 1965–1970." *Journal of Broadcasting* (Spring 1976), 20:147–58.

Balswick, Jack O. "Theology and Political Attitudes Among Clergymen." *Sociological Quarterly* (Summer 1970), 11:397–405.

"Battle of Conscience." *Newsweek* (November 15, 1965), 66:78.

Bennett, John C. "Christian Realism in Vietnam." *America* (April 30, 1966), 114:616–17.

—— "End the War Now!" *Christianity and Crisis* (October 27, 1969), 29:261–63.

—— "From Supporter of War in 1941 to Critic in 1966." *Christianity and Crisis* (February 21, 1966), 26:13–14.

—— "It Is Difficult to Be an American." *Christianity and Crisis* (July 25, 1966), 26:165–66.

—— "The Place of Civil Disobedience." *Christianity and Crisis* (December 25, 1967), 22:299–302.

—— "The President's Folly." *Christianity and Crisis* (May 11, 1970), 30:94–95.

—— "Questions About Vietnam." *Christianity and Crisis* (July 20, 1964), 24:141–42.

—— "Where Are We Headed in Vietnam?" *Christianity and Crisis* (March 8, 1965), 25:29–30.

Berger, Peter L. "Indochina and the American Conscience." *Commentary* (February, 1980), 69:29–39.

Berkowitz, William R. "The Impact of Anti-Vietnam Demonstrations Upon National Public Opinion and Military Indicators." *Social Science Research* (March 1973), 2:1–14.

"Berrigan." *New Yorker* (April 9, 1966), 42:34–35.

Blast, Diane Carol. "Conscience Comes to the Classroom." *Christian Century* (March 5, 1986), 103:239–40.

Blevins, Kent B. "Southern Baptist Attitudes Toward the Vietnam War in the Years 1965–1970." *Foundations* (July–September 1980), 23:231–44.

"The Bombing of America." *Christianity and Crisis* (May 15, 1972), 32:115.

Branfman, Fred. "Unselling the Air War." *American Report,* June 9, 1972, p. S1.

Brickner, Balfour, "On Calley . . . and Silence." *American Report,* May 28, 1971, p. 5.

—— "Vietnam and the Jewish Community." *Christian Century* (April 29, 1970), 87:531–34.

Brockopp, Jon, and Ron Freund. "No Nukes in the Windy City." *Progressive* (August 1986), 50:15–16.

Brown, Robert McAfee. "Benisons on Bennett." *Christian Century* (May 27, 1970), 87:663–64.

—— "The Church and Vietnam." *Commonweal* (October 13, 1967), 87:52–55.

—— "Dissent in the Great Society." *Christianity and Crisis* (May 15, 1967), 27:104.

—— "In Conscience, I Must Break the Law." *Look* (October 31, 1967), 31:48–52.

—— "An Open Letter to Spiro T. Agnew." *Christian Century* (October 14, 1970), 86:1213–17.

—— "An Open Letter to the U.S. Bishops." *Commonweal* (February 17, 1967), 85:547–49.

—— "Treating Dissent Seriously." *Christianity and Crisis* (April 18, 1966), 26:75–76.

—— "Vietnam: Crisis of Conscience." *Catholic World* (October 1967), 206:5–10.

Brown, Sam. "The Defeat of the Antiwar Movement." In Anthony Lake, ed., *The Vietnam Legacy,* pp. 120–27. New York: New York University Press, 1976.

Burstein, Paul. "Senate Voting on the Vietnam War, 1964–1973: From Hawk to Dove." *Journal of Political and Military Sociology* (Fall 1979), 7:271–82.

Burstein, Paul, and William Freudenburg. "Changing Public Policy: The Impact of Public Opinion, Antiwar Demonstrations, and War Costs on Senate Voting on Vietnam War Motions." *American Journal of Sociology* (July 1978), 84:99–122.

—— "Ending the Vietnam War: Components of Change in Senate Voting on Vietnam War Bills." *American Journal of Sociology* (March 1977), 82:991–1006.

Burton, Michael G. "Elite Disunity and Collective Protest: The Vietnam Case." *Journal of Political and Military Sociology* (Fall 1977), 5:169–183.

"Business — 'Internal' and 'External.' " *Christian* (November 17, 1968), 106:9–11.

"The Business of the Christian Church." *Christian* (October 5, 1969), 107:14–15.

"CALC Chapters and the National Office: Conflict or Symbiosis?" *CALC Report* (August/October, 1985), 11:14–16, 13.

"CALC Circulating NARMIC Slide Show." *American Report,* February 25, 1972, p. 7.

"CALC Corporate Campaign Aimed at Major Military Contractors." *American Report,* April 14, 1972, p. 12.

"CALC Renews Antiwar Push." *American Report,* September 3, 1971, pp. 1, 8.

"CALC Takes Lead in Unsell Campaign." *American Report,* November 5, 1971, p. 1S.

"CALC vs. Honeywell." *American Report,* March 24, 1972, p . 2.

"A Call to Resist Illegitimate Authority." *New Republic* (October 7, 1967), 157:34–35.

"Call to Vigil on Vietnam." *Christian Century* (May 12, 1965), 82:605.

"Catholic Bishops Speak Out on Vietnam, Birth Control." *Lutheran* (December 21, 1966), 4:24–25.

"CCSA Protests Bombing, Urges Negotiation." *United Church Herald* (September 1966), 9:32.

"CCSA Takes Stand on Vietnam." *United Church Herald* (April 1, 1965), 8:26.

"Church and Society." *Presbyterian Survey* (August 1968), 58:21–24.

"Church and Society Papers." *Presbyterian Survey* (June 1969), 59:19–24.

"Churches Asked to Provide Draft Counseling." *Presbyterian Life* (June 15, 1969), 22:14–15.

"Churches Continue to Call for Vietnam Peace." *Lutheran* (June 21, 1967), 5:24.

"Churches: Dimensions of Dissent." *Time* (January 26, 1968), 91:62.

"The Churches: 'What Should We Say?' " *Newsweek* (July 10, 1967), 70:81–82.

"Churchmen View Escalation in Vietnam." *Presbyterian Life* (August 1, 1966), 19:28.

"Churchmen Welcome Pope Paul's New Year's Plea for Peace." *Lutheran* (January 17, 1968), 6:25–26.

"Clergy Concerned About Vietnam." *Christian Century* (January 26, 1966), 83:99–100.

"Clergy in Politics." *New Republic* (February 17, 1968), 158:11.

"Clergy Mobilize for Peace." *Christian Century* (January 4, 1967), 84:5.

Coffin, William Sloane, Jr. "Civil Disobedience, the Draft, and the War." *Christianity and Crisis* (February 5, 1968), 28:8–11.

Collins, John. "CALC Transformed." *CALC Report* (August–October 1985), 11:7–8.

"Concerned and Committed." *Christian Century* (February 15, 1967), 84:197–98.

"A Conscience-Quickening Document." *Christian Century* (February 21, 1968), 85:219–20.

"Convention Roundup." *American Baptist* (June 1971), 169:22.

Converse, Philip E., and Howard Schuman. " 'Silent Majorities' and the Vietnam War." *Scientific American* (June 1970), 222:17–25.

"Council Scores Draft Evasion." *United Church Herald* (November 15, 1965), 8:29.

Cox, Harvey. "Amnesty for America's Exiles." *Christianity and Crisis* (November 25, 1968), 28:286–88.

—— "The 'New Breed' in American Churches: Sources of Social Activism in American Religion." *Daedalus* (Winter 1967), 96:135–50.

"The Dallas Assembly." *Christian* (November 13, 1966), 104:4–13.

DeBenedetti, Charles. "A CIA Analysis of the Anti-Vietnam War Movement: October 1967." *Peace and Change* (Spring 1983), 9:31–41.

—— "Lyndon Johnson and the Antiwar Movement." In Robert A. Divine, ed., *The Johnson Years: Vietnam, the Environment, and Science.* Vol. 2. Lawrence, Kansas: University Press of Kansas, 1987.

—— "On the Significance of Citizen Peace Activism: America, 1961–1975." *Peace and Change* (Summer, 1983), 9:6–20.

"A Declaration of Conscience." *Presbyterian Life* (June 15, 1967), 20:24–25.

"The Dissent Ahead." *Commonweal* (May 19, 1967), 86:252.

"The Dying Continues." *American Report,* November 5, 1971, p. 1.

"Ecumenical Meeting of Churchmen Urges End to Vietnam War." *Presbyterian Life* (February 15, 1972), 25:28–29.

Elegant, Robert. "How to Lose a War." *Encounter* (August 1981), 57:73–90.

Elston, Gerhard A. "Vietnam: Some Basic Considerations." *Catholic World* (May 1967), 205:78–82.

"Emergency Ministry Initiated for Services to Veterans." *Presbyterian Life* (February 15, 1972), 25:42.

"End the War Ads Available for Use on Local Stations." *American Report,* October 1–8, 1971.

Erskine, Hazel. "The Polls: Freedom of Speech." *Public Opinion Quarterly* (Fall 1970), 34:483–96.

—— "The Polls: Is War a Mistake?" *Public Opinion Quarterly* (Spring 1970), 34:134–50.

"Excerpts from the Resolutions at Boston." *Crusader* (September 1968), 23:7.

"Excerpts from the Resolutions at Pittsburgh." *Crusader* (June 1967), 22:7.

"Face-Saving or Life-Saving." *Engage* (June 1972), 4:2–4.

Fairclough, Adam. "Martin Luther King, Jr. and the War in Vietnam." *Phylon* (March 1984), 45:19–39.

Falk, Richard A. "The Inner Circle of Responsibility." *Nation* (January 26, 1970), 210:77–82.

Farren, Pat. "The Honeywell Corporation Learns About Nuremberg." *American Report,* June 10, 1974, pp. 13, 15.

Fernandez, Richard. "The Air War in Indochina: Some Responses." *Christian Century* (December 1, 1971), 88:1404–5.

—— "CALCAV's Contributions to the Anti-War Efforts." *CALC Report* (August/October, 1985), 11:9–11.

Fernandez, Richard, and Trudi Young. "CALC After Ann Arbor: Peace Efforts Renewed." *American Report,* September 3, 1971, p. 6.

"Fifth General Synod Sets Forward Course." *United Church Herald* (August 1, 1965), 8:12–18.

Finn, James. "The Debate on Vietnam." *Catholic World* (May 1966), 203:76–80.

—— "Vietnam Balance Sheet." *New Republic* (June 1, 1968), 158:31.

Furlow, Frances. "General Assembly Highlights." *Presbyterian Survey* (August 1967), 54:13–14, 16–17, 19–24.

Garrett, William R. "Politicized Clergy: A Sociological Interpretation of the 'New Breed.' " *Journal for the Scientific Study of Religion* (December 1973), 12:383–99.

Gelb, Leslie H. "Dissenting on Consensus." In Anthony Lake, ed., *The Vietnam Legacy,* pp. 102–19. New York: New York University Press, 1976.

"Getting Close to Home." *Presbyterian Life* (June 15, 1967), 20:13–17.

Gitlin, Todd. "Seizing History: What We Won and Lost at Home." *Mother Jones* (November, 1983), 8:33–38, 48.

Granberg, Donald. "Jewish-Nonjewish Differences on the Vietnam War: A Study of Social Psychologists." *American Sociologist* (August 1973), 8:101–6.

Gray, Francine du Plessix. "Profiles: Acts of Witness." *New Yorker* (March 14, 1970), 46:44–121.

—— "To March or Not to March." *New York Times Magazine,* June 27, 1976, pp. 6–7, 31–39.

Gumbleton, Thomas J. "War Never Again!" *New Catholic World* (September–October 1972), 215:203–5.

Hahn, Harlan. "Correlates of Public Sentiments About War: Local Referenda on the Vietnam Issue." *American Political Science Review* (December 1970), 64:1186–98.

Halberstam, David. "The Second Coming of Martin Luther King." *Harper's* (August 1967), 235:39–51.

Hall, Mitchell K. "A Time for War: The Church of God's Response to Vietnam." *Indiana Magazine of History* (December 1983), 79:285–304.

Hallin, Daniel C. "The Media, the War in Vietnam, and Political Support: A Critique of the Thesis of an Oppositional Media." *Journal of Politics* (February 1984), 46:2–24.

Haselden, Kyle. "Concerned and Committed." *Christian Century* (February 15, 1967), 84:197.

"Hawks in the Pews." *Christianity Today* (April 12, 1968), 12:36.

"Herbster Explains Synod Actions on War Service." *United Church Herald* (November 1967), 10:4.

"Honeywell Campaign: An Update." *American Report,* March 12, 1973, pp. 15–16.

"Honeywell Responds." *American Report,* May 5, 1972, p. 9.

Horner, Charles. "America Five Years After Defeat." *Commentary* (April, 1980), 69:50–58.

"Houston Church Threatens to Withdraw from Denomination." *United Church Herald* (November 1967), 10:32–33.

"Issues at General Synod." *United Church Herald* (August 1969), 12:10–11.

Johnson, Barry. "Seminarian in 'The Resistance.' " *Christian Century* (January 3, 1968), 85:15–17.

Katz, Milton S. "Peace Liberals and Vietnam: SANE and the Politics of 'Responsible' Protest." *Peace and Change* (Summer 1983), 9:21–39.

Katz, Milton S., and Neil H. Katz. "Pragmatists and Visionaries in the Post-World War II American Peace Movement: SANE and CNVA." In Solomon Wank, ed., *Doves and Diplomats: Foreign Offices and Peace Movements in Europe and America in the Twentieth Century,* pp. 265–88. Westport, Conn.: Greenwood Press, 1978.

Kernodle, John. "Update on Honeywell." *American Report,* October 23, 1972, pp. 14–15.

Kuttner, Robert L. "Recharging the Peace Movement." *Commonweal* (February 28, 1969), 89:669–70.

Lachman, Seymour P. "Barry Goldwater and the 1964 Religious Issue." *Journal of Church and State* (Autumn 1968), 10:389–404.

"LCA 3rd Biennial Convention." *Lutheran* (July 20, 1966), 4:6–9, 25–28, 44.

Lecky, Robert S. "From Emergency Committee to Protracted Struggle." *American Report,* September 3, 1971, pp. 6, 9.

—— "Requiem of an Editor." *American Report,* November 20, 1972, p. 3.

Leo, John. "News and Views." *Commonweal* (February 24, 1967), 85:580.

Lewis, Robert A. "A Contemporary Religious Enigma: Churches and War." *Journal of Political and Military Sociology* (Spring 1975), 3:57–70.

Lichty, Lawrence W. "The War We Watched on Television." *American Film Institute Report* (Winter 1973), 4:30–37.

"Listening to Some New Voices." *Presbyterian Life* (June 15, 1970), 23:4–7.

"Local Groups Press Honeywell to 'Cease and Desist.' " *American Report,* May 5, 1972, p. 8.

Luce, Don. "How CALC Humanized the War." *CALC Report* (August–October, 1985), 11:12–13.

"Luce Named CALC Director." *American Report,* July 22, 1974, p. 2.

Lunch, William L., and Peter W. Sperlich. "American Public Opinion and the War in Vietnam." *Western Political Quarterly* (March, 1979), 32:21–44.

"Lutheran World Relief to Aid Refugees in South Vietnam." *Lutheran* (February 16, 1966), 4:24.

MacKaye, William R. "Clergy in the Capital." *Christianity and Crisis* (March 4, 1968), 28:36–37.

Mandelbaum, Michael. "Vietnam: The Television War." *Daedalus* (Fall 1982), 111:157–69.

Marshall, David F. " 'We Have Opened Another Door.' " *United Church Herald* (August 1967), 10:12–19.

Maurer, Robert. "Religious Convocation for Peace." *American Report,* January 1–15, 1973, pp. 8–9.

McCorkle, Henry L. "Pain and Promise." *Episcopalian* (December 1966), 131:21–26.

McDermott, Patrick P. "Round II: Peace Movement vs. Vietnamization." *Catholic World* (April 1971), 213:6–12.

McGraw, James R. "Unselling of the Pentagon." *American Report,* June 9, 1972, p. S3.

"A Message to United Presbyterians." *Presbyterian Life* (July 1972), 25:38–39.

"Mission Board Urges Candor on Viet Nam." *Together* (April 1967), 11:8.

Mitchell, Michael C. "Television and the Vietnam War." *Naval War College Review* (May–June 1984), 37:42–52.

"Mobilizing for Peace." *Newsweek* (February 17, 1969), 73:68–69.

Morse, Stanley J., and Stanton Peele. "A Study of Participants in an Anti-Vietnam War Demonstration." *Journal of Social Issues* (1971), 27(4):113–36.

Mueller, John E. "Trends in Popular Support for the Wars in Korea and Vietnam." *American Political Science Review* (June 1971), 65:358–75.

Nelson, J. Robert. "Vietnam Summer." *Christian Century* (May 24, 1967), 84:678–79.

Neuhaus, Richard John. "American Religion and the War." *Worldview* (October 1967), 10:9–13.

—— "The Good Sense of Amnesty." *Nation* (February 9, 1970), 210:145–48.

—— "Super-General Hershey." *Commonweal* (January 19, 1968), 87:456–67.

—— "The War, the Churches, and Civil Religion." *Annals of the American Academy of Political and Social Science* (January 19770), 387:128–40.

"New Ads Offer Alternatives to 'Selling of the Pentagon.' " *American Report,* November 5, 1971, p. 1S.

Novak, Michael. "Alive and Well in Paris." *Commonweal* (November 22, 1968), 89:276–78.

—— "Rights and Wrongs." *New Republic* (February 10, 1973), 168:31–32.

—— "Vietnam's Tomorrow." *Commonweal* (October 10, 1969), 91:45–47.

O'Brien, James. "The Anti-War Movement and the War." *Radical America* (May–June, 1974), 8:53–86.

"On the Antiwar Front." *Christian Century* (February 5, 1966), 83:132–33.

"On War, Peace, and Dissent." *Presbyterian Life* (June 1, 1970), 23:6–7.

"The Opinion Poll on Vietnam." *Presbyterian Life* (April 1, 1968), 21:22–23.

Page, Benjamin I., and Richard A. Brody. "Policy Voting and the Electoral Process: The Vietnam War Issue." *American Political Science Review* (September 1972), 66:979–95.

Palms, Charles L. "Peace and the Catholic Conscience." *Catholic World* (June 1966), 203:145–52.

" 'Peace' Priest Muzzled." *Christian Century* (December 8, 1965), 82:1500–1.

"A Plea for Openness and Flexibility." *Presbyterian Life* (January 15, 1967), 20:32–33.

"Preparing for Protracted Struggle." *American Report,* November 5, 1971, pp. 1, 6.

"Presbyterian Group to Help Returning Vietnam Servicemen." *United Church Herald* (April 1972), 15:12–13.

"Protest: The Banners of Dissent." *Time* (October 27, 1967), 90:23–29.

"Protest Trends in Foreign Policy." *Christian Century* (July 7, 1965), 82:861–62.

Quinley, Harold E. "The Protestant Clergy and the War in Vietnam." *Public Opinion Quarterly* (Spring 1970), 34:43–52.

Ranck, Lee. "The Atlanta Pinata." *Engage* (June 1972), 4:6–18.

"Religious Groups Call for Withdrawal." *American Report,* March 5, 1971, p. 1, 6.

Rieke, Tom. "Honeywell's Annual Meeting." *American Report,* May 7, 1973, pp. 7, 15.

Robinson, John P. "Public Reaction to Political Protest: Chicago 1968." *Public Opinion Quarterly* (Spring 1970), 34:1–9.

Roche, John P. "The Impact of Dissent on Foreign Policy: Past and Future." In Anthony Lake, ed., *The Vietnam Legacy,* pp. 128–38. New York: New York University Press, 1976.

Roddy, Joseph. "Case of the Jail-Bound Jesuit." *Look* (April 15, 1969), 33:63–65.

Rose, Stephen C. "Busted Flat in Washington, Waiting. . . ." *Christian Century* (May 31, 1972), 89:625–26.

—— "From Viet Nam to Empire." *Christianity and Crisis* (March 3, 1969), 29:44.

—— "The Coming Confrontation on the Church's War Investments." *Christian Century* (October 14, 1970), 86:1209–11.

Schreiber, E. M. "Anti-War Demonstrations and American Public Opinion on the War in Vietnam." *British Journal of Sociology* (June 1976), 27:225–36.

Schuman, Howard. "Two Sources of Antiwar Sentiment in America." *American Journal of Sociology* (November, 1972), 78:513–36.

"A Second Selma." *Christian Century* (March 8, 1967), 84:301–2.

"A Sense of Freedom, Joy, and Rightness." *Time* (February 23, 1970), 95:54.

Shapiro, Fred C. "God and That Man at Yale." *New York Times Magazine,* March 3, 1968, 30–31, 52–62, 73–74.

Sharp, Frank A. "Denver Wrap-Up." *American Baptist* (June 1972), 170:14–17.

Sheerin, John B. "The Bishops and the Vietnam War." *Catholic World* (January 1967), 204:196–97.

—— "Bishop Shannon, Exile?" *Catholic World* (August 1969), 209:194–95.

—— "A Cease-Fire Now in Vietnam." *Catholic World* (November 1969), 210:50–51.

—— "From Vietnam to Isolation?" *Catholic World* (November 1967), 206:50–51.

—— "Is Peace Coming Tomorrow?" *Catholic World* (April 1967), 205:4–6.

—— "The Limits of Civil Disobedience." *Catholic World* (July 1968), 207:146–47.

—— "The Morality of the Vietnam War." *Catholic World* (March 1966), 202:326–30.

—— "Must Conscientious Objectors Be Pacifists?" *Catholic World* (January 1968), 206:146–47.

—— "Silent Church and the Endless War." *Catholic World* (February 1968), 206:194–95.

—— "The Vietcong as Negotiators?" *Catholic World* (April 1966), 203:6–10.

—— "War Crimes in High Places." *Catholic World* (July 1971), 212:163–64.

—— "Who Speaks for the Church on Vietnam." *Catholic World* (November 1966), 204:72–76.

"Silent March." *Newsweek* (February 19, 1968), 71:58.

Slemp, John C. "Be Disciples . . . Make Disciples." *Missions* (June 1966), 164:15–18.

—— "San Francisco, 1965." *Missions* (June 1965), 163:15–18.

Small, Melvin. "The Impact of the Antiwar Movement on Lyndon Johnson, 1965–68: A Preliminary Report." *Peace and Change* (Spring 1984), 10:1–22.

Smylie, James H. "American Religious Bodies, Just War, and Vietnam." *Journal of Church and State* (Autumn 1969), 11:383–408.

Starr, Jerold M. "Religious Preference, Religiosity, and Opposition to War." *Sociological Analysis* (Winter 1975), 36:323–33.

Stauderman, Albert P. "Editor's Opinion." *Lutheran* (March 27, 1968), 6:50.

"Too Much, Too Little." *Episcopalian* (July 1970), 135:13–15, 30.

"Toward Caesarism." *Christian Century* (May 3, 1967), 84:579–80.

"Trying to Level Scales of Political Commentary." *Broadcasting* (February 7, 1972), 82:54.

Tygart, Clarence E. "Social Movement Participation: Clergy and the Anti-Vietnam War Movement." *Sociological Analysis* (Fall 1973), 34:202–11.
"UCC Minister Brings Letters from American POWs." *United Church Herald* (March 1972), 15:7.
"A Union . . . and Much More." *Together* (July 1968), 12:5–7, 9–16.
" 'Unsell the War' Ads." *American Report,* pp. S4–S7.
" 'Unsell the War' Ads are Unveiled." *Advertising Age* (June 19, 1972), 43:123.
"Unsell TV Spot Wins Ad Award." *American Report,* July 7, 1972, p. 2.
"Uphold Right to Protest." *Together* (January 1966), 10:9–10.
"U.S. Policy in Vietnam: A Statement." *Christianity and Crisis* (June 14, 1965), 25:125–26.
Verba, Sidney, et al. "Public Opinion and the War in Vietnam." *American Political Science Review* (June 1967), 61:317–33.
Verba, Sidney, and Richard Brody. "Participation, Policy Preferences, and the War in Vietnam." *Public Opinion Quarterly* (Fall 1970), 34:325–32.
"Vietnam Report: Looking Toward the Future." *Presbyterian Life* (June 15, 1968), 22:14–16.
"Vietnam Statement Causes Anguish." *Presbyterian Life* (June 15–July 1, 1971), 24:14–15.
Walzer, Michael. "The Peace Movement." *New Republic* (February 10, 1973), 168:24–26.
"The Washington Fast." *New Yorker* (March 7, 1970), 46:32–33.
Webber, George. "CALC: The Anti-War Years." *CALC Report* (August–October, 1986), 11:4–6.
"Wednesdays in Washington." *Christian Century* (April 27, 1966), 83:518.
"Weighty Unanimity." *Christian Century* (December 22, 1965), 82:1564–65.
"We Protest the National Policy in Vietnam." *Christianity and Crisis* (March 7, 1966), 26:33–34.
"We Resolve." *Christian* (December 3, 1967), 105:11–13.
Whalen, Jack, and Richard Flacks. "Echoes of Rebellion: The Liberated Generation Grows Up." *Journal of Political and Military Sociology* (Spring 1984), 12:61–78.
"What Did We Actually Do?" *Episcopalian* (November 1967), 132:39–45.
"When Compromise Is Progress." *Lutheran Witness* (August 1967), 86:6–7.
Willis, Jeannie. "A Summary of General Convention Actions." *Episcopalian* (December 1970), 135:13–15, 56.
Withers, Leslie. "CALC Chapters and the National Office: Conflict or Symbiosis?" *CALC Report* (August–October, 1985), 11:14–16.
Woodward Kenneth L. "A Foretaste of Eternity." *Newsweek* (January 8, 1973), 81:50.

UNPUBLISHED MANUSCRIPTS

Carl, William J., III. "Old Testament Prophecy and the Question of Prophetic Preaching: A Perspective of Ecclesiastical Protest to the Vietnam War and the Participation of William Sloane Coffin, Jr." Ph.D. dissertation, University of Pittsburgh, 1977.
Colenback, Don F. "Christian Moral Argument and United States Policy in Viet Nam." Ph.D. dissertation, Yale University, 1975.
Hensley, William E. "The Vietnam Anti-War Movement: History and Criticism." Ph.D. dissertation, University of Oregon, 1979.
Long, Ellis E. "Communication and Social Change: The Verbal and Nonverbal Protest of Selected Clerical Activists Opposed to the Vietnam War, 1965–1970." Ph.D. dissertation, Florida State University, 1971.

INDEX

Church of the Brethren, 60
Citizen's Conference on Ending the War in Indochina, 110
Civil disobedience, 21, 44, 53, 55-60, 76, 99-100, 109-11, 125, 154, 160
Civil rights movement: and religious community, 5-6, 112; and antiwar movement, 21, 27, 70, 185n65; King's Riverside speech, 41-44; and ecumenism, 171; and social disruption, 175
Clark, Albert T., 125
Clark, Ramsey, 156, 159
Clergy and Laity Concerned (CALC), see Clergy and Laymen Concerned About Vietnam
Clergy and Laymen Concerned About Vietnam (CALCAV): origins, 1, 13-16; profile of leadership, 16-20, 115; tactics, 20-21, 25, 53, 55-57, 60, 67, 86-87, 99, 110, 125-26, 155, 174; local chapters, 21-22, 28-29, 60, 68-70, 91, 100-1, 115, 120-22, 139-40, 143, 157-58, 162, 165, 167-68; support for social activisim, 22, 48-49; and U.S. policies, 23, 30, 34, 48, 50, 61, 77, 79, 87, 96-97, 102, 160; and morality of Vietnam War, 24, 34, 51, 61, 77, 79; becomes permanent, 26; national office, 27-28, 32, 34, 47, 60-61, 67, 69, 73, 75, 85, 94, 99, 101, 104-6, 108, 111, 114-16, 121-22, 129, 131, 138-39, 157-58, 167-68; relations with antiwar movement, 27, 31-32, 45, 49, 59, 89, 93-95, 97-98, 105, 108-11, 114, 121, 124-27, 159, 168, 175; name change, 27, 116, 157; motives for joining, 29, 186n14; first Washington mobilization, 33-38; relations with U.S. government, 37, 51, 54, 64-65, 89, 92, 124-25, 160; and religious community, 39-40, 47, 65, 73, 90-91, 94, 100-1, 112, 114-16, 121, 131-36, 141, 144-45, 150, 162, 166, 171-72, 174; Riverside speeches, 41-43; size of organization, 47, 64, 78, 156, 158, 169; second Washington mobilization, 60-64; financial problems, 61, 104-6, 129, 139, 150, 166-67; and public opinion, 66; and corporations, 68, 87-88, 122, 131-41, 143-45, 147, 149-52; field staff, 69-70, 106, 115; 1968 presidential campaign, 70-72; and amnesty, 73-75, 79,

161-65; third Washington mobilization, 78-81, 86; and war resisters, 81-85, 92; and war crimes, 99, 111-12; internal tensions, 99, 108, 115-16, 120, 122-24, 157, 170; field development committee, 122, 135, 139, 158; and Vietnamization, 153; 1972 presidential campaign, 156-57; medical aid, 165; leadership transition, 167; postwar activities, 168-69; impact of, 171-77; opposition to, 173-74; see also Air Force Academy; American Report; "American Report Radio"; Ann Arbor Conference; Cambridge Conference; Local CALCAV chapters; Presidio Mutiny; Unsell the War
Clergy Concerned About Vietnam, see Clergy and Laymen Concerned About Vietnam
Clergymen's Emergency Committee for Vietnam, 9
Cleveland Area Peace Action Coalition, 92
Clifford, Clark, 71
Coffin, William Sloane: as CALCAV spokesman, 1; view of New Left, 13; profile, 18; and CALCAV leadership, 21, 27; defends CALCAV's role, 22, 24, 65; CALCAV Washington mobilizations, 36-37, 62-63, 80; and local CALCAV chapters, 38, 60, 157; and Martin Luther King, Jr., 42; and civil disobedience, 56-58, 61; fund raising, 61, 104; and Johnson's bombing halt, 72; and November (1969) mobilization, 93-95; and American Report, 108; and February (1971) mobilization, 110; and CALCAV transition, 115-16; "American Report Radio," 129; and May (1972) demonstration, 155; January (1973) convocation, 159; and amnesty, 161; Hartford Statement, 170; and Vietnamese commitment, 175
Columbia University, 20, 61, 67
Commager, Henry Steele, 42
Commentary, 7
Committee for Daniel Berrigan, 15
Committee for Noviolent Action (CNVA), 2, 12
Committee of Liaison, 97-98, 127
Commonweal, 7, 15
Communist Party, 2, 124

Conference of Catholic Bishops (U.S.), 31, 39, 80, 91, 134
Congress; and draft card burning, 4; and civil rights, 10; lobbied by antiwar movement, 11, 125, 156, 159, 166; lobbied by CALCAV, 35-36, 38, 60-62, 65, ,80, 166; antiwar sentiment in 37, 51, 176; and Martin Luther King, Jr., 44; criticizes antiwar movement, 54; and deescalation, 175
Conlon, Thomas, 3
Conscientious objection, see Selective conscientious objection
Continental Baking Company, 139
Conyers, John, 89
Cooper-Church Amendment, 101
Corporate Responsibility, 118-19, 122, 132, 143, 147, 149
Corrigan, Daniel, 9
Council for Corporate Review, 134, 149
Council on Economic Priorities, 132
Counterculture, 55, 115, 123, 159, 168, 173, 175
Cousins, Norman, 44
Cox, Harvey: and U.S. policy, 9, 154; and civil disobedience, 56; and amnesty, 74; Allenwood service, 75; and U.S. exiles, 81; Ann Arbor conference, 118-19; and Air Force Academy, 125-26; and Honeywell campaign, 148; and European religious community, 166; Boston Affirmations, 170; links CALCAV to faith, 176
Cronin, John, 36
Cupples, John, 70, 136, 167
Cushing, Richard cardinal, 16

Daily Death Toll, 118-19, 125, 141-42
Deats, Richard, 69-70
DeBenedetti, Charles, 55, 173, 175
Dellinger, Dave, 59, 81, 98, 118, 127
Democratic Farmer Labor Party, 163-64
Democratic National Convention (1968), 72-73, 87, 93
Democratic Party, 146
Dewey, USS, 54
Diem, Ngo Dinh, see Ngo Dinh Diem
Dirksen, Everett, 36
Disciples of Christ: and selective conscientious objection, 31, 65; and U.S. escalation, 46; and CALCAV, 60; and

the draft, 91; and Vietnam veterans, 154; and amnesty, 162
Dispatch News Service, 91
Docherty, George, 36
Dow Chemical Company, 67-68, 87-88, 98, 132-33, 145
Draft resistance, 4, 44, 54, 58, 64, 68, 74, 81, 84, 90, 92, 154, 161, 189n5
Drinan, Robert, 62, 89
Drolet, Brian, 121
Dudley, Carl S., 38

Easter Peace Walk, 2
Ecumenical Witness for Peace, 154
Eisendrath, Maurice, 16, 62
Eliot United Church of Christ (Newton, Mass.), 28, 101
Ellsberg, Daniel, 129
Elston, Gerhard: and CALCAV mobilizations, 34, 80; and Vietnam Summer, 46; and U.S. ideals, 50; and civil disobedience, 56; and Socialist Workers Party, 94; and NCC, 104; and American Report, 108
Episcopal Church: and American religion, 5; and CALCAV, 16; and U.S. policies, 31, 46, 102; South Bend convention, 90; and Honeywell, 144; and social issues, 147, 151; and amnesty, 162, 165
Episcopal Peace Fellowship, 82, 132
Evangelical churches, 5, 66
Exxon, 150

Fain, Irving, 61
Falk, Richard, 99, 123, 136, 146
Farnham, Philip, 68, 84, 86, 120-21
"Fast for the Rebirth of Compassion," 38-39
Faulk, John Henry, 129
Federal Bureau of Investigation (FBI): and Martin Luther King, Jr., 44; and antiwar movement, 54, 78, 125, 160; and CALCAV, 64, 74, 92, 124-25, 160
Fellowship of Reconciliation (FOR): and antiwar movement, 2, 12, 27, 125; and U.S. policy, 9, 10; relations with CALCAV, 36, 70, 74, 88, 97-98, 109, 121, 125, 159
Ferber, Michael, 58

Human Rights Party, 146
Humphrey, Hubert, 24, 72-73
Hunter, David: and CALCAV, 16, 27; and civil disobedience, 56; and NCC, 104; Air Force Academy, 125-26; and General Electric, 138

Independence, USS, 54
Indochina Peace Campaign, 156
"Indochina: The Aftermath," 160-61
Inside North Vietnam, 62
Internal Revenue Service, 105-6
International Days of Protest, 3
International Telephone and Telegraph Corporation (ITT), 133, 138-39
Interreligious Committee on Vietnam, 9
Inter-Religious Task Force on Amnesty (ITFA), 161-62
Inter-University Committee for a Public Hearing on Vietnam, 3
In the Name of America, 61-62, 111
"In the Name of America II," 99
"In the Public Interest," 129-30, 163
Issues and Actions, 92, 99, 107

Jehovah's Witnesses, 75
Jewish Theological Seminary, 19, 21
Johnson, Barry, 53
Johnson, Lyndon B.: and bombing of Vietnam, 2, 126; 1964 election, 8; and Vietnam policies, 9, 70, 72-73, 95; and Martin Luther King, Jr., 10, 41; and antiwar movement, 14, 38, 45, 51, 54, 75, 175; and CALCAV, 20, 37, 80; and peace initiatives, 25; support for, 40; and "wise men," 71
Joint Chiefs of Staff, 26
Jones, William A., 14
Jordan, Robert, 86
Jorden, William, 35, 37
Judaism: and ecumenical movement, 5; branches of, 6, 17, 19; and religious nationalism, 6; and religious press, 7; and antiwar movement, 12, 96, 171; and CALCAV, 14, 17, 19, 162; and *American Report,* 108; *see also* Religious community

Kahin, George M., 3
Katzenbach, Nicholas, 14
Keating, Francis, 15
Kennan, George F., 12

Kennedy, Edward, 129
Kennedy, John F., 1
Kennedy, Robert, 61, 71-72
Kent State University, 100, 102, 109
Kenyatta, Muhammad, 117-18
Kerry, John, 128
Kilfoyle, Daniel, 15
Killmer, Richard, 85, 91, 161
King, Coretta Scott, 4, 67, 80-81
King, Martin Luther, Jr.: and civil rights, 6, 10, 39; and U.S. policy, 9-10, 51; opposition to, 11, 43-44, 188n78; and CALCAV, 17, 43, 60-61, 63, 171; Riverside speech, 41-44; April (1967) rally, 44; and Vietnam Summer, 45; death of, 67; as presidential candidate, 70
Kissinger, Henry, 80, 89, 100, 145, 153
Kittlaus, Paul: Ann Arbor conference, 117; and CALCAV, 120, 122-23; Honeywell campaign, 135, 143
Korea, 2, 23
Kuttner, Robert, 86
Ky, Nguyen Cao, *see* Nguyen Cao Ky

Laos, 43, 95, 110
LaPorte, Roger, 4
Lecky, Robert, 107-8, 129-30
Lenten-Passover Fast Action Project, 97-98
Light, Timothy, 21, 25, 40
Lindsay, John, 67
Local CALCAV chapters: Philadelphia, 21, 69; Cleveland, 21, 140; Memphis, 21; Wichita, Kan., 21; Austin, Tex., 21; Chapel Hill, N.C., 21; Grinnell, Iowa, 21; Maine, 21, 91; Vermont, 21; Delaware, 21; Portland, Ore., 21, 69-70; Boston (Committee of Religious Concern for Peace), 21, 28, 69-70, 85, 136, 140-44, 149-50; Seattle, 29, 69, 85, 158; Palo Alto, 38; Minneapolis, 38, 113-14, 136, 149, 162; Buffalo, 38, 85, 149; Anderson, Ind., 60; Indianapolis (Hoosiers for Peace), 60, 149; Madison, Wis., 60; Chicago, 68-69, 149; Medford, Ore., 68; Denver, 68, 125, 134, 149-50; San Francisco (Northern California, Ecumenical Peace Institute), 68-69, 86, 120-22, 149, 158, 165-66; New Haven, 69; Kansas City, Mo., 69; Dallas, 69-70,

91, 143; Los Angeles (Southern California), 69, 120, 140, 150, 162; San Jose, 69; Detroit, 85, 144, 149, 162; Iowa, 100-1; San Diego, 120; Houston, 138, 158; Amherst, Mass. (Western Massachusetts), 140, 149, 165; Louisville (Kentuckiana), 140, 149; Greenville, S.C., 140, 144, 149, 162; Schenectady, N.Y., 143; Tempe, Ariz., 143; Ann Arbor, Mich. (Interfaith Council for Peace), 145-47, 149; Worcester, Mass. (Central Massachusetts), 149, 162; Washington, D.C., 149; Lincoln, Neb. (Nebraskans for Peace), 158

Lowenstein, Allard, 42, 62, 70
Luce, Don, 89, 167
Lutheran, The, 66
Lutheran Church in America, 5, 16, 31, 65, 80
Lutheran Church—Missouri Synod, 16-17, 19, 46, 90
Lutheran Peace Fellowship, 121
Lutheran World Relief, 30

McCall, David B., 127
McCarthy, Eugene, 37-38, 60-62, 70-72
McDonough, John R., 58, 64
McGee, Vincent, Jr., 64
McGovern, George, 78-79, 94, 156-57
McIntire, Carl, 35-36, 62-63, 80
McNamara, Robert, 37, 62
McQuire, Mathew, 63
McSorley, Richard, 81
Mainstream churches: origins, 5; response to Vietnam, 11, 51; relations with U.S. government, 38; and public opinion, 66; and CALCAV, 115, 171; *see also* Religious community
Mao Zedong, 13
March Against Death, 93-94
March on the Pentagon, 55, 58-59
Marquette University, 15
Marty, Martin, 56
Maslow, Robert, 129-30
Mattison, Lynn, 130
Meacham, Stewart, 93, 98
Medical Aid to Indochina Committee, 165
Melman, Seymour, 61-62, 79
Mennonite Central Committee, 30
Mennonites, 60

Methodist Church: mainstream, 5; and CALCAV, 16-17; agencies of, 31, 46; see also United Methodist Church
Miller, David, 3, 54, 75
Miller, Jack, 101
Miller, James, 37
Miller, Susan, 93
Milwaukee Fourteen, 80
Minister's Vietnam Committee, 8
Minnesota Council of Churches, 163
Minnesotans for Amnesty, 162-64
Mitchell, John, 87
Moore, Paul, Jr., 36
Moore, Phillip, 149
Moratorium Committee, see Vietnam Moratorium
Morgenthau, Hans, 3, 64
Morley, Michele, 164
Morrison, Norman, 4
Morse, Wayne, 37
Morton, Thruston, 62
Movement and Revolution, 77
Mullen, Peg, 101
Muste, A.J., 11, 31, 33
Mutual Broadcasting Network, 129
My Lai massacre, 99, 111-12, 126

Nation, 99
National Action/Research on the Military-Industrial Complex(NARMIC), 135, 138, 140-41, 146
National Association for the Advancement of Colored People (NAACP), 44
National Committee for a Sane Nuclear Policy, *see* SANE
National Conference of Concerned Democrats, 70
National Coordinating Committee to End the War in Vietnam, 3-4, 11
National Council for Universal and Unconditional Amnesty (NCUUA), 161
National Council of Churches in the United States (NCC): formation, 5; and U.S. policies, 10, 46, 102; relations with CALCAV, 19, 21, 28, 104-6, 124, 133, 171, 206*n*3; and refugees, 30; relations with U.S. government, 38, 187*n*51; and war resisters, 85; and FBI, 124; Corporate Information Center, 138; and Unsell the War, 156; and amnesty, 161; criticism of, 170

National Council to Repeal the Draft, 89
National Emergency Committee of
   Clergy Concerned About Vietnam, see
   Clergy and Laymen Concerned About
   Vietnam
National Liberation Front (NLF): and
   U.S. refusal to negotiate, 23; contacts
   with antiwar movement, 81, 110, 119;
   and South Vietnamese, 97; and Paris
   agreement, 145, 172; support for, 168;
   commitment of, 175; see also Vietcong
National Mobilization Committee, 44,
   55, 67, 74, 78, 87, 92
National Peace Action Coalition
   (NPAC), 109-10,124
National Religious Convocation and
   Congressional Visitation for Peace,
   159
National Student Association, 144
Negotiation Now, 44-45
Nelson, Carole, 162, 164
Nelson, Gaylord, 129
Nerken, Ira, 127-28
Neuhaus, Richard John: defends dissent,
   14, 49; and Daniel Berrigan, 15; and
   CALCAV leadership, 16, 25, 27; pro-
   file, 19; New York peace march, 24;
   July (1966) fast, 29-30; and Washing-
   ton mobilizations, 37, 62, 80-81; and
   civil disobedience, 56; and American
   society, 59, 77; and Democratic con-
   vention, 72; and amnesty, 74; and
   U.S. exiles, 81-82; Cambridge confer-
   ence, 91; and U.S. policies, 97; and
   American Report, 107-8; February
   (1971) mobilization, 110; Ann Arbor
   conference, 114; breaks with CAL-
   CAV, 123, 166; and corporations,
   135; Hartford Statement, 170
New Approach, 107
New Left, 2, 4, 13, 168
New Mobilization Committee to End
   the War in Vietnam, 92-95, 97, 100,
   102
New Republic, 161
New York Times, 43, 64, 80
Ngo Dinh Diem, 2
Ngo Dinh Nhu, Mme., 2
Nguyen Cao Ky, 59
Nguyen Thi Binh, Mme., 119
Nguyen Van Thieu, 59, 96, 145, 148,
   159, 166, 168

Niebuhr, Reinhold, 8-9, 20, 30, 72
Nixon, Richard: and Vietnam War, 73;
   election of, 76, 157; and antiwar
   movement, 78, 96, 125, 175; and
   CALCAV, 80, 86; "secret plan," 87,
   156; and Vietnamization, 90, 95, 135,
   152, 155; and Cambodia, 99, 102; and
   bombing of Vietnam, 126, 154; Paris
   Agreement, 145; and negotiations,
   153; and amnesty, 161; and Israel, 171
North Vietnam: U.S. bombing of, 2-4,
   26, 32, 43, 154, 159; bombing halt,
   20, 34, 38; invasion of South Vietnam, 40; and peace negotiations, 71,
   145, 153, 159; and U.S. prisoners, 74,
   97-98, 127; contact with antiwar
   movement, 81, 110, 124, 167; military
   offensive (1975), 168; commitment of,
   175; see also National Liberation Front;
   Viet Cong
Novak, Michael; and CALCAV mobili-
   zaton, 37; author, 47; and racism, 51;
   and U.S. exiles, 74, 81; and antiwar
   movement, 96; and South Vietnamese, 97, 99; and American Report, 107;
   and bombing of Vietnam, 154; and
   Vietnam War, 159; break with CAL-
   CAV, 166
November 5-8 Mobilization Committee, 31
Nuremberg obligations, 146-47
Nuremberg principles, 61, 148, 151
Nystrom, Kristina, 84

Oglesby, Carl, 4
Oleo Strut, 69
Oline, Dale, 138
Operation Chaos, 160

Paris Agreements (1973), 150, 153, 159-
   61, 167-68
Paris peace talks, 80-81, 145
Paul VI, Pope, 166
Peace Walkers, 113-14
Pemberton, John, 89
Pentagon Papers, 160
People's Coalition for Peace and Justice
   (PCPJ), 109-10, 124-25
Percy, Charles, 101
Playboy, 128
Portland Council of Churches, 70
Powers, Thomas, 3, 43

Presbyterian Church, 5, 16, 20, 132; *see also* United Presbyterian Church
Presbyterian Church of the United States, 46, 65, 90
Presidio mutiny, 85–86
Price, Robert, 62
Prisoners of war, 65, 74, 98, 127, 154, 159, 176
Progressive Labor Party, 44
Project Air War, 126
Project on Corporate Responsibility, 149
Prokosch, Erik, 146
Public opinion, 17, 32, 52, 65–67, 112, 161, 165, 172-73, 175, 191*n*57

Quaker Action Group, 87
Quakers, 4, 12, 93
Quinley, Harold, 16

Ransom, Louise, 53, 89, 95, 164
Ransom, Mike, 53, 89
Ransom, Robert, 89, 106
Raskin, Marcus, 55, 58
Rauch, Tom, 126, 167
Rauh, Joseph, Jr., 44
"The Reconciliation We Seek," 79
Reed, Robert, 37
Reid, Duff, 62
Reis, Pat, 129
Religious community: and antiwar movement, 5, 11, 94; and social issues, 6–7; and religious press, 7; and ecumenical actions, 14, 36, 39, 153–54; and CALCAV, 33, 37, 51, 91, 101, 112, 171-72; and selective conscientious objection, 55; Vietnam War, 90, 153–54, 184*n*51, 192*n*58; and corporate investment, 147
"The Religious Community and American Politics," 73
"The Religious Community and Politics 1968," 62
"The Religious Community and the Draft," 62
"The Religious Community and the War in Vietnam," 34-35, 47
Religious Convocation and Congressional Visitation for Peace, 165
Republican Party, 146-47, 163
Resistance, the, 54, 58

Resor, Stanley, 86
Reston, James, 13
Reuther, Victor, 44
Richter, Edward, 107
Rivers, Mendel, 54
Robinson, Eric, 70
Robinson, John, Jr., 74
Rockeye II, 137-38, 146, 148
Rogers, Carl, 116, 128
Roman Catholic Church: religious nationalism, 5–6; and religious press, 7; and antiwar movement, 12, 28, 39–40, 51, 171, 187*n*57; and Daniel Berrigan, 15; and CALCAV, 17, 33, 40; "just war" doctrine, 40; *see also* Religious community
Romney, George, 102
Rose, Sharon, 98
Rose, Stephen, 132
Rostow, Walt, 35, 37
ROTC (Reserve Officers Training Corps), 55, 165-66
Rowan, Carl, 44
Rowland, Sue, 86
Rubin, Jerry, 55

Ste. Angelle, Jhonnye, 138
St. John's University, 15
SANE (National Committee for a Sane Nuclear Policy): and antiwar movement, 2, 4, 12, 27, 44-45; and civil disobedience, 13; relations with CALCAV, 33, 166; and McCarthy campaign, 70
Scalapino, Robert, 3
Scharper, Philip, 64
Schlesinger, Arthur M. Jr., 3, 44
Schoenerr, Walter, 136
Schomer, Howard, 151
Scott, Hugh, 101, 125
Seattle *Times,* 29
Second International Days of Protest, 11
Second Vatican Ecumenical Council (Vatican II), 6
Securities and Exchange Commission, 133, 136, 138, 145
Seeger, Pete, 95
Seitzman, Bea, 83
Selective conscientious objection, 46, 51, 55-56, 59, 65, 79-80, 90, 154
Selective Service System, 12, 65, 68